AVID

READER

PRESS

BEN & ME

IN SEARCH OF A FOUNDER'S FORMULA
FOR A LONG AND USEFUL LIFE

ERIC WEINER

AVID READER PRESS

NEW YORK   LONDON   TORONTO   SYDNEY   NEW DELHI

AVID READER PRESS
An Imprint of Simon & Schuster, LLC
1230 Avenue of the Americas
New York, NY 10020

First Avid Reader Press hardcover edition June 2024

AVID READER PRESS and colophon are trademarks of Simon & Schuster, LLC

Simon & Schuster: Celebrating 100 Years of Publishing in 2024

For information about special discounts for bulk purchases,
please contact Simon & Schuster Special Sales
at 1-866-506-1949 or business@simonandschuster.com.

The Simon & Schuster Speakers Bureau can bring authors to your live event.
For more information or to book an event, contact the
Simon & Schuster Speakers Bureau at 1-866-248-3049
or visit our website at www.simonspeakers.com.

Interior design by Ruth Lee-Mui

Manufactured in the United States of America

1   3   5   7   9   10   8   6   4   2

Library of Congress Cataloging-in-Publication Data

Names: Weiner, Eric, 1963- author.
Title: Ben & me : in search of a founder's formula for a long and useful life / Eric Weiner.
Other titles: Ben and me
Identifiers: LCCN 2023058232 (print) | LCCN 2023058233 (ebook) | ISBN 9781501129049
(hardcover) | ISBN 9781501129056 (paperback) | ISBN 9781501129070 (ebook)
Subjects: LCSH: Franklin, Benjamin, 1706–1790. | Franklin, Benjamin, 1706–1790—Homes and
haunts. | Statesmen—United States—Biography. | Weiner, Eric, 1963—Travel.
Classification: LCC E302.6.F8 W546 2024 (print) | LCC E302.6.F8 (ebook) |
DDC 973.3092 [B]—dc23/eng/20240206
LC record available at https://lccn.loc.gov/2023058232
LC ebook record available at https://lccn.loc.gov/2023058233

ISBN 978-1-5011-2904-9
ISBN 978-1-5011-2907-0 (ebook)

For Sharon

The noblest question in the world is *What good may I do in it?*
—BENJAMIN FRANKLIN

Benjamin Franklin is the founding father who winks at us.
—WALTER ISAACSON

Contents

Author's Note

It was common practice in the eighteenth century to capitalize most nouns. This can confuse the contemporary reader and create distance between us and Benjamin Franklin. That is not, I think, what he would want, so I have modernized most capitalization and spelling. I have retained the use of ampersands, contractions ("fix'd" instead of "fixed," for instance), and other stylistic touches to retain the flavor of Franklin and his time.

INTRODUCTION

ALIEN BEN

The dust is what I remember most. Chunks of reddish-brown earth adhered to my skin and my microphone and my silly correspondent's vest and the few tufts of hair remaining on my prematurely bald head. Kabul was barren, a city of darkness and despair, and I, a young journalist in way over my head, was the greenest thing around.

It was 1996. The Afghan capital had just fallen to the Taliban: religious zealots who passed the time cruising Kabul's muddy, cratered streets in Toyota pickups, with grenade launchers perched atop the flatbeds. Music was banned. Women, on those rare occasions they ventured onto the streets, were required to wear burqas, head-to-toe coverings with only a small mesh window for the eyes and, incongruously, a royal blue colorway that made them look like faceless apparitions. The soccer stadium had been converted into a site for public executions.

I faithfully produced stories for NPR, waving my microphone as if it were a wand and hoping misery conveyed was misery diminished.

One day, I decided to take a break from the grimness and dipped into a local carpet shop. Here was an art form still permitted under Taliban rule. I spotted the rug I wanted—a Bukhara beauty, featuring a tight maroon weave—and reluctantly haggled (I hate haggling) with the shopkeeper, a rotund man with a hearty laugh and wry smile. We settled on a price; then I retrieved a wad of US dollars, a mix of tens and twenties, from the money belt strapped to my belly.

"No," he said, the smile fading from his face, his voice growing agitated. "Only Franklins! Only Franklins!"

Much of the world knows Ben Franklin this way: the face on the hundred-dollar bill. (Two-thirds of all hundred-dollar bills circulate *outside* the United States.) This is how I thought of Franklin too—if I thought of him at all. When I did, cartoonish images sprang to mind. Franklin manning his printing press. Franklin signing the US Constitution. Franklin flirting with the ladies of Paris. And, of course, Franklin flying his electrified kite.

A restless soul, I've always been drawn to the wisdom of strangers: Gandhi, Confucius, Nietzsche, and many others. I had always assumed true wisdom resided far away and spoke a foreign tongue. I inhaled the history of others even as I remained ignorant of my own. This disturbed me, but not enough to do anything about it. I had a war to cover, a world to see, so I stashed my remaining Franklins into my money belt and didn't give him another thought.

Until I did.

Fast-forward three decades. I am no longer young. I am a man of a certain age, with all the uncertainty and apprehension that entails. I am approaching what Plato called the threshold of old age. I am not old, to be clear, but I am no longer young. I occupy an uncomfortable bardo state, somewhere between middle age and early-bird-special age. A birthday is approaching. A big one, where the number six features prominently. I've tried ignoring it. At first, this proved easy enough. The birthday was a tiny speck in the big sky, like an airliner at cruising altitude or a hot-air balloon floating high above the badlands of South Dakota.

Gradually, though, the unnamed birthday grew larger until it filled my field of vision. I began to take stock of my life, and I didn't like the inventory. What did all my endless, mindless striving amount to? What good have I done?

That's when Franklin reappeared in my life. He snuck in when I wasn't looking. My editor suggested I write a book on aliens—one UFO encounter in particular that may or may not have happened over the Berkshire Mountains in Massachusetts in 1969. I didn't want to write a book on aliens, but I did want to keep my editor happy, so I promised to look into it.

The Berkshire incident struck me as problematic, even more so than most UFO encounters. It involved bright lights, an abduction of an entire family, and insect-like creatures. I sighed. (I am a big sigher.) My antipathy for the whole UFO idea hardened. I told myself I'd do a tad more research, then call my editor and recuse myself. No UFO book for me. Then I stumbled across an article that changed everything.

It was titled "Our Founders, Alien Obsessed." Intrigued, I began to read. Apparently several of America's founders believed in the possibility of intelligent life in the universe. In 1639, John Winthrop, first governor of the Massachusetts Bay Colony, noted the appearance of strange objects in the sky over Boston—UFOs, in other words. Then there was Benjamin Franklin, who, as a young man, wrote, "I stretch my imagination thro' and beyond our system of planets, beyond the visible fix'd stars themselves, into that space that is every way infinite, and conceive it fill'd with suns like ours, each with a chorus of worlds."

A chorus of worlds! Now my interest was piqued—not about UFOs but about Benjamin Franklin.

He is not an obvious source of inspiration for someone like me, a fan of foreign lands and peoples, a man of art, not science, but if I've learned anything from my travels, it is to always question assumptions, to always ask: What if? What if I've been looking in all the wrong places? What if wisdom resides a lot closer than I think?

The more I learned about Ben Franklin, the more I suspected he just might be the mentor, the guide to ageing and to living, I've been seeking. The last third of his life was by far the most interesting, and the first two-thirds were downright fascinating. It was in his closing act, a time when he could have been doing the colonial equivalent of golfing in Florida, that he accomplished the most and changed the most. This was when Franklin the

Loyalist became Franklin the Rebel and, later, when Franklin the Enslaver became Franklin the Abolitionist. This was when he charmed the French into supporting the American cause. It was also, paradoxically, when Franklin found the almost Buddha-like serenity that had long eluded him.

Franklin was the most corporeal of the founding fathers. Jefferson, Adams, and Washington all had good heads on their shoulders, but that's the problem—they were all head. I have no idea what Jefferson's gut looked like (did he have one?) or Washington's buttocks. Ah, but Franklin. Now here was a founder in full! "Fleshly, worldly, fluid, and ungodly," as one scholar put it.

Yes, I thought, reading those words, and thank goodness, for this most fleshly and fluid of founders was also the most human. He's the founder we want to have a beer with. I can't imagine calling Thomas Jefferson "Tommy" or James Madison "Jimbo," but I feel comfortable calling Franklin Ben, or even Benny, as he was known in his youth.

Benjamin Franklin is the best-known president who wasn't president. He achieved so much it's hard to know where to begin. He was the most famous American of his time and the only founder who would have been famous even if there had never been a Revolutionary War. Franklin was a printer, publisher, satirist, scientist, philanthropist, humorist, diplomat, inventor, legislator, meteorologist, memoirist, postmaster, editor, traveler, debunker, and enthusiast. He was also an influencer, perhaps the first. He signed all four documents leading to the founding of the new republic, the only person to do so. He invented the lightning rod, bifocals, a new kind of stove, the matching grant, a musical instrument called the glass armonica, and a chair that doubles as a step stool. And that list is only partial. In Philadelphia, he founded many of the civic organizations we now take for granted: public libraries, hospitals, volunteer fire departments, neighborhood watches. He was at once practical *and* visionary, a rare combination.

My résumé is considerably less impressive. I have invented nothing, founded nothing. I am not the most famous American of my time. I have won no wars, signed no declarations.

As I dig, though, I unearth a few ways we are alike, Ben and me. I too need to lose more than a few pounds. I too believe the best way to a person's heart is through their funny bone. Franklin, like me, was a traveler. He journeyed farther and longer than any other American of his time. He crossed the Atlantic eight times, and during an age when reaching one's destination was not guaranteed and in-flight service was even worse than today. He spent a third of his long life abroad, living in London and Paris and visiting Canada, Ireland, Scotland, Germany, the Netherlands, and, for three glorious days, the Portuguese island of Madeira. The region's wine was one of those small pleasures that Franklin cherished; amass enough of them, he believed, and the result was outsized happiness.

Franklin is the most misunderstood of the founders. Despite his business success and his visage gracing the hundred-dollar bill, he was no money-grubbing capitalist. He was, I've discovered, more Buddhist than banker. He wrestled with the imponderables of life: morality, mortality, God, bliss, love. Despite his reputation for coldness, Franklin was no automaton.

Was he perfect? Absolutely not. Franklin disappoints me at times, infuriates me at others. He was, as one historian said, "the perfect model of sanity," and I can think of nothing more annoying than that. He could be too literal and pedantic, and too cautious. He could be ethnocentric and bigoted. So, yes, he was flawed, but so am I.

Like me, Ben loved nothing more than telling a good tale. Just as we need oxygen to breathe and water to drink, we humans need stories to tell ourselves, especially about three essential questions. How did we get here? Where do we go when we die? What should we do in the meantime? On the first two questions, Franklin is not much help; he had no time for idle speculation. But on the third question, he has much to offer. He is a good guide, and I sure could use one.

At a time when everyone, including me, is struggling to create better versions of themselves, Franklin, America's original self-help evangelist, reminds us it is easier than we think. At a time when the tapestry of our union is fraying, Franklin reminds us there is something uniquely uplifting and admirable about the American experiment. At a time when opinions have calcified, Franklin reminds us that changing your mind is not only a noble act; it is also an American one.

Unfortunately, Ben Franklin resides in the past, and that is not a locale we Americans care to visit. Sure, we like a good museum gift shop or Civil War reenactment, but as a young nation, we find the future, replete with both promise and dread, far more compelling than the past. Yet it is the past—the eighteenth century, in particular—where I've had my head firmly inserted for the past few years. It was not a bad place to have had a head, provided said head was not Black or Native American or female or any head, really, except a white male one that spoke with the right accent.

A while ago, the late social critic Neil Postman wrote *Building a Bridge to the 18th Century*. His thesis: the eighteenth century was a pivotal time when many of our modern ideas were born, and we'd be wise to revisit it. "To forget our mistakes is bad," he wrote, "but to forget our successes may be worse." We're so worried about repeating the past that we overlook the hidden treasures it contains. I find that notion mighty appealing. If I am anything, it is a treasure hunter.

My curiosity about Franklin and his times slow-simmered at first but soon reached a rolling, roiling boil with an intensity and persistence that surprised me. The result of my Franklin fixation is the book you are holding in your hands. You will, alas, find no aliens in these pages, but will, I hope, see what I now see in Benjamin Franklin: a fleshly and fluid founder who has much to teach us about something as enticing as it is elusive—the secret to living a long and useful life.

ONE

RESTING BEN

A man is not completely born until he be dead.

—BENJAMIN FRANKLIN

We begin, naturally, at the end. It is only here, at life's terminus, where the journey makes sense. Taking the measure of a life still being lived is like reviewing a movie you're still watching or a meal you're still eating. Your verdict is bound to be incomplete at best, foolish at worst.

Every ending is different but none are happy. Benjamin Franklin's final chapter, unfolding at his Philadelphia home in spring 1790, was no exception. The closing scene was faithfully recorded by Polly Stevenson, who was like a second daughter to Franklin. In London, they lived under the same roof for many years and shared a fierce curiosity about the natural world. His "dear little philosopher," he called her.

In the last year of his life, Ben rarely left his bedroom. He rigged a means to close the door from bed by using a series of cords and pulleys. Suffering from gout, kidney stone, and pleurisy, he was in pain, despite the laudanum, a tincture of opium mixed with alcohol he was taking in increasing doses. Still, reports Polly, "No repining, no peevish expression ever escaped him," nor an iota of self-pity.

Eighty-four years old, Benjamin Franklin had enjoyed a long life, especially considering the numerous, often colorful ways one could meet their
demise in the eighteenth century. Franklin survived multiple illnesses, two
wars, eight ocean crossings, and a botched experiment involving a lethal
electrical charge and a turkey. Everyone marveled at Franklin's longevity and
none more so than Franklin himself. "I seem to have intruded myself into the
company of posterity, when I ought to have been a-bed and asleep," he told
a friend. "Yet had I gone at seventy it would have cut off twelve of the most
active years of my life, employed too in matters of the greatest importance."
That is an understatement. The last decades of Franklin's life were his busiest
and his happiest.

After a lifetime of kinetic activity, Benjamin Franklin accomplished
what had long eluded him: repose. By 1788, his various public obligations
discharged, he could sit back and enjoy "the leisure I have so long wish'd for."
Here was Franklin at rest, or as close to rest as possible for such a restless
man. There was still much to do: an autobiography to finish, a life to assess,
and a house to look after, a small compound on Philadelphia's Market Street
now known as Franklin Court.

Ben spent his final years reading and writing, meeting old friends, and
entertaining guests. He was an amiable, if quirky, host, serving simple fare
of beer and russet potatoes. One visitor, the Reverend Manasseh Cutler, recalled how he arrived expecting to meet American royalty but instead found
"a short, fat, trunched old man in plain Quaker dress, bald pate, and short,
white locks, sitting without his hat under the tree." Franklin's ordinariness
was perhaps his most extraordinary quality.

Franklin loved to show visitors his inventions and curiosities: a two-
headed snake, a glass contraption demonstrating the human circulatory system, an early version of today's copier, a "long-arm" device that enabled him
to reach the top shelves of his many bookcases. Franklin Court resembled, if
nothing else, an eighteenth-century version of the Sharper Image—a world
apart from the simple two-room house young Ben had shared with nearly a
dozen family members in his native Boston.

•   •   •

Toward the end, in early April 1790, he briefly rallied, raising hopes, but two weeks later an abscess in one of his lungs burst, filling them with fluid. "A calm lethargic state succeeded," reports John Jones, the attending physician. Then, on April 17 at 11 p.m., "he quietly expired, closing a long and useful life of eighty-four years and three months."

The doctor's choice of words is important—not merely a long life, but a long *and useful* one. Usefulness mattered a lot in the eighteenth century. The greatest test of an idea, any idea, was its utility. Did it promote the greatest happiness of the greatest number?

The truth is that we are ambivalent about leading useful lives. We claim it's what we strive toward, yet complain that so-and-so is "just using us." Being the kind of person whom others regularly use is seen as a character flaw. But maybe it is the highest compliment. Rather than avoiding being used, perhaps I should invite it. *Yes, please. Use me.*

Usefulness was especially important to Franklin. The word appears nearly thirty times in his autobiography. It motivated him. It defined him. He was a useful printer, a useful statesman, a useful scientist, a useful writer, and a useful friend. And he was a useful revolutionary—arguably the most useful, second only to George Washington.

Am I useful? I have my doubts. When I compare myself to others, I come up short. My father was a doctor. He saved lives. My mother was a teacher. She shaped lives. My friend James leads guided meditations. He calms lives. Me? I scratch words onto a page, and some days not many of those. So, no, I am not useful, certainly not compared to Benjamin Franklin.

This realization triggers a low-grade melancholy that has shadowed me for years. Ben suffered no such despondency. He retained a sanguine outlook and never lost hope, even when others did. When asked if something could be done, or done better, he always replied, in so many words, "Why the heck not?"

Benjamin Franklin was not a pragmatist. He was what neuroscientist

David Eagleman calls a "possibilian." The pragmatist asks, "What can we do about this now?" The possibilian imagines what might be done in the future, no matter how improbable. The possibilian is infinitely patient. The possibilian always perseveres, and never sighs.

Might there be a possibilian lurking inside me, too?

TWO

BABY BEN

For much of his long life, Benjamin Franklin was known as "Dr. Franklin." It wasn't exactly a lie, but it wasn't entirely truthful. While Franklin did display an intense interest in and knowledge of medicine, he was not a medical doctor. And while he was widely read and conversant in several languages, he never earned a PhD, or any other degree for that matter, not even a high school diploma. The title was honorary, bestowed first by St. Andrews University in Scotland and later by Oxford University. Dr. Franklin was not a "real" doctor.

I am not a real doctor either. Yet hanging in my office is a diploma granting me the title of Doctor Honoris Causa. It's set in elegant typeface and accompanied by the requisite medieval motifs and sprinkling of Latin. I look at the framed diploma often, probably too often.

My honorary doctorate is not from Oxford or any other university you might have heard of. It is from St. Cyril and St. Methodius University of Veliko Tarnovo, the second-most prestigious university in all of Bulgaria. It took me a full week of continual practice to wrap my American lips around the Bulgarian syllables, but I mastered them, as well as fourteen other words: *Izvinete, no Bŭlgarskiyat mi ne e mnogo dobŭr, taka che shte govorya na Angliĭski.* "Excuse me, but my Bulgarian is not very good, so I shall speak in English."

That is what I told an audience of several dozen faculty, students, and journalists gathered one spring day at the university. I will never forget that moment. Draped in a black and purple robe, clutching my diploma like a talisman, I experienced what I imagine Franklin did when he received one of his honorary doctorates: a complex admixture of pride and validation, laced with trace elements of embarrassment. Do I deserve this? Have I earned it?

Most of all, I experienced relief. The good people of Veliko Tarnovo removed a large and debilitating chip from my shoulder. Unlike my wife and several friends, I had not attended an Ivy League school. I was a lazy, disengaged student. No Rhodes Scholar, I was a road warrior. Flitting from one place to the next, I was a compulsive wanderer and unrepentant neurotic. Now I was a doctor too and had the documentation to prove it.

I have a recurring fantasy. I am on an airplane—in first class, naturally (this *is* a fantasy)—sipping a Bloody Mary and nibbling on warmed nuts when a flight attendant makes an announcement.

"Attention passengers. Is there a doctor on board? If so, please press your call button."

I press my call button, and the flight attendant rushes to my seat.

"Sir, you are a doctor?"

"Why, yes, I am, though technically it's an honorary doctorate from the second-most prestigious university in Bulgaria. How can I help?"

I have a theory. Everyone is famous somewhere. Benjamin Franklin and Jerry Lewis were more famous in France than in America. The Germans worship David Hasselhoff. Thanks to the luck of the draw, I got Bulgaria.

Bulgarians love me. They love me even more than they love Michael Bolton, which is *a lot*. When I visited Sofia, the Bulgarian capital, I turned a corner and saw an eight-story-high billboard of the fading pop icon. They have a saying in Bulgaria: "Rock stars rise in the West and set in the East."

I'm not sure why Bulgarians love me when, truth be told, there are days I don't love myself. Now that I think about it, maybe that explains it. Bulgarians are among the least happy people in the world, so perhaps they relate to my Eeyore-ish sensibility. Or perhaps it is my dark humor that resonates with them. In any event, I'm not complaining. Unsolicited affection is a gift and, like all gifts, is best not questioned. It's a lesson Franklin learned early in life.

The education of "Dr." Franklin is on my mind as I walk the streets of old Boston one cold and rainy January day. I have a destination in mind. It's a short walk from my hotel, only five minutes, but along the way I bump into Ben twice. I pass Franklin Street (all fifty states have at least one) and then a sign featuring his portly visage, the same one that appears on the hundred-dollar bill. "Benjamin Meet Blockchain," it reads. The ad's implication: Franklin would approve of blockchain and crypto and other financial wizardry cooked up in a Wall Street skyscraper or Bahamian villa. I'm not so sure. Ben loved innovative technologies but only useful ones, and these "innovations," in my mind, don't make the grade.

I arrive at my destination: 17 Milk Street. It's a six-story brick building, not unlike the dozens of others nearby, but this building—or, to be more precise, this location—is special. I look up and there is Ben, sandwiched between a dental office and a marijuana dispensary called Cannabist. ("How do you want to feel today?" asks the sign in the window.) He's perched above the second-floor window, wondering how the hell he got up here and why the good people at Cannabist don't treat him to the occasional free sample.

The small bust, so discreet no one but me seems to notice it, marks where Franklin was born on January 17, 1706, less than a century after the death of Shakespeare and only thirteen years after the infamous Salem witch trials. Baby Ben arrived just in time to witness the dawn of a new era, the Age of Enlightenment. Old superstitions were dying out, replaced by a more rational and hopeful worldview. Franklin was born in the right time though not quite the right place, an oversight young Ben would correct. But not now, not yet. Boston was not done with Ben Franklin, nor was he done with Boston.

The actual house where Franklin was born is long gone. It burned to the ground in 1810, but thankfully a neighbor had sketched the house shortly before the fire. I retrieve a copy of the drawing from my backpack. I see a simple, two-story cottage with clapboards in front and large, rough shingles on the sides. Inside, space was at a premium, with only one room on the main floor and not many more upstairs. Two windows fronted the street while others faced a small yard and garden in the rear.

I look up from the drawing and gaze across twenty-first-century Milk Street. I see a coffee shop. It is cooler than I am, the kind of place where no one would ever, *ever*, use the word *cool* unless they were talking about the weather. Coffee shops were also plentiful in Franklin's time, though less artisanal. Next to the coffee shop is Sulgrave News, a small store that sells lottery tickets and high-octane energy drinks but no actual newspapers or magazines. Ben would no doubt mourn the slow-motion death of print. Printer's ink was in his blood.

Next to the newsstand that is not a newsstand is a church that is not a church. It is a sturdy green-steepled brick building sided with rows of white-framed arch windows. The Puritans didn't consider the physical building where people gathered to worship a church. The "church" was the congregation, the people. When they weren't congregating at these buildings—called meeting halls—they lent the space to others, presumably for weddings and bar mitzvahs.

Founded in 1669, the Old South un-church was a plucky upstart, a breakaway from the more established North un-church, that particular Puritan congregation apparently too puritanical for the likes of Josiah Franklin, Ben's father, and many other Bostonians. Old South was where Boston's intellectuals congregated. It may be just a building, in the Puritan mind, but what a building! Here one of the judges overseeing the Salem witch trials publicly apologized, accepting "the blame and shame of it." Here Phillis Wheatley, the first enslaved African American poet, worshipped. Here Samuel Adams and other members of the Sons of Liberty hatched the plot for the Boston Tea Party.

And here baby Ben Franklin was baptized. Reverend Samuel Willard performed the ceremony. He was a kind man, a friend of the Franklins. Sprinkling icy water on the newborn's head, the reverend recited the

Puritan blessing: "In the name of the Father, and of the Son, and of the Holy Ghost . . . a sign and seal of the covenant of grace." These words, among the first Franklin heard, were meant to consecrate the life of a devout Christian, a Puritan. Ben was Josiah Franklin's tenth son, and he intended to steer him "to the service of the church." Young Ben was to become a man of the cloth.

Today, the Old South Meeting Hall is a small museum. I step inside and take in the wooden rafters and neatly arranged pews. A display case contains a chart of the old seating assignments. I lean closer to read the tiny print. There it is: "Franklin." The seats weren't bad—not primo, but not nose-bleed territory either. Josiah Franklin was a simple tradesman, a maker of soap and candles. How could this "leather apron," as such manual workers were known, manage to score such good seats?

"He might have provided the church with candles," suggests Delaney, the friendly tour guide.

"A kind of barter?" I say.

"Exactly."

That is certainly possible. Bostonians loved to barter; they put the quo in quid pro quo. But there is another, more noble explanation. Josiah Franklin may have been a poor man, but he was rich in character and reputation. Townspeople came to the elder Franklin for advice and to mediate disputes. In Boston, unlike England, a candlemaker was respected for such traits and could play a role in political life. "Private virtue assured a public role," as one historian put it.

I walk a few blocks from the Old South Meeting Hall to the Granary Burying Ground. A light snow has begun to fall, coating the tombstones with a thin layer of white fluff. Cemeteries always look better in the snow. Many luminaries from the Revolutionary War era are buried here: Paul Revere, John Hancock, Samuel Adams. Their graves are marked with simple headstones. The same cannot be said of the towering, phallic obelisk in the center of the cemetery. In large letters, it reads: "FRANKLIN."

It's an oddly ostentatious memorial for Ben's parents, people who were, by all accounts, reserved and unassuming. Ben remembers his father as a wise and gentle man who exercised his authority judiciously. (He had considerably less to say about his mother, noting only that she was "a discreet and virtuous woman.") When young Ben and his friends were caught stealing stones from a construction site, Josiah Franklin didn't "correct" (read "whip") young Ben like the other fathers did to their sons, but instead taught him the memorable lesson "that nothing was useful which was not honest." Again that word: *useful*. Franklin's passion for it, I realize, was born not in his adopted town of Philadelphia but here in his birthplace.

I climb the few stone steps that lead to the obelisk platform and notice that, as often happens at Franklin pilgrimage sites, people have left pennies, and a few quarters, though no hundred-dollar bills. It's touching and understandable, I suppose, but misses the point of Ben Franklin's life and that of his parents, whose headstone lies before me now, the words written by their son Benjamin.

> *Josiah Franklin*
> *And Abiah his Wife*
> *Lie here interred.*
> *They lived lovingly together in Wedlock*
> *Fifty-five Years.*
> *Without an Estate or any gainful Employment,*
> *By constant labour and Industry,*
> *With God's Blessing,*
> *They maintained a large Family*
> *Comfortably;*

Ben then suggests his parents' lives were not only long but also useful, a model for those of little means.

> *From this Instance, Reader,*

> *Be encouraged to Diligence in thy Calling,*

> *And distrust not Providence.*

I get the diligence part. That was pure Franklin. It is through sustained and focused effort that we get ahead. But his admonition to "distrust not Providence" surprises me. He was not a man who bent to the whims of chance. "He that waits upon fortune, is never sure of a dinner," he once said. Was this nod to providence a gesture of respect for his pious father—or something more? There's no denying Ben's lucky breaks, including one that happened years before he was born.

When Josiah Franklin arrived in Boston in 1683, he was just another religious dissenter looking to start anew in John Winthrop's "city upon a hill." In England, Josiah was a successful dyer, but Boston had no textile industry and no need for Josiah's skill, so he pivoted and learned a new trade: tallow chandler. He was something of an alchemist, transforming animal fat into useful products such as soap and candles. His youngest son would go on to perform his own kind of alchemy, converting theories, scientific and political, into useful inventions and practices.

Ben's father was strong and athletic. Cultured, too. He could "draw prettily," Franklin recalls, and had a "a clear pleasing voice." He played the violin. A pious man, he often quoted scripture to his children, especially these words of Solomon's: "Seest thou a man diligent in his calling, he shall stand before kings." Josiah likely never imagined his youngest son would one day stand before four kings and dine with a fifth.

Josiah Franklin was a model of probity and restraint, traits Ben would inherit. Like his father, he could be friendly, warm even, but there was always part of him that remained separate and aloof. Was it protective, I wonder? Was he afraid of getting too close to people and getting hurt? It's a common defense mechanism, then and now. My own father had mastered it. If someone slighted him, or he imagined they had, he wrote them off promptly and in perpetuity. He did not have many friends. So determined was he to protect himself that he forfeited much intimacy, forgetting that even the most timid turtle pokes his head out of his shell now and then.

I have inherited my father's aversion to confrontation and avoid it whenever possible. It doesn't matter whether it is a large or small conflict; if anything, it is life's smaller tussles that unnerve me the most. A confrontation, a *perceived* confrontation, with an airline agent or a barista can send me into a prolonged funk. I'm not sure why, and years of therapy and a library of self-help books have shed little light on my affliction. I know my conflict avoid-ance comes at a cost, one I willingly pay. After all, who wants to get ensnared in a kerfuffle or, worse, a brouhaha? I worry, though, that I might end up like my father: safe but friendless.

Franklin also dreaded direct confrontation, but that is where we part ways. I deploy the covert hostility of the passive-aggressive, quietly seething and hoping my adversary discerns the source of my silent anger. It's a feck-less tactic. Friction unacknowledged is friction unresolved. Franklin took a different approach.

At a young age, he realized that being "saucy and provoking," as he put it, wasn't getting him anywhere, so he softened his language and adopted a strategy of "modest diffidence." He jettisoned definitive words, such as *cer-tainly* and *undoubtedly* and instead deployed softer phrases, like "*I conceive, I apprehend,* or *I imagine* a thing to be so or so." This way, he made his point without alienating his interlocutor. Maybe this soft language could work for me too and help me overcome my conflict-aversion. *It appears to me* it just might, Ben.

Franklin's Boston, population eight thousand, was more town than city, a co-lonial outpost perched on the edge of the British Empire. Distance, though, is a blessing as well as curse. Some of the era's greatest advances in science and governance were made not in London but in faraway America. David Bushnell's submarine, dubbed "the *Turtle.*" Eli Whitney's cotton gin. Ad-vances made not despite the distance from the mothership but because of it. Distance is liberating, as any teenager taking their first parent-free trip will tell you.

Boston was a town of brightly painted houses packed into a narrow pen-insula, exposed to wilderness and sea. Life was hard. Open sewers ran down the middle of the streets. During the long winters, firewood and fresh water were scarce. Epidemics, such as smallpox, surfaced with alarming regularity. One in four newborns died within a few days.

Assuming you survived infancy, the hazards didn't stop there. Every few weeks, the local newspaper reported raids by Native Americans. There was rampant piracy, and frequent public hangings of captured pirates. Most Britons thought of Boston as a feral and dangerous place, if they thought of it at all. In the calculus of British imperialism, Boston was a rounding error.

Yet it was remarkably well educated. The literacy rate was 98 percent among men and 62 percent for women. And Boston, while small, was still larger than New York and Philadelphia. The archetype of the snooty "Boston Brahmin" was already taking shape, and that shape looked and sounded a lot like John Adams. Writing in his diary shortly after visiting Philadelphia for the first time, Adams lays on the Boston exceptionalism thick: "The morals of our people are much better, their manners are more polite, and agreeable . . . our language is better, our persons are handsomer, our spirit is greater, our laws are wiser, our religion is superior, our education is better. We exceed them in every thing."

Adams was right about at least one thing: Boston was no ordinary town. Like the Blues Brothers, it was on a mission from God. Founded by the Puritans in 1630, it was a biblical commonwealth, where God and country were intertwined. On the streets, you'd hear, along with chitchat about the weather and town gossip, this common question: "Are you saved?" Bostonians observed the Sabbath with uncommon rigor. The only recognized church was Puritan New England Congregationalism. The Massachusetts authorities persecuted Quakers and other sects. Early eighteenth-century Boston was not quite a theocracy, but it came close.

Despite the religious zealotry, Boston society was fluid, at least when it came to your choice of profession. As long as you didn't offend the governing clergy, you could do more or less as you pleased. Bostonians started businesses. They published books. And a surprising number chose to join the Native Americans, abandoning the town altogether for a more bucolic life.

The beauty of this time and place is you didn't have to choose one profession. This was the age of the hyphenated career. Boston was populated by physician-farmers, lawyer-poets, preacher-scientists, and printer-journalists. Such hybrid lives were possible in a way they are not today.

One reason people could master more than one trade is that there was less to master. The eighteenth century was perhaps the last time in human history when it was possible for one person to know everything that had come before. Specialized knowledge has its benefits, of course, but it has drawbacks too, and I for one mourn the passing of the hyphenated career. I wouldn't mind being a barber-physicist or maybe a deejay-doctor. I think that's why I decided to become a journalist. The profession enabled me to try on different personas. By shadowing an airline pilot for a day, I was an airline pilot for a day, and similarly with firefighters and Wall Street traders.

Boston, a city of merchants and tradesmen, imported much from England, including dangerous ideas such as those of John Locke, the ideological godfather of the American Revolution. Franklin's Boston wasn't yet the defiant hotbed of Samuel Adams and his fellow Sons of Liberty, but the roots of rebellion were already visible. Bostonians regularly ignored Parliament's Acts of Trade and Navigation, which naturally favored Great Britain.

Boston may have been a Puritan city, but that doesn't mean it was joyless. People knew how to have fun (provided it wasn't Sunday, of course). "[Bostonians] dressed as elegantly as their budgets allowed, in spite of their pastors' objections," write historians Claude-Anne Lopez and Eugenia Herbert, noting that people also "drank heartily: homemade cider for the poor, rum for the better off; imported wine for the wealthy." Near the Franklin house was the city's best-known tavern, the Green Dragon, and, around the corner, a house of prostitution run by a woman known as "the Little Prude of Pleasure," which is, I think, the perfect name for a Puritan madam.

It was the fluid nature of colonial Boston that enabled young Ben to mold his identity into new and unusual shapes. From a young age, he refused to accept the choices offered him. He ordered off-menu. More than that, he created an entirely new menu, one for future generations to peruse. None of this would have been possible had his father not taken a huge risk and sailed for parts unknown.

I'm beginning to appreciate the compactness, the human scale of old Boston. Nothing is more than ten minutes away by foot, and it's only a short walk from the Granary Burying Ground to School Street. Here I find another version of Ben Franklin, this time in bronze. He is cradling a hat in one arm, a walking stick in the other, and looking more regal than he actually was. Franklin's gaze is directed slightly downward toward . . . something. Following his line of sight, I spot a colorful sidewalk mosaic. Installed in 1983, it's worn by forty years of passing shoes but is still bright and legible.

Rendered in the style of a hopscotch game, it depicts children doing childlike activities: flying kites, jumping rope, playing marbles, turning cartwheels, swinging from trees, drawing. The mosaic marks the original location of the Boston Latin School. Founded in 1635, it is the oldest public school in America. Young Ben was a student here. For a while.

I'm looking at the school motto, in Latin naturally: *Labor Omnia Vincit. Omnibus opportunitas.* "Work Conquers All—Opportunity for All." It's a sentiment Franklin, even at age eight, shared. Hard work was his passport to a better life.

Franklin was a good student, rising to the top of his class and even moving up a grade. It was, by all accounts, a happy time for Ben. The schoolhouse was light and airy, and when the windows were opened on warm spring days, the students could hear the sounds of the nearby waterfront humming with activity. Boston Latin offered the best secondary education in the colonies.

The curriculum was ambitious, but Ben mastered it easily. Soon he was performing scholarly feats like translating Aesop's fables into Latin. Most of the students, from backgrounds more privileged than Ben's, were destined for Harvard and then, most likely, a career in the clergy.

But after only a year, Ben's father withdrew his son from the prestigious Latin School and enrolled him in a markedly less prestigious school where the subjects taught included dancing, embroidery, violin, flute, and "English and French quilting." A year later, Josiah Franklin pulled Ben out of that school too, thus marking the end of Benjamin Franklin's formal education. He was ten years old.

That must have stung. In a way, getting a taste of school was worse than none at all. The prospect of a learned life had been dangled in front of Ben, then yanked away. Why did Josiah Franklin deny his youngest son an education?

The conventional explanation, one posited by Franklin himself, is that his father couldn't afford it. That theory doesn't hold up, though. There was no tuition at the Latin School, and other expenses (a few shillings for firewood) were minimal. His father could have afforded to keep Ben in school. It was not the money but the faith—specifically, Ben's lack of it—that was the problem.

From a young age, Franklin was a skeptic. "I began to doubt of Revelation itself," he recalled. He was also prone to poking some good-natured fun at religious traditions. One day, when his father was saying grace yet again over a meal, Ben offered a helpful suggestion: "I think, father, if you said *grace* over the whole cask—once for all—it would be a vast *saving of time.*" Josiah Franklin knew the ministry would never accept a smart-ass skeptic like Ben into their fold. Providing him an education, so tied to the clergy, seemed pointless.

Franklin's aborted education—far scantier than that of most other founders—explains a lot. It explains the sizable chip on his shoulder, every bit as burdensome as mine. It explains why he decried the excessive use of Latin and ancient Greek, "the quackery of literature," in school curricula. It explains his allergy to even a whiff of snobbery. Most of all, it explains his nimble and resourceful mind. Josiah Franklin's decision to pull young Ben out of school was, in hindsight, the best thing that ever happened to him. *Distrust not providence.*

Life is best understood backward but must be lived forward, observed the Danish philosopher Søren Kierkegaard. Maybe we would trust providence more if we could watch our lives in reverse, like a home movie played backward. Maybe providence is always working in our favor, but we're too close to appreciate it. Only time provides the distance needed to admire its handiwork.

THREE

BOOKISH BEN

Young Ben's schooling may have ended at age ten, but his education had only begun. The venue merely shifted from the classroom to his father's small library or his brother's print shop or under a tree by Mill Pond or in bed late at night when everyone else was asleep. The curriculum was international. Faculty included Daniel Defoe, John Locke, Plutarch, Xenophon, Pliny the Elder, and the Third Earl of Shaftesbury. The subjects were as rich and varied as those offered at any school, from mathematics and philosophy to the classics and French literature.

Franklin had the good fortune of being born into a bookish community. There was a library in Boston even before there was a Boston. In 1629, a year before the launch of the *Arabella*, the ship that carried the first Puritans from England to Salem, the fledgling Massachusetts Bay Company acquired a collection of some fifty volumes. They were mostly theological works, of course, but there were also grammar books and, for reasons unclear, an odd little volume called *The French Country Farm*. It is testament to the Puritans' love of reading that on a ship with hardly a spare inch of cargo space, they made room for books. Once on dry land, Puritan leaders like Cotton Mather urged residents to use their free time wisely. "Be *not fools*, but *redeem* this time to your own advantage. . . . Give *thyself* unto reading." Say what you like about the Puritans, they loved their books.

So did Ben Franklin. His long and useful life was intimately intertwined with books. He read them, wrote them, bought and sold them, borrowed and lent them, edited them, printed them, gifted them, collected them, loved them. In Philadelphia, at age twenty-five, he founded the first lending library in America. He read there for at least an hour or two each day, "and thus repair'd in some degree the loss of the learned education my father once intended for me." By the time of his death in 1790, he had amassed a collection of 4,276 volumes, among the largest private libraries in the young United States.

It's difficult to overestimate the importance of print at the time. Other than the spoken word, the printed page was the only medium for conveying information and writing the only form of communication. If you wanted to learn something, you either had to hear about it or read about it. You were what you read, and no one knew this better than Benjamin Franklin.

Years later, dining with friends in Paris, one of Franklin's dinner companions, the Abbé de Raynal, asked those gathered a deceptively simple question: "What description of men most deserves pity?" One by one, they answered. When Franklin's turn came, he replied, "A lonesome man [on] a rainy day, who does not know how to read."

Books had—and still have—a magical quality. They are time machines, enabling us to leap across centuries. In Franklin's time, they provided a means, the only means, really, for an ordinary tradesman, one of the "middling sort," to gain entry to the upper echelons of society.

If it is possible for books to save a life, they saved Ben Franklin's. They enabled young Ben, adrift in Puritan Boston, to connect with a larger world bursting with possibility. Franklin loved reading for the same reason he loved any activity: it was pleasurable *and* useful, and in more or less equal measure.

Franklin always had a "bookish inclination," as he put it. He couldn't remember a time when he could *not* read. He read the Bible at age five. Soon he was spending the little money he had on books. He became a vegetarian in part so he could save money to buy books.

He read anything and everything he could get his hands on. He started with his father's collection of "polemic divinity," but soon discovered he also owned a copy of Daniel Defoe's *An Essay upon Projects*. The 1697 book, Defoe's first, proposes clever and farsighted schemes for improving people's lives: a network of local banks, a college for children of the working class, a pension fund for widows. In his preface, Defoe seems to be speaking to young Ben: "Books are useful only to such whose genius are suitable to the subject of them; and to dedicate a book of projects to a person who had never concerned himself to think that way would be like music to one that has no ear." When it came to useful projects, Franklin had a virtuoso's ear.

Later, working at his brother's print shop and newspaper, Ben had access to what must have felt like the library of Alexandria: Pliny's *Natural History*, Aristotle's *Politicks*, George Sandys's *Travels*, Shakespeare's complete works as well as St. Augustine's, Jonathan Swift's *A Tale of a Tub*, Giovanni Marana's *Letters Writ by a Turkish Spy*, and Thomas Tryon's *The Way to Health* (the inspiration for Ben's vegetarianism).

The first book young Ben purchased was John Bunyan's hugely popular *The Pilgrim's Progress*. I see why the story appealed to young Ben. The protagonist, Christian, is an everyman who thirsts for a larger life, one free of the "slough of despond," and courageously journeys to find it.

More than the story, it was Bunyan's writing style that grabbed Franklin: animated and conversational, lean. "Honest John," as Franklin called Bunyan, was the first author he'd read who mixed narration and dialogue, engaging the reader "who in the most interesting parts finds himself as it were brought into the company and present at the discourse."

Franklin cherished his copy of *The Pilgrim's Progress* but was willing to part with it to afford other books. His library, like his life, was fluid, adapting to circumstances, always seeking the most expeditious course, the most useful path. Once he had juiced the usefulness from a book, he'd sell it or gift it to someone he thought might benefit.

Franklin soon traded Bunyan's fictional pilgrim for tales of actual adventurers. These came in the form of chapbooks, compact and inexpensive volumes sold by wandering peddlers who traveled up and down the Eastern

Seaboard. Written in a lively, accessible tone, chapbooks recounted tales of derring-do or shed light on what today we call "secret histories." They had snappy, enticing titles like *Unfortunate Court Favourites of England* and *Female Excellency, or The Ladies' Glory: Worthy Lives and Memorable Actions of Nine Famous Women* and *The Surprising Miracles of Nature and Art*.

Young Ben was looking for role models, and he found them in the chapbooks—up to a point. They proved too lightweight for him. He craved meatier fare, and you don't get any meatier than *Plutarch's Lives*. Written in the second century AD, the book traces the lives of notable Greeks and Romans. No ordinary history, it is less concerned with events than with lessons gleaned from these extraordinary lives. Plutarch's aim, he said, was to make "the virtues of these great men serving me as a sort of looking-glass, in which I may see how to adjust and adorn my own life."

I see why young Ben was drawn to the book. It portrays these men as models not only of heroism but of usefulness. They possessed traits anybody, even a "leather apron," or working-class person, could emulate. Pericles of Athens, for instance, is described as a nimble leader, able to "change and shift with the greatest ease to what he himself shall judge desirable." It is a lesson Franklin imbibed.

For Franklin, there was something furtive, almost subversive, about reading. Snuggled under the blankets late at night or at his brother's print shop on a Sunday morning when everyone else was at church, he felt like a spy—or a rebel. Working in cahoots with bookshop apprentices, he surreptitiously borrowed books, taking great care to return them unmolested, as if they hadn't been borrowed at all. For Franklin, reading was a conspiracy between author and reader, and he didn't need anyone's permission to take part.

Ben didn't merely read books. He conversed with them. This conversation often unfolded in the margins, the place where reader and author meet. Franklin was an enthusiastic underliner, notetaker, and denizen of the margins. He read widely and wisely. He chose books plump with wisdom but also brought his own sagacity to the encounter. He read skeptically but with an open mind. A possibilian from a young age, he possessed the one personality trait most closely associated with creative genius: openness to experience. And for Franklin, reading was just that: an experience.

Franklin loved books and he loved the people who loved them. Describing his earliest friends, he says little about their occupations and instead simply notes that they were "all lovers of reading." Books also opened doors for Franklin. The royal governor of New York met with young Ben simply because he heard he had an impressive collection of books.

Ben was generous with his books, lending them to friends who seldom returned them. Writing to his British friend Jonathan Shipley, he apologizes for not sending a certain book sooner, but it had gone missing. "I suppose I have lent it, and do not yet recollect to whom." This happened often. He once ran an ad in his own newspaper, the *Pennsylvania Gazette*, asking the person—whoever that might be—who had borrowed a book from him to please return it. Generosity comes at a price, one Ben Franklin happily paid.

Franklin was well read but rarely called attention to his erudition. He was no name-dropper. This was due in part to his anti-elitism, but I think there is another reason too. Support is most effective when it is invisible—the unseen beam reinforcing a building, the barely perceptible pause between notes, the deep yet invisible ocean of research that buoys an argument. True erudition doesn't call attention to itself—or, as Franklin said, "He's a fool that cannot conceal his wisdom."

After a short walk through Boston's Copley Square neighborhood, I arrive at my destination, a place that loves books as much as Franklin did. With its domed ceiling and religious iconography, the Boston Public Library feels less like a repository for books and more like a cathedral where you go to worship them. Our Lady of the Printed Word. I take the glass elevator to the third floor and the sanctum sanctorum: the Special Collections Department.

You don't simply walk into the room. There are procedures to follow, rituals to perform. Only a few items are permitted inside: laptop, cell phone, reading glasses. No pens or notebooks or, heaven forbid, coffee. Before entering, I'm told to wash my hands, which I do with uncommon rigor. I feel like a doctor scrubbing before surgery.

I am buzzed into the clean room where a librarian directs me to my assigned seat, then gently places the book I've requested into a foam cradle. I am to turn the pages slowly, she explains, and hold them open not with my hands, scrubbed though they may be, but with string weights. These are exactly what they sound like: weighted strands less likely to damage a page than human hands, especially my beefy ones.

I feel eyes on me. Librarian eyes. I'm afraid to touch the book, worried I'll make a mistake, fumble the weighted string maybe, and this precious volume that has survived more than three centuries will crumble in my hands and I will be banished, excommunicated, from the Special Collections Department for the rest of my days.

So for a long while I just look at the book. Brown and leather-bound, it is more compact than I expected. This is silly. It is just a book. I gently lift it. It is lighter than I expected. Slowly, using the weighted strings as instructed, I turn the pages. They feel sturdy and rough in my hands, with a satisfying heft. I turn to the title page. Set in a flowery typeface, it's a real doozy: *Bonifacius: An essay upon the good, that is to be devised and designed, by those who desire to answer the great end of life, and to do good while they live.* Today it's known simply as *Essays to Do Good.*

Franklin owned a copy, published in the same year as the one I'm holding: 1710. Franklin's copy was secondhand and missing a few pages, but it moved him. Years later, he recalled how the book "gave me a turn of thinking that had an influence on some of the principal future events of my life." The author, the Reverend Cotton Mather, was not an obvious source of inspiration for Ben.

Mather was pure Puritan. He was involved, albeit indirectly, with the notorious Salem witch trials. He believed in demonic possession and exhorted his fellow citizens not to indulge in stage plays or games of chance. Yet he was no narrow-minded Puritan—not by a long shot. He wrote 450 books; was inducted into the Royal Society, the most prestigious scientific body of its day; and could write in seven languages. His library held some three thousand volumes and occupied the largest room in his large house on Boston's Hanover Street. The collection included the expected theological works, but also books on geography, medicine, physics, astronomy, botany, political and military history, the classics (in Greek and Latin), as well as works on practical subjects like navigation and commerce. Mather was constantly expanding his library, begging and borrowing books shamelessly, just like Franklin.

Mather was especially well versed in the field of medicine and more knowledgeable than many of Boston's physicians. He had a good bedside manner and was among the first to identify the link between emotions and illness. "*Tranquility of mind* will do wonderful things towards the relief of bodily maladies," he wrote, advising doctors to converse with their patients to determine the source of their anxiety and find ways to relieve it. And when a smallpox epidemic descended on Boston in 1721, it was Cotton Mather, not the town's medical establishment, who advocated for a new, and controversial, method of inoculation.

I never thought of the Puritans as great scientific thinkers, but many were. "No religion has ever been less hostile to science than Puritanism," says historian Arthur Tourtellot. Of the nine colonial Americans elected to the Royal Society in the early eighteenth century, eight were Puritans. True, these preacher-scientists had very specific reasons for exploring and explaining the natural world—to appreciate God's works and thus glorify him—but there is no denying their scientific and philosophical chops. At the time, reason and faith had not yet parted ways.

I open Mather's three-hundred-year-old book with the same care my wife deploys in her daily contact lens ritual ("performing microsurgery," I call it). I find the book surprisingly upbeat, and not only for a Puritan. Right up front, Cotton Mather makes his case. The world is a mess and in desperate need of people who do good—a statement that, sadly, applies equally today. Anticipating the 1960s, Mather says, in so many words, you are either part of the solution or part of the problem. "He is unworthy to be considered as a man, who is not for doing good among men."

Mather portrays good deeds not as a burden but a privilege. "It is an invaluable *honor* to do *good*; it is an incomparable *pleasure.*" Mather, a man who never met an italic he didn't like, succinctly connects good deeds and godliness. "A *workless faith* is a *worthless faith.*"

Doing good can be daunting, he concedes. Where to begin? Why not start with improving the lives of those closest to you: your family. As he writes in an unintentional pun: "One way to prove ourselves *really good,* is to be *relatively good.*"

I can imagine young Ben reading Mather by candlelight and getting fired up. Surely this sentence resonated: "Perhaps thou art one who makes but a *little figure* in the world, a *brother of low degree.*" And I can see young Ben, the son of a soap maker, nodding. *Why yes, I am, Cotton. Tell me more.* I can practically hear Mather's thundering voice: "Behold, a vast encouragement! . . . It is possible the *wisdom of a poor man* may start a proposal that may *save a city,* serve a nation!"

A good book—and Mather's is a good book—always stirred Ben Franklin's fertile mind, no matter the author's background or peccadillos. Ben cared more about what a book had to say than who wrote it. Sadly, this is not our way today. We read the author, not the book. Rather than interrogating a new and possibly life-changing idea, we interrogate the source instead and, more often than not, accept or reject it on that basis alone. In doing so, we forfeit much wisdom.

Whatever lingering animosity Franklin may have had toward Cotton Mather evaporated and, if anything, his fondness for the Puritan preacher grew with time. Years later, he fondly recalled one visit in particular to Mather's North Boston home. On his way out, Franklin navigated a narrow staircase with a low ceiling. "Stoop!" Mather called to him. Ben, not reacting quickly enough, bonked his head on a beam. Mather, making a bigger point, added, "Let this be a caution to you not always to hold your head so high; stoop, young man, stoop—as you go through the world—and you'll miss many hard thumps." Franklin needed to check his pride, lest he get conked on the head. Stoop so you can rise. It is advice he followed, or tried to at least.

Years later, when Cotton Mather was long dead, Franklin wrote to the reverend's son, Samuel, about the influence his father's book had on him. "I have always set a greater value on the character of a *doer of good*, than on any other kind of reputation; and [if] I have been . . . a useful citizen, the public owes the advantage of it to that book."

I sense a shadow, a hovering presence. I look up and see the librarian. She is smiling, but she is not happy. She reprimands me, politely, quietly, for a biblio-transgression, something about improper page turning and failure to use the foam cradle correctly. I apologize, then decide not to push my luck. Better to leave the sanctum sanctorum voluntarily before I am evicted. I return *Essays to Do Good* to the librarian and wish it another three hundred years of health and intactness.

I ride the glass elevator to the lobby, exit onto Boylston Street and, looking up at the bright and hopeful sky, head east, toward the water.

FOUR

EMPIRICAL BEN

A plane departing Logan International roars overhead, and I'm reminded how Franklin regretted being born too soon: "It is impossible to imagine the height to which may be carried in a thousand years the power of man over matter. We may perhaps learn to deprive large masses of their gravity & give them absolute levity, for the sake of easy transport."

Nailed that one, Ben. I, on the other hand, regret being born too late. The future is a phantom, a mirage, tantalizingly close but always just out of reach, like those fifteen pounds I need to lose. No, when I'm able to purchase my portable solar-powered time machine on Amazon—*order within the next three hours and receive it yesterday!*—it is the past, not the future where I'll be heading. I yearn for a time when there were still uncharted lands to explore, genuine adventures to be had, a time before Google Maps and packaged tours and selfies.

The part of me drawn to the past is the same part drawn to travel. Both are illuminating, clarifying experiences. Spending a single day in a foreign land reveals more about the place than reading a dozen books. Sadly, we can never truly know distant times. We forever remain outsiders, pressing our noses against the windows of the past. "The past is a foreign country," said British writer Leslie Hartley. "They do things differently there."

The uneasy relationship between past and present is on my mind as I snake my way to Boston's waterfront, passing statues of Paul Revere and other Revolutionary heroes who populate the city's Freedom Trail. To my left stands a phalanx of red brick condominiums and, to my right, a small flotilla of fiberglass-hulled sailboats. Straight ahead lie the frigid waters of Massachusetts Bay. Reaching into the time traveler's bag of tricks, I squint and try to erase the condominiums and sailboats, imagining the bay as it looked during Franklin's time.

The year is 1718. Boston is a water world. Life revolved around the sea and bay, as well as the many rivers and estuaries, ponds and lakes. The town had an excellent harbor, the largest in British North America. On any given day, a ship might arrive from some distant port of call: Brazil, Madeira, Barbados, Madagascar, and, of course, England. Loitering at the harbor, young Ben no doubt heard tales of nautical adventures. It must have been heady stuff for a boy who had never roamed more than a few miles from home. No wonder he yearned to "break away and get to sea." But his father soon nixed the idea. Josiah Jr., one of Franklin's many brothers, had become a sailor and was never heard from again. Josiah Sr. was not about to lose another son to the sea.

So Ben contented himself with exploring amphibious Boston. He was fond of Mill Pond, a salt marsh on the edge of the broad mouth of the Charles River. (Sadly, it is long gone, now the site of TD Garden, the arena where the Boston Celtics and Bruins play.) He spent a lot of time there, just like the other boys. But unlike these boys—and most other Bostonians, for that matter—Ben didn't merely row on the water or fish in it. He dove in and swam.

He'd swim for hours at a time. He'd swim on and under the water and perform aquatic tricks that delighted onlookers. His upper-body strength was impressive. Modern bathing suits did not yet exist, so Franklin, like all boys and men of the day, swam naked. Women did not swim, at least not in public.

During the Classical Age, the ability to swim was considered a mark of education and common sense. The Romans had an expression: a good-for-nothing was someone who had not learned to read or swim. Swimming then fell out of favor for many centuries. During Ben's time, few people, not even sailors, could swim. Colonial newspapers carried reports of regular drownings. There was, I think, another reason Franklin enjoyed swimming. It was a mildly subversive activity, prohibited on the Sabbath and seen as almost preternatural. The test for witches was whether they floated or sank. Mortals sank. Witches floated.

Franklin's aquatic childhood didn't just happen, of course. He had to learn how to swim, and there were no schools for that. He turned to a book, an odd little volume called *The Art of Swimming Illustrated by Proper Figures with Advice for Bathing*. It's not exactly a bestseller these days, but I managed to get ahold of a copy, a reprint of the 1696 original.

On page 1, the author, a Frenchman named Melchisédech Thévenot, explains the book is intended for sailors and others who earn their living on the water but also those who want to swim for pleasure. What grabs my attention are not the words but the woodcut illustrations. They depict naked men striking various awkward poses and above the water. A few look as though they might have something to do with swimming, but I can't be sure. How, I wonder, did Franklin learn to swim by reading this book?

He didn't. Ben knew when to read—and when to stop reading. He loved books but recognized their limitations. Book knowledge, valuable as it is, is imperfect. It is always, by definition, secondhand. By recognizing this, Franklin avoided the trap that befalls many book people. We confuse books with humans and, given a choice, would rather spend time with a book. It's understandable. Unlike people, books don't bully you or shame you. A book can't break your heart. Ensconced between the covers, nobody can hurt you.

I wonder, if it wasn't a book that taught Franklin to swim, what was it? I decide to return to the sidewalk mosaic commemorating the Latin School. I have a nagging feeling I missed something. I look closely and, sure enough, there it is: a quote from the school's most famous dropout: "Experience keeps a dear school, but fools will learn in no other."

Experience. The word, the concept, mattered a lot to Franklin. It mattered as much, or more, than another word: *experiment.* No, that's not quite right. In Franklin's mind, the two words were nearly identical. So, too, in the dictionary. In most languages derived from Latin, the words *experience* and *experiment* are the same. Both entail, Merriam-Webster informs me, the "testing of possibilities." But a diehard possibilian like Benjamin Franklin didn't need a dictionary to tell him that.

Franklin was an empiricist. He believed all knowledge is acquired, not innate. We are born with hardware only, no preinstalled software. We obtain knowledge via our senses. The French philosopher René Descartes famously wrote, *cogito ergo sum*, "I think therefore I am." Franklin and his fellow empiricists didn't buy this. "I sense therefore I am" was their unofficial motto. What does this approach to life look like in action? Franklin liked to answer a question with a story, so I will too.

One of Franklin's more ingenious experiments involved water and oil. He discovered you can calm turbulent waters by adding a small amount of oil. One day at a pond, he met a skeptic. How was such a thing possible? Franklin then demonstrated the "trick," and with a showman's flamboyance. The man was stunned.

"But what, sir," he stammered, "should I derive from all this?"

"*Nothing*," replied Franklin, "but what you see."

Empiricism in a nutshell. For Franklin, experience wasn't flimsy or trivial. It was another form of knowledge. Books can take you only so far. Not so with experience. You can question a book's validity but not that of an experience. You can argue with a book. You can't argue with an experience.

Consider happiness. How do researchers studying the emotion determine if someone is happy? They don't deploy brain scans or any other technology. Instead, they ask people, "How happy are you these days, on a scale of one to ten?"

Many people find this approach suspect. Aren't such self-reports subjective? Absolutely, but that doesn't render them any less valid. Only the person *experiencing* happiness or sadness, or any other emotional state, is qualified to assess the intensity of these states. The term "subjective data" is not an oxymoron. A doctor, a good one at least, won't dismiss a patient's pain even if the MRI shows nothing amiss. We are all experts of ourselves, the author of our own book. It is a tale told one experience at a time, legible only to us.

I need to remind myself of this truth constantly. A case in point: my troubled relationship with my smartwatch. At first, we got along swimmingly. It could do everything: track my steps, calories, and sleep. It monitored my stress levels, my blood oxygen saturation, and my "body battery," how much juice remained in my tank. It even told time.

But our relationship soon soured. It started with sleep tracking. Every morning, I'd wake to a sleep score that was alarmingly low. "You slept poorly last night," my watch scolded. I felt like a failure before I brushed my teeth, a completed task my smug watch failed to acknowledge. Scrolling down, I learned of the dire consequences of my below-par sleep: "Your body did not recover very well," my watch chided. "You will likely feel tired today."

My watch was right. I did feel tired that day, but was it because I was truly tired or because my scheming watch had planted the idea in my mind?

"I slept terribly last night," I'd tell my wife morning after morning. She was mildly sympathetic, but one day she snapped.

"How do you know you slept terribly?"

"My watch told me."

She shot me *that look*, delivering an unspoken message: Are you going to trust a piece of technology strapped to your wrist or your own body?

She was right. I had outsourced my sense of well-being to an alien device. Who is to say whether my sleep was restorative or not? If I *feel* that I had a restful night's sleep, isn't that what matters? Franklin would answer yes. My experiential data are every bit as valid as my smartwatch's data—more valid in fact.

Still, like a lover who can't bear to say goodbye, I couldn't part with my smartwatch. I craved its calorie counts and vibrating alarms. I craved its outside validation, even if it made me feel worse about myself. I'd wear it for a week, then stash it in a desk drawer the following week. And so it went for several months, until one day I discovered the hybrid watch: the mechanical hands of an analog watch combined with some of the tracking of a smart one. Like all hybrids, it is an imperfect compromise but I, an imperfect man, can live with that.

Young Ben trusted his taut and muscular gut. Waist-deep in the Mill Pond, naked and smartwatch-less, he experienced and experimented. Using Thévenot's book as a guide, he mastered the simple strokes, then invented a few of his own, "aiming at the graceful and easy, as well as the useful." I love that. It neatly sums up Franklin's philosophy of life. Any activity worth doing must meet those two criteria: grace and utility. It is a rare combination, but when the graceful and the useful do merge, it is something to behold. Roger Federer's backhand comes to mind. Not only is it powerful and graceful; it is powerful *because* it is graceful.

Can I swim? If managing not to drown qualifies as swimming then, yes, I can swim. My preferred stroke? The doggie paddle. It's not the exertion part of swimming that trips me up but the water part. The truth is I don't like water, never have. I wonder what this hydro-aversion says about me. Nothing good, I fear. The math is troubling. We humans are 60 percent water, so if I dislike water, does that mean I like only 40 percent of myself?

When I recall my early swimming lessons in suburban Baltimore, I get a queasy feeling. I remember only two details: the acrid hospital smell of chlorine, which to this day makes my heart race, and a particularly dreadful exercise called the "survival float." The instructor told us to float on our stomachs, face down, with our arms outstretched above our heads. We were to raise our heads for oxygen as little as possible. No wonder I despise the water. How you learn to do something determines not only whether you master it but whether you enjoy it.

Young Ben, free from such draconian instruction, toyed with various ways of propelling his muscular body through the water more efficiently. Humans are well designed for swimming, with two exceptions: the palms of our hands and soles of our feet are too small, limiting our ability to generate power. Young Ben set about to remedy these hindrances. He constructed two oval boards that resembled painter's palettes and added a hole for the thumb so he could affix them securely. "I pushed the edges of these forward, and I struck the water with their flat surfaces as I drew them back," he recalled.

It worked. He swam faster! He was less successful when he fitted his feet with "a kind of sandals," an early version of flippers. Franklin had the right idea but unfortunately was ahead of his time. Flexible rubber had not yet been invented.

Then there was his most daring aquatic experiment. One day, he wondered what would happen if he married his love of swimming with his love of kites. He waded into a local pond and launched the kite, while holding tight and lying on his back. "I was drawn along the surface of the water in a very agreeable manner," he recalled. He had just invented an early form of windsurfing (or wind-swimming). He did not accomplish this by reading a book but by trial and error, by regularly attending the school of experience.

By inventing these new forms of water propulsion he had also invented *new experiences*, and it is these, not any newfangled device, that are the true product of all ingenuity. The greatest invention to emerge from the eighteenth century was not Thomas Newcomen's steam engine or Eli Whitney's cotton gin but an idea: happiness. Not in some nebulous afterlife, but happiness here and now. It is an idea that Franklin had much to say about.

FIVE

MASKED BEN

I decamp from the waterfront and head west. I jog north onto Hanover Street, then turn onto a narrow lane where, in the shadow of the North Church, Cotton Mather's parish, I find what I'm looking for: a colonial-era print shop called Edes & Gill.

The print shop is closed. I am disappointed. No one likes disappointment, of course, but it hits me especially hard. It's as if I'm missing the gauge other people have, the one that distinguishes minor setbacks from major calamities. An audit from the IRS or a parking ticket. A concussion or a paper cut. It's all the same to me—all equally disappointing. I don't know why. I hope you can help, Ben. You were, after all, the "perfect model of sanity." How did you do it? How did you prevent those minor disappointments, and God knows you had plenty, from ballooning? How did you avoid sinking into John Bunyan's slough of despond, that bottomless bog of melancholy?

I press my nose against the shop window and peer inside. I see a large wooden contraption, the printing press, and the metal balls used to spread ink evenly and the composition stick to arrange the metal type. Printing was intricate, grueling work. A single page in a newspaper might take twenty-five hours to produce. It was a noble vocation, though. The printing press was a powerful, almost mystical force, converting perishable spoken words into something that endures. No ordinary machine, it was the engine that powered the Enlightenment.

I can picture young Ben, eleven years old, his little nose pressed against a window like this one. At the time, he was working at his father's soap and candle shop and hating every minute. It was difficult, dirty work, with none of the intellectual stimulation he craved. In the little spare time he had, he read and swam and loitered at Boston's handful of print shops. I can see the appeal. Now here was real work, at once physical and intellectual—useful, too, in a way soap and candles were not.

Fortunately for young Ben—*distrust not providence*—his brother James, nine years his senior, ran a print shop. It was a competitive business, but James, like most of the other Franklins, was talented and determined. Ben's father sensed his youngest son's fascination with printing and his bookish inclination and persuaded James to take on Ben as an apprentice.

The apprentice system was serious business. Apprentice and mentor entered a legally binding agreement, with a commitment of about seven years. The apprentice worked, without pay, side by side with his mentor and even lived in his house. The apprentice was indentured, financially beholden, to the master craftsman. Leaving before you had completed your term of apprenticeship was a crime, punishable by imprisonment.

The arrangement worked for both parties, provided apprentice and mentor got along. James and Ben Franklin did not get along. They argued frequently. Yet it was in this tense and cramped print shop on Boston's Queen Street where young Ben taught himself to write.

He had access not only to a generous collection of books but also periodicals such as Addison and Steele's *Spectator*, a spicy London journal. Ben developed a unique way of teaching himself. After reading an essay, he'd jumble passages, then attempt to reconstruct them. He was learning by imitation, but with a twist: he mimicked the writer's technique then added his own flourishes. "There is much difference between imitating a good man, and counterfeiting him," he'd later say. The imitator honors the good man. The counterfeiter defames him.

This is how I learned to write too, though I was older than Ben. I read writers I admired: Jan Morris, Pico Iyer, Italo Calvino, John Steinbeck, Paul Theroux. I constructed sentences like theirs. At first, too much like theirs. I was counterfeiting. Eventually the sentences I crafted were like theirs yet not theirs. They were mine. I was imitating.

My first public piece of writing appeared in the newsletter of the local Red Cross chapter of Madison, New Jersey. It was about a blood drive, or maybe tips for flood preparation. I do remember the frisson of pleasure I felt when I first laid eyes on the finished product. Here were my words, *mine*, and in print with *my name* attached. I was nineteen years old—ancient by Franklin standards.

Young Ben was only twelve when he wrote two poems. Both had maritime themes. One was about the capture and execution of the infamous pirate Blackbeard. The other was a ballad, "Light House Tragedy," a grim account of the drowning of a lighthouse keeper and his family. It was rather dark material for a twelve-year-old, but even then, Ben knew a good story when he heard one.

Ben hawked the poems at the waterfront like popcorn or cotton candy, and they sold well. Before he could get too excited, though, his father squashed any dreams his son might have harbored about pursuing a career in poetry. "Verse-makers were generally beggars," the elder Franklin opined, a statement that, sadly, has aged well. Ben was grateful for this piece of fatherly advice, he recalled, for he "escap'd being a poet, most probably a very bad one."

I'm not so sure. Franklin had more than a touch of the poet's sensibility. He read poetry throughout his life and used it to teach himself to write. He'd convert prose to verse, then back to prose again. Cadence mattered to Franklin. He wrote for the ear more than the eye. (That is why his writing contains so many italics; he is trying to mimic the emphasis found in speech.) He continued to write poetry all his life, mainly to sharpen his prose, and he advised young writers to begin with verse. He found poetry useful, as do I. When my writing gears jam, as they often do, I crack open a book of poetry and, sure enough, they start turning again.

Ben's big writing break came in 1721. His brother James decided to launch a newspaper, the *New England Courant*. There were already two newspapers in Boston, but they were gutless rags that toed the government line. The *Courant* was going to be different. Its mission, as articulated by James Franklin, was to "expose the vices and follies of persons of all ranks and degrees" and to do so "without fear of, or affection to any man." It's safe to say the *New England Courant* was America's first "real" newspaper.

The competition wasn't exactly thrilled about this upstart. The *Boston News-Letter* described its new rival as "a notorious, scandalous paper . . . full freighted with nonsense, unmannerliness, raillery, profaneness, immorality, arrogancy, calumnies, lies, contradictions, and whatnot, all tending to quarrels and divisions, and to debauch and corrupt the minds and manners of New England." Then they got nasty. The *Courant's* enemies dubbed James Franklin and his writer friends the "Hell-Fire Club." They did not mean it as a compliment, though I suspect James Franklin and his scribes took it that way.

James Franklin launched his newspaper in the midst of a smallpox outbreak. This was not fortuitous, though it did give James plenty to write about. The *New England Courant* took a stance against a controversial new smallpox inoculation. This position strikes me as odd, given the Franklin family's pro-science stance, but James's position was based on animus, not science: Cotton Mather favored the new procedure, so James Franklin was against it. (Ben Franklin would go on to become a vocal advocate of smallpox inoculation.)

It was in the midst of this atmosphere of rancor and fear when, one morning, James Franklin woke to find a sheath of papers slipped under his door. It was a letter, an essay of sorts, from a woman named Silence Dogood. She was fond of the newspaper's readers, she said, and hoped to "add somewhat to their entertainment." Intrigued, James Franklin continued to read.

Silence Dogood was born at sea, en route from old world to new. Tragically, and in a twist, her father had died during his daughter's birth. He was standing on deck, rejoicing at her birth, when "a merciless wave entered the ship, and in one moment carry'd him beyond reprieve." Once in Boston, life didn't get any better for Silence. Her mother and husband died too, leaving her orphaned and widowed.

Silence ends her missive with a promise to write again, and a disclaimer: she knows she can't please all her readers "but I would not willingly displease any; and for those who will take offense, where none is intended, they are beneath the notice of your Humble Servant, Silence Dogood."

James Franklin liked what he read. On April 2, 1722, he published Silence Dogood's essay on the front page of the *New England Courant.* Unbeknownst to him, he had just launched his sixteen-year-old brother's writing career.

Ben had hoped to write for his brother's newspaper, but he knew that was unlikely. He was too young, too green, not to mention saucy and provoking. So he invented Silence Dogood, disguising his handwriting and his identity.

The name was a nod to Cotton Mather. It was partly ironic—Mather was incapable of silence—but mostly serious. The name "Dogood" was not meant as a pejorative. The trope of the nosey, obsequious do-gooder didn't exist yet. Doing good was noble, not suspect. Over the course of the next several months, Silence Dogood, alias Ben Franklin, wrote thirteen more essays, all published in the *Courant.*

I return to 17 Milk Street, Franklin's birthplace. There's a Greek restaurant on the ground floor, directly below the Franklin bust. I order a salad and coffee, find a quiet seat and, between bites of grilled halloumi, read Silence Dogood.

Silence is anything but silent. She brims with observations and opinions, which she delivers in a snappy, accessible style. She is smart and feisty. Hers is a homespun, tell-it-like-it-is wisdom.

In her second essay, Silence lays out what she likes and what she doesn't in a passage that reads less like a description and more like a warning. "*Know then,* that I am an enemy to vice, and a friend to virtue. I am one of an extensive charity, and a great forgiver of *private* injuries: a hearty lover of the clergy and all good men, and a mortal enemy to arbitrary government and unlimited power."

When Silence (that is, Franklin) wrote those words, open revolt against

British rule was more than half a century away, yet Franklin's rebel colors are visible, even if they were worn by a take-no-prisoners widow named Silence Dogood. "I am naturally very jealous for the rights and liberties of my country; and the least appearance of an encroachment on those invaluable privileges, is apt to make my blood boil exceedingly."

Over the next dozen essays, Silence Dogood's blood boils often. She attacks religious hypocrites, ridicules Harvard men and hoop petticoats ("monstrous topsy-turvy *mortar-pieces*"), and rebukes town drunks. She touches on themes that would occupy her puppeteer Ben Franklin's long and useful life: education, religious zealotry, arbitrary power, the status of women, elitism.

She is no mere scold. She is solution oriented, suggesting civic projects to improve the lives of all Bostonians. She argues for freedom of speech and education for girls. She wants to curb bad habits such as excessive drinking and cultivate good ones such as philanthropy. She is not modest: "I never intend to wrap my talent in a napkin." It was not she but Franklin who was wrapping his talent in a napkin, and behind a mask.

Masking is as old as civilization—older, even. Humans have worn masks, in one form or another, for at least 30,000 years. We mask during wartime and peace, festivities and funerals, fertility rites and theatrical performances, parades and pandemics.

Masks conceal. We hide behind them. Masks also reveal. From behind a mask, we are free to express ideas and opinions otherwise forbidden. The word *person* comes from the Latin *persona* meaning *mask*, as in the mask worn by actors on the Greek and Roman stage. For the ancients, a person is not the human behind the mask. They *are* the mask. We are not playing roles. We *are* our roles. We wear masks all the time. We're just not aware of it.

When indigenous peoples, such as the Nuxalk of British Columbia, don a ceremonial mask, they are not impersonating anyone or anything. They transform into another version of themselves. Masking, as Ralph Ellison said, is "a play upon possibility."

That playfulness extends to gender. There is a long tradition of men masquerading as women. In some cultures, men mask as women to ensure a good harvest or many children. In others, men pose as women to express a feminine side otherwise off-limits to them. Some Roman warriors masked as women to tap into female fierceness. They would don a helmet featuring the face of an Amazonian in hopes of channeling her ferocity.

Masks were part of colonial American culture too. At masquerades, masked women were free to proposition men at will, and without harming their reputations. In Charleston, South Carolina, women donned masks when traveling outside to shield themselves from the wind and sun. These masks also freed them to "look where they pleased and to make whatever facial expressions they chose, all without social consequences." Another word for masking is experimenting.

Submerged in the Silence Dogood essays, I surface every now and then and remind myself these essays were written not by a middle-aged widow but by a sixteen-year-old boy. So convincing was Franklin that several readers wrote to the newspaper proposing marriage to Silence Dogood. Yet Franklin had about as much in common with his invented Silence Dogood as I have with Dwayne "The Rock" Johnson. Franklin was not a woman, nor was he middle-aged nor was he from the countryside. (He had never spent a single day in a rural setting.) Writing so credibly in the voice of Silence Dogood demanded boatloads of imagination and empathy.

The use of pseudonyms was common in the eighteenth century, but it was rare for a man to write in the voice of a woman. This was Franklin's "androgynous imagination," as John Updike called it, at work. He also reveals the first inkling of his proto-feminism. Even at this young age, he clearly agreed with Daniel Defoe, who believed women were treated unfairly and could, in fact, outperform men in many cases. Throughout his life, Franklin argued for a woman's right to a proper education, even if he denied such an education to his own daughter. Franklin was many things. Consistent was not one of them.

In an ideal world, writers wouldn't need a mask. The reader would judge their words on their merits. But Franklin's world wasn't any more ideal than ours is. He knew masks mattered and must be chosen carefully. By conjuring

Silence Dogood, he chose well. The residents of eighteenth-century Boston weren't about to listen to a semieducated printer's apprentice with a sharp tongue and penchant for swimming. But they would listen to a wise country woman, a straight talking but compassionate soul with a genuine interest in improving the community. As a woman, Silence Dogood could criticize people and institutions that Franklin could not.

Silence Dogood was Franklin's first mask but by no means his last. Masking became a lifelong habit. "Let all men know thee, but no man know thee thoroughly," said Richard Saunders. Only it wasn't really Richard Saunders. He didn't exist. Nor did Alice Addertongue or Polly Baker or Caelia Shortface or Jethro Standfast or Anthony Afterwit or Ephraim Censorious or Martha Careful or dozens of other invented characters.

Franklin's masks came in many forms. They might be rich or poor, common or aristocratic, male or female, young or old. He wrote as a Native American chief, an enslaved African, an Algerian emir. He wrote as a pregnant single woman and as the king of Prussia. He wrote from the perspective of the letter Z, a deformed leg, a mayfly, and his own gout.

Franklin had a theatrical bent and once compared life to "a dramatic piece." He could slip in and out of roles as fluently as Tom Hanks. In London, he played the part of the English gentleman. In France, donning a marten fur cap on his wigless head, he played the role of the backwoodsman philosopher. The French couldn't get enough of this Ben.

Why did Franklin wear so many masks? For starters, it was fun. He enjoyed fooling people. His fictitious characters were so convincing some readers mistook them for real people. After reading the words of Sidi Ibrahim, the "Algerian emir," people searched bookstores and libraries for the works from which they were supposedly extracted. When Polly Baker, the woman charged with birthing children out of wedlock, ran logical circles around the male magistrates judging her in a courtroom, she was so convincing many Europeans thought she was real and refused to believe otherwise. As has been observed, it is easier to deceive people than to convince them they've been deceived.

Then there was the king of Prussia, who supposedly wrote an edict announcing his intention to make all Britons Prussian subjects. When the article ran in a London newspaper, many readers worried a Prussian invasion was imminent. "Here's the king of Prussia, claiming a right to this kingdom!" exclaimed the writer Paul Whitehead at a posh London gathering with Franklin also in attendance. "Damn his impudence," cried another man. "I dare say, we shall hear by next post that he is upon his march with one hundred thousand men to back this." Franklin, overhearing these comments, smiled knowingly.

Later, writing to his sister Jane, he explained why he had written the spoof. "I have held up a looking-glass in which some [British] ministers may see their ugly faces, and the nation its injustice." Peering into a mask we see our own reflection, and more clearly than in any mirror.

Franklin's masking was useful in other ways. It helped Ben launch his many projects, from hospitals to schools. He rarely attached his name to these proposals. Instead, he'd pen an anonymous essay attributing the idea to "a number of friends" or "some public-spirited gentlemen." Only later, when the proposal had garnered support, would Franklin come forward, and then merely as a fellow participant, not the driving force behind the project.

Franklin's masks freed his friends to critique his writing honestly. His audience found a masked Ben useful too, for "it relieved readers of the unpleasant experience of taking advice from Benjamin Franklin." As for Richard Saunders, the pseudonymous author of *Poor Richard's Almanack*, they were happy to take advice from him. This subterfuge still works today; many advice columnists use pseudonyms.

Masking also enabled Franklin to act older and wiser than he was. From the middle-aged Silence Dogood to the wizened Father Abraham, truth-teller in *The Way to Wealth*, he regularly donned the cloak of the wise and the old. So accustomed was he to playing the part of the aged sage that when his time came, he slipped into the role effortlessly.

Masking is not free. It comes at a price. Franklin's serial masking raised suspicions about him. One critic, writing in 1740, carped that Franklin was "never at a loss for something to say, nor for somebody to say it for you, when you don't care to appear yourself." John Adams was less kind: "I can have no dependence on his word. I never know when he speaks the truth, and when not." (Adams and Franklin often butted heads.)

All this masking, I confess, makes me uneasy. Who was the man behind the mask? Or was Ben Franklin all mask? Biographers have combed through every follicle of the historical record looking for the "real Benjamin Franklin." They have yet to find him. He is the stealth founder. "Who can do more than guess about this man?" said Franklin biographer Edmund Morgan. This from an esteemed Yale scholar who spent a lifetime studying Franklin and editing the forty-three volumes (at last count) of *The Papers of Benjamin Franklin*. What chance do I have?

Maybe Franklin was just a more extreme example of a charade we all engage in. We all wear masks. Perhaps I am just as veiled as Franklin. At home, I wear the Husband Mask and the Dad Mask. Out in the world, I wore my Journalism Mask for many years. It was a good mask, a useful one—up to a point. It was excellent at concealing, enabling me to feign impartiality and report effectively, but not so good at revealing. I exchanged it for my Writer Mask, which is more useful, albeit extremely fragile. Then there is my Extrovert Mask, nearly as brittle and in need of constant recharging. I suspect I wear other masks as well, covert ones I'm not even aware I'm wearing. Maybe it is not me writing these words but a masked version of me. Does this make me a phony, as some labeled Franklin, or is it the anti-maskers who are duplicitous while Ben practiced a kind of masked authenticity?

There is the word that lies at the heart of all these vexing questions: authenticity. We're told it is the highest ideal, that our essential task is to live an authentic life, to find our real self, as if it has gone missing like our car keys or a wayward sock. To call someone "inauthentic" is to accuse them of acting in "bad faith," as the philosopher Jean-Paul Sartre said, and suggests they are somehow immoral.

Our "cult of authenticity," as one scholar calls our obsession with finding our true self, can be traced to Polonius, the character in Shakespeare's *Hamlet* who dispensed fatherly advice to his son. "To thine own self be true," he said. The cult really gathered steam in Franklin's time. The philosopher

Jean-Jacques Rousseau argued that society is to blame for this inchoate feeling of disconnectedness. So heavily coated are we with social norms and
cultural conventions that we've lost touch with our true nature. Our task,
Rousseau said, is to strip away this artificial veneer and reconnect with our
authentic, presocial self.

So seemingly self-evident is the primacy of authenticity that we rarely
question it. But what if it is not true? What if there is no authentic self to find,
only a collection of masks in various shapes and sizes? What if the Buddhists
are right and there is no authentic self because there is no self? The notion
that we possess a fixed identity is an illusion. All is flux, including us.

This aspect of Buddhist philosophy unnerves me. I may be a neurotic
person prone to bouts of melancholy, but I always thought of myself at least
as a person, a solid self. Now I'm told this is an illusion. "I don't like this," I
think, but who is the "I" that is doing the thinking? If there is none, then how
am "I" supposed to get out of bed in the morning? What prevents my nonself
from floating off into the ether? And, crucially, if there is no self, then who
has been shelling out all that money to my therapist?

The philosopher and 1960s guru Alan Watts offered a way out of this
metaphysical maze. Stop fretting about this illusory authentic self and instead be a "genuine fake." Genuine fakes are not con artists and they are not
deluded. Genuine fakes so fully inhabit their role, their *roles,* there is no distance between part and person, mask and face. What matters is not the kind
of masks we wear but how well they fit. Ben Franklin's masks fit well. He was
a genuine fake.

Franklin subscribed to an "as if" philosophy. Live your life as if it were
good and, before you know it, it *is* good. Treat your fellow humans as if they
were good and, in due course, they are good, or at least better. As Franklin said, speaking through one of his masks, Richard Saunders, "What you
would seem to be, be really."

In the latter half of 1723, Ben Franklin's many masks, and his life, began to
unravel. His brother had discovered Silence Dogood's true identity. James
Franklin was angry, and when he got angry, he often got violent. He beat

his younger brother on more than one occasion. Their relationship deterio-
rated, and Ben's writing days ended, at least for a while. By giving voice to
Silence Dogood, Franklin had silenced himself.

One day, he absconded from his brother's print shop. James Franklin responded by ensuring no other printer in Boston would hire him. Ben's indis-
creet religious utterances didn't help his standing in town. He was "pointed
at with horror by good people, as an infidel and an atheist," he recalled. For
Franklin, a social animal, there was no worse punishment. He yearned for the
embracing fold of people who understood him. He knew what he needed to
do. He needed to flee Boston.

I can relate. Franklin felt about Boston the way I feel about Baltimore: a
place you run away from, as far and as fast as possible. I can't point to any one
event or person that prompted me to abscond. My parents divorced when
I was six years old, an especially brittle age for such familial ruptures—not
that there is a "good age," of course. Mine was a frequently sad childhood but
never an abusive one. No, it was the stale, claustrophobic air of our suburban Baltimore neighborhood that I needed to escape. The fault, I know, was
partly mine. I was, and it pains me to say it, unremarkable: athletic but not
athletic enough, smart but not smart enough. I feared I was falling into a dark
and bottomless chasm of mediocrity.

I needed to begin anew somewhere else. I needed to flee. So I did, first
to New York, then New Delhi. Just as Franklin devoted himself to "forgetting
Boston as much as I could," I've attempted to do the same with Baltimore.

It is a futile endeavor, this perpetual escaping, as both of us learned. We
never forget where we came from. Our hometown remains a part of us, and
more so as the years tick by. Childhood looks better when viewed through
the gauzy lens of time. Writing in 1788, at the age of eighty-two, Franklin recalls "the innocent pleasures of youth" and pines to visit his hometown once
more. "The Boston manner, turn of phrase, and even the tone of voice and
accent in all please, and seem to refresh and revive me." As for me and Baltimore, I still love crabs, still pronounce water "wa-der" and still experience a
satisfying pang of familiarity whenever I visit the city. It's not far, only forty
miles from where I live now. The pull of home is stronger than we suspect.

.   .   .

Franklin left Boston, but Boston never fully left him. He retained the Puritan passion for projects, for callings; he just transformed that impulse into a secular vision. Boston taught Franklin the value of self-discipline and of conversing with people from all walks of life, be they revered preachers or grizzled dockworkers, renowned scholars or common candle makers. And it was in Boston where, in 1743, he watched a performance that would change his life, an electrical demonstration by an itinerant and hyphenated showman-scientist named Archibald Spencer.

Franklin didn't turn his back on Boston, not exactly. He turned sideways, rejecting some of what the Puritan city offered (see Puritans) but accepting much else (see books), and transforming still more. He took the Puritan devotion to God and added an extra "o," concluding that "the most acceptable service of God is doing good to man." That was going to be his life's calling. That much he knew. The only question was where.

Franklin's father had come to Boston to retreat from the world. His youngest son saw the town, and especially its bustling port, as something else: a gateway. The sea was his way out. In late summer 1723, he sold a few of his precious books to pay the ship's captain; then, one September day, Benjamin Franklin, all of seventeen years old and with only a few coins in his pocket, boarded a sloop bound for New York and the wide and wondrous world that lay beyond.

SIX

GROUNDED BEN

Today Benjamin Franklin and Philadelphia are conjoined, as insepara-ble as cheese and steak, but that was not always the case. They nearly missed hooking up. The love affair happened by chance. *Never distrust providence.*

When the ship docked in New York, Ben looked for work as a printer. William Bradford, one of the few printers in town, dashed the seventeen-year-old's hopes. There was no work to be found in New York. Philadelphia is where he should go. And so he did.

Whew, I think, as I read about this close call. At the time, New York was the lesser city. Comparatively uncultured, it was a haven for pirates and plunderers, smugglers and slave traders. Money was the only metric that mattered. As one pamphleteer said, "The wisest man among us without a fortune, is neglected and despised . . . while every wealthy dunce is loaded with honours." Had Ben found work in New York rather than Philadelphia, he probably would not have flourished, and today we may not know the name Benjamin Franklin. History is not only shaped by great people like Benjamin Franklin but also by great coincidences.

To reach Philadelphia, Franklin needed to traverse New Jersey, as treacherous an undertaking then as it is today. Everything that could go wrong, did. The crossing from Manhattan to Perth Amboy normally took two hours. Ben's journey took more than thirty, as the gusty winds and rough seas nearly "tore our rotten sails to pieces." A passenger fell overboard and would have drowned had Franklin not rescued him. Franklin and his shipmates spent a sleepless night off Long Island, the spray from the water soaking everyone onboard. There was nothing to eat or drink except "a bottle of filthy rum."

He reached Perth Amboy the following day, but then endured a fever and a fifty-mile trek to Burlington, New Jersey, today a suburb of Philadelphia. It rained the entire way. He arrived soaked and despondent, "beginning now to wish I had never left home."

Franklin nevertheless soldiered on. In Burlington, a local woman took pity on the filthy and disheveled Ben, serving him a hearty meal of ox cheek and accepting only a pot of ale for payment. So began a pattern that would repeat throughout Franklin's life. He always welcomed kindness but never counted on it. That evening, he climbed aboard a small boat heading to Philadelphia via the Delaware River. There was no wind, so the passengers took turns rowing. Exhausted, and with darkness coming, they stopped for the night along a creek, huddling by a fire on the cold October evening. The next morning, the boat docked at Philadelphia's Market Street wharf. Young Ben felt as if he had arrived in the promised land.

Just as each of us has a soulmate, we also have a soulplace. Your soulplace is where you know, just *know* you were meant to be. Like a soulmate, your soulplace brings out the best in you and nurtures abilities you didn't know you had. Just as you can have many partners but only one soulmate, you can love many places but have only one soulplace.

You don't find your soulplace any more than you find your soulmate. It finds you. Timing is essential. So is luck. For me, both aligned unexpectedly, miraculously, one autumn day a long time ago.

I was working for NPR as an economics reporter. I didn't want to be an economics reporter. I wanted to be a foreign correspondent, and I reminded the network's foreign editor, a sanguine woman named Elizabeth Becker, of this every chance I had. One day, she called me into her office.

"So you want to go overseas?" she asked rhetorically.

"More than anything," I replied.

"Okay, let's see," she said, gazing at a world map taped to her wall. Her eyes alighted on London. *Oh, yes, London,* I thought, *that would be great.* Then her gaze traveled south, across the English Channel to Paris. *Paris would totally work,* I told myself. *I don't speak French, but I'll learn.* Her eyes, though, were not finished migrating. They hurtled eastward, past Italy and Greece and, picking up speed, traversed the entire Middle East before coming to an abrupt and unexpected stop at the Indian subcontinent.

"How about Delhi?" she asked.

I had never been to India, never been anywhere near India. I did not speak any of its hundreds of languages and knew little about the country. As I was thinking about all the reasons Delhi made no sense, would be an unmitigated disaster, professionally and personally, my mouth hijacked my brain. "Absolutely," I heard my mouth say. "I would love to go to India."

India, it turned out, was my soulplace. My timing was good. India in 1993 was reforming its economy, opening to the outside world, and transforming how others saw it. Gone were the cartoonish images as a land of snake charmers and swamis. India was a nation on the move, and in transition. Just like me.

My arrival in India was fraught. I had traveled by way of Nepal, where I had agreed to co-teach a crash course in business journalism. It was not until day 5 that I realized my students did not understand much English. The evening before my flight from Kathmandu to Delhi, I felt ill. At first, I had just a few aches, but soon these flowered into severe chills and a fever of 104 degrees. The next morning, I felt even worse, but I was determined to make it to New Delhi. I shivered the entire flight, then shivered at the immigration line and in the taxi and while checking into my hotel. The clerk looked worried and summoned a doctor. I'd spend the next five days bedridden. No matter. I had arrived.

Soulplaces don't coddle. They make demands of us. India demanded

I slow down and practice acceptance on a regular basis. Either that or go insane. The choice was mine.

Being separated from your soulplace is just as traumatic as being separated from your soulmate. In 1864, at the height of the Civil War, Confederate forces captured a Union soldier named Abner Small and held him as a prisoner of war. His fellow captives were dying, though their injuries didn't seem that serious. In his diary, Small speculated why. "*They became homesick* and disheartened. They . . . were dying of nostalgia."

In his memoir, Salman Rushdie recalls how his family's nanny, Mary, grew despondent when they brought her from Bombay to London in the 1960s. Her heart ached for home—at first metaphorically, then physically. She developed cardiac ailments. When she moved back to India, her heart problems disappeared and never returned. She lived to more than one hundred. "The idea that you might actually be in danger of dying from a broken heart was something to write about," Rushdie says. I agree. So is the idea that your heart might break if ripped from its soulplace.

Franklin's heart ached every time he left "my dear Philadelphia." Franklin was to Philadelphia as Socrates was to Athens, Dickens to London, and Cher to Las Vegas. Franklin loved Philadelphia, and it loved him. Philadelphia shaped Franklin, and Franklin shaped Philadelphia. Though he left many times, he always returned.

When Franklin first arrived in 1723, Philadelphia was a young city, more of a town, really, with a population of only about six thousand. Like any youngster, it had many needs and made many demands. It was brimming with potential but required someone to unlock it. That someone was Benjamin Franklin. When Franklin arrived, Philadelphia had no fire department, paved or lighted streets, sanitation department, night watch, hospital, or circulating library. Three decades later, it possessed all of these, and more. Franklin had a hand in each of these projects, even if sometimes it was an invisible one.

As Oliver Wendell Holmes said, greatness depends, in large part, on simply being in the right place. Franklin was and, crucially, at the right time.

Philadelphia was the New York of the eighteenth century, a kinetic, quixotic place where anything seemed possible. Boston attracted the devout. Philadelphia attracted the determined. New Englander John Adams grudgingly acknowledged this reality when he called Philadelphia "the pineal gland" of America. (The man could make anything sound unsexy.)

Philadelphia was born as payback, the settling of a debt. The year was 1681. King Charles II owed William Penn's family a sizable sum. Rather than shelling out cash, the king suggested a barter. *How would you, William, like some grade A primo property in North America?* Penn, a Quaker, and thus persecuted in England, was looking for new digs. He took the deal.

It was love at first sight. In a letter to a friend, he described the region, now known as Pennsylvania, as a kind of Eden. "The air proveth sweet & good, the land fertile, & the spring many & pleasant."

If ever there was a city birthed by one man, it was Philadelphia. William Penn named it, chose the site, devised the street plan, and set the tone. A utopian at heart, Penn was determined his would be no ordinary colony. Pennsylvania was a "holy experiment" and its city Philadelphia "a seed of a nation."

William Penn was as contradictory as his new colony. He was a Quaker but dressed like a dandy—no drab clothes or wide-brimmed hat for him. He preferred tailored suits, accessorized with a blue silk sash and ceremonial sword. And he was ambitious.

Philadelphia was America's first planned community. Penn laid out his city in a neat grid. He envisioned a verdant country town, a soulplace with elbow room. High (now Market) Street was one hundred feet wide, broader than any boulevard in seventeenth-century London. Streets, initially named for prominent settlers, were renamed for local trees: Cedar, Pine, Spruce, Walnut, Chestnut, Mulberry, Sassafras, and Vine—all part of William Penn's green, orderly city.

That was the idea. But no urban plan survives first contact with actual people. Within a few years, dozens of alleyways had sprouted. People didn't build their homes spread out across the city, as Penn had hoped, but clustered along the waterfront. Coveting waterfront property is an ageless pastime. William Penn's bucolic paradise was soon one of the most congested towns in America.

The other pillar of Penn's "holy experiment" proved more successful. Philadelphia was to be a spiritual refuge where all Christians—and even non-Christians—were welcome. In keeping with Quaker pacifism, Penn demilitarized the city. There were no fortifications, no city walls, no garrisons or soldiers. At first, there was no municipal government either, and therefore, Penn hoped, no factional politics. William Penn's city was unlike any other in the world.

But it was no utopia for the Delaware, or Lenni Lenape, the Native Americans who inhabited the site of Philadelphia. Penn intended to live in peace with them, and for a while, he did. Rather than confiscating their land, he purchased it from them and vowed to negotiate honorably. Although Penn was more enlightened than other colonists, he still held a patronizing view of Native Americans and hoped to convert them to Christianity.

The slave trade in Philadelphia was nearly as old as the city. In 1684, two years after the city was founded, the *Isabella* docked at the waterfront, carrying 150 enslaved Africans. They were sold "to eager Philadelphia buyers." By 1700, one Philadelphian in ten was enslaved. William Penn himself was an enslaver. Philadelphia was also home to some of colonial America's most ardent abolitionists. The city contained multitudes.

The business of Philadelphia was business. A visitor from my home state of Maryland—apparently a land of loafers—marveled at how Philadelphia shops opened at 5 a.m. and how the central market dwarfed those found in other colonies. Andreas Rudman, a Swedish pastor, observed in 1700 that anyone first stepping foot in Philadelphia "would be astonished beyond measure" that it was founded less than a decade ago. "All the houses are built of brick, three or four hundred of them, and in every house a shop, so that whatever one wants at any time he can have, for money." Philadelphians could order newspapers, books, and pamphlets by mail.

Quaker Philadelphia was a lot more fun than Puritan Boston (an admittedly low bar to clear). Billiards and bowling were allowed. There was a dance school. The playful spirit was even evident in the city's barbershops, as visiting physician Alexander Hamilton (not *that* Alexander Hamilton) attests: "I was shaved by a little finical, humpbacked old barber, who kept dancing round me and talking all the time . . . and yet did his job lightly and to a hair." Competent *and* fun. That was the Philadelphia way.

William Penn's Philadelphia was far more tolerant than John Winthrop's Boston. Here was the true city upon a hill. All were welcome: Germans, Scots, Irish, Welsh, Swiss, Swedes, Huguenots, and, of course, the English. Philadelphia was one of the most multicultural cities in the world. Dr. Hamilton describes dining at a local tavern and admiring how religiously diverse the clientele were. Sitting side by side were Roman Catholics, Methodists, Quakers, Seventh Day Adventists, "and one Jew." Said one resident: "We are a people, thrown together from various quarters of the world, differing in all things—language, manners and sentiments." And yet somehow it worked.

It worked especially well when the ale was flowing. Philadelphia was a city of taverns. More than one hundred dotted the streets, or one for every dozen adult men. There was a tavern for every taste and budget, from the sailors' dive bars by the wharves to the elegant City Tavern. Book lovers convened, naturally, at the Library Tavern, artists at James's Coffee House (which served more than coffee), explorers at the Bull's Head. For a while, there was even a tavern attached to the local jail. One visitor said an hour at a tavern taught you more about Philadelphia than a week walking its streets.

Philadelphia was no paradise, though. Crime was rampant. Waste disposal consisted of hogs gorging on trash. A stench hung in the air. Punning on its name, some people began to call the young town "Filthy-dirty."

Not Franklin. He loved the city, loved every bit of it from the moment he stepped onto Market Street that sunny autumn day three centuries ago. He had no clean clothes. His pockets were stuffed with dirty shirts and socks. He smelled. Tired and hungry, he had only a single Dutch dollar and a shilling's worth of copper. When Ben offered the shilling to the owner of the boat that carried him from New Jersey, he declined to accept it; after all, Franklin had rowed. But he insisted the boat owner take it, "Man being sometimes more generous when he has but a little money than when he has plenty," he recounts in his autobiography. This generosity of the impoverished, Franklin speculated, might be because the destitute want to retain some scrap of pride. Perhaps, but there is another explanation: those poor in money are often rich in empathy.

Franklin walked up Market Street and, in one of the most iconic scenes of American letters, approached a bakery and asked for threepenny worth of bread. In Boston, that sum would buy a single roll, but the Philadelphia baker handed Franklin "three great puffy rolls." Walking away, one roll under each arm while he nibbled on the third, Franklin marveled at the generosity of spirit, the overflowing abundance that was Philadelphia. This was home.

He passed by the door of the Reed family and caught the eye of young Deborah Reed, his future wife, knowing he made "a most awkward ridiculous appearance." Returning to the Market Street wharf, where his boat had docked, he splashed himself with water from the Delaware River. Refreshed, he spotted a line of people streaming toward somewhere, so he followed them. They were headed to the great Quaker Meeting House, the largest building in town. Sitting among the worshippers, in complete silence, he dozed for several hours. "This was therefore the first house I was in or slept in, in Philadelphia," he recalled.

And so went the Philadelphia adventures of Franklin the Possibilian. He found work as a printer's assistant with a grouchy oddball named Samuel Keimer and lodging next door with the Reed family. He soon found friends, like-minded leather-apron men and bibliophiles. They went for long walks, swam in the Schuylkill River, and held poetry contests.

Life was good, even if the work was less than satisfying. His boss, Keimer, was a second-rate printer working with "an old shatter'd press." He passed himself off as a Quaker (he was not) and had strange ideas about religion. He even schemed to found his own sect, attempting to recruit Franklin. Ben demurred and, instead, toyed with Keimer, suggesting his new faith include a vow not to eat meat. The two men abstained for three months. "I went on pleasantly," recalled Franklin, "but poor Keimer suffer'd grievously, tir'd of the project, long'd for the flesh pots of Egypt, and order'd a roast pig."

·   ·   ·

Time and chain stores have blurred the sharp differences that once distinguished American cities. Today an insipid sameness fuses Seattle and Atlanta, Boston and Philadelphia, at least on the surface. Scratch a little, and the old differences reappear, like discovering a vestigial tail. It's no coincidence that Boston's signature dish is clam chowder, a tidy meal you eat slowly with a spoon, while Philadelphia's is the cheesesteak sub, a messy mélange you gobble with your hands.

Philadelphia's Old City possesses the same cozy compactness as Boston's. As in Boston, there is colonial merch to buy here—pointy hats, founder bobbleheads, snow globes—and you might bump into a Jefferson or Washington lookalike. That is where the similarities end. Boston wears its history dry-cleaned and pressed. Philadelphia wears its history like a pair of baggy jeans that haven't seen a washing machine, let alone a dry cleaner. In Boston, Franklin's statue is discreetly perched next to a dentist's office or on the spot of the old Boston Latin School. In Philadelphia, he's mounted above bridges and on billboards. He sells cheesesteaks and beer and roots for the 76ers.

I walk down Chestnut Street, heading toward the waterfront. I wonder what Ben would think of his "dear Philadelphia" today, three hundred years since his arrival. Would he recognize it? What would he make of the storefronts advertising chakra healing and psychic readings? Dr. Franklin would approve, up to a point. Fascinated by the medicinal arts, he was open to new methods of healing, provided they could be empirically verified. And while he was definitely a futurist, he was less interested in predicting the future than shaping it. Fortune favors fortitude.

Walking farther, I pass a beauty parlor with "handmade artisanal soaps" displayed in the window. I can see Ben cringing, transported to those dark days making soap in his father's shop. I move on. I pass the "Nauti Mermaid Crab House and Piano Bar. More Oysters, Fewer Clams." The restaurant is boarded. Out of business. That's a shame. Ben would appreciate the humor—and the oysters.

What would Ben make of the young man I see on Market Street, wearing a red T-shirt and sneakers, cradling a Styrofoam cup and a cardboard sign that reads, "Homeless and Hungry. Please help?" Franklin would feel sympathy for the man and might offer to help him find work, but he would not drop any coins in the cup. Franklin was opposed to handouts, fearing they create dependency and "encourage idleness and prodigality . . . thus multiplying beggars, instead of diminishing them." He fell in the teach-a-man-to-fish camp. "I think the best way of doing good to the poor, is not making them easy *in* poverty, but leading or driving them out of it."

If you're thinking this stance makes Franklin a Reagan Republican, not so fast. He also held views that would tickle a modern liberal's bleeding heart. He opposed private ownership of "superfluous property." He thought taxation (with representation, of course) was a good idea and a civil obligation. "He can have no right to the benefits of society who will not pay his club towards the support of it." He thought elected officials should work for free, and prisons should be humane. There's something for every political persuasion in Franklin's words and life.

I turn onto Third Street, around the corner from Franklin Court, and it's all dogs. There's an obedience school called Opportunity Barks and another called Ruff Life and, not far away, the Paws Adoption Center. Ben would approve. He liked dogs and was especially fond of his son William's Newfoundland. He had a soft spot for turkeys. He thought they and not the bald eagle should be the national bird of the young United States. He also liked squirrels. One in particular captured Ben's heart: Mungo. Mungo was a peripatetic squirrel. With Franklin's help, he traveled from America to England and the Hampshire estate of Franklin's friend Jonathan Shipley. There, Mungo led a happy life under the kind and loving care of the Shipleys' young daughter, Georgiana, at least until Mungo got into a losing tussle with a neighborhood dog.

I turn down an alleyway, and am catapulted clear of the touristy Old City into a working-class neighborhood. Leather-apron country. I spot a ramshackle store—"Mr. Bar Stool. Thousands in Stock"—and a construction site where a melody of salsa mingles with a backbeat of buzz saws and hammers. These are Franklin's people. Even when he was wealthy and world famous, Franklin still saw himself as a leather-apron man. "He that hath a trade, hath an estate."

Franklin and Philadelphia were a perfect fit. Placemates. Both were young and in a hurry. Both possessed a generous spirit and boatloads of gumption. Both were scruffy, unpolished. Both craved, but never achieved, orderliness.

Philadelphia provided Franklin what he needed most: anonymity. Having broken the apprenticeship with his brother, Franklin was technically a runaway and could be arrested. But that was unlikely. Not in Philadelphia. No one cared where you came from or what your name was. What can you *do*? That was the question foremost on people's minds.

Here was a place where the church didn't dictate how you lived. Here was a place where a filthy, nearly penniless runaway was welcomed. Here was a place in need of good deeds. The perfect place for a fresh start.

SEVEN

WANDERING BEN

Sometimes we don't appreciate our soulplace until we leave it.

It was 1723, and Franklin was underemployed and unhappy. Restless, too. One day, while working at the Philadelphia printing house with his miserable boss, Franklin saw Sir William Keith, the lieutenant governor of Pennsylvania, dressed impeccably, approach the door and knock. It was not Keimer who the lieutenant governor had come to see but Franklin. He had heard good things about the teenager from Boston and suggested they decamp to a local tavern for some fine Madeira.

That is the kind of place Philadelphia was at the time. The kind of place where an ambitious young runaway with a mere two years' education and hardly a farthing to his name finds himself sitting down at a local pub downing a bottle of excellent wine with the colony's lieutenant governor.

Keith saw something in young Ben and suggested he establish his own printing business. Ben sailed for Boston and, chastened, asked his father for a loan. The elder Franklin, unimpressed with the scheme, turned him down. Back in Philadelphia, the smooth-talking William Keith suggested Franklin travel to London, where Keith assured Ben that Keith's own good credit would enable Ben to stock up on the equipment needed to launch his print shop.

So on November 5, 1724, eighteen-year-old Ben Franklin boarded a sailing ship, the *London Hope*—an ironic name, he'd soon learn—and watched as the waters of the Delaware River receded, giving way to the Delaware Bay and, soon, the vast and unforgiving expanse of the North Atlantic. The seas were rough, the weather bad. Six weeks later, on Christmas Eve, the *London Hope* entered the English Channel.

Ben and I have this in common: we were both bitten by the travel bug at a young age—me growing up in 1970s Baltimore, Ben in 1710s Boston. I watched the planes overhead, en route to Friendship Airport (now Baltimore-Washington International), and dreamed of becoming a pilot. Ben watched the ships arriving at Boston Harbor and dreamed of becoming a sailor. That wasn't in the cards, so young Ben traveled in his mind, gazing at the four world maps his father had pinned to the walls of their tiny house, reading travelogues and chatting with arriving sailors at Boston Harbor.

Soon, he no longer needed his father's permission to travel—so he did, logging 42,000 miles over the course of his life. As deputy postmaster, he traveled the entire length of the Northeast and at age seventy embarked on an arduous journey to Montreal. At age seventy-six, he considered traveling through Italy before realizing the stagecoach ride would probably kill him. He could be cocky about his travels, bragging to friends about his mileage count or his iron stomach, which never failed him even when other passengers were hurling overboard.

For Franklin, travel was not optional. If he didn't take his annual summer excursion, he grew irritable. "I am as well as I can be without my usual journey," goes a typical letter to his wife, Deborah, "but I begin to feel the want of it, and shall set out in a few days." Travel enabled Franklin to cast his gaze beyond Puritan Boston and still-parochial Philadelphia. It was also "one way of lengthening life." With the right mindset, he said, two weeks in Paris felt like six months anywhere else.

Travel enabled Ben to pause and think. He did some of his best writing and experimenting while on the road or at sea. It was on a bumpy carriage ride from Philadelphia to Albany, New York, in 1754 when he composed his brilliant and prescient plan for colonial unity. It was on an Atlantic crossing to London in 1757 when he wrote his famous "Father Abraham's Speech," later retitled "The Way to Wealth."

It is a truism that travel broadens our horizons. But like most truisms, it is only partly true. Yes, travel expands our world, but it does so by shrinking it. Life on the road is circumscribed and manageable, and that is why I find it so appealing. For me, a pared-down life is a better, happier life.

The dirty little secret of travel is that it's a parlor trick, a mind game. We are the same person on the road as we are at home. You may feel more romantic in Paris or more relaxed in Rio de Janeiro, but those cities, wonderful as they are, can't take all the credit. So why the transformation? Because out there, you give yourself permission to be romantic or relaxed, or whatever else, and so you do. Everything you experience while traveling you could experience at home too. It's just a lot harder. Parlor tricks and a little self-deception are useful. No one knew this better than Franklin, a man John Adams once called the "Old Conjurer." Adams didn't mean it as a compliment—he was referring to Franklin's alleged duplicity—but I bet Ben smiled at the moniker.

From a young age, Franklin was a fussy traveler. He knew what he liked and what he didn't. Had Tripadvisor existed then, he would have been every hotelier's worst nightmare. In France, he argued with innkeepers over matters small and smaller. In England, he described a Portsmouth hotel as a "wretched inn," where even the stationery was shoddy. He called the town of Gravesend "a *cursed biting* place" whose inhabitants expertly relieved travelers of their money. "If you buy any thing of them, and give half what they ask, you pay twice as much as the thing is worth," wrote Franklin, before delivering the coup de grâce: "Thank God, we shall leave it tomorrow."

It's difficult to pin down when Franklin grew suspicious of Governor Keith's promises. Perhaps it was when the ship's captain denied him access to Keith's letters of credit until they reached English waters. Perhaps it was when Ben discovered there were no such letters. No doubt he knew he had been duped when the merchants he approached in London had nothing good to say about Keith and tended to swear a lot when his name was mentioned. Franklin's inevitable conclusion: the governor had not given him letters of credit because he had no credit to give. Ben wondered why Keith chose to dupe a hapless young man, but he had more immediate concerns.

Put yourself in Benjamin Franklin's shoes. You are eighteen years old. You've never seen a city larger than one with ten thousand inhabitants. Now, hoodwinked by a trusted elder, you find yourself in a sprawling metropolis of more than half a million restless souls, a "great and monstrous thing," as Defoe called London. You are unemployed and broke. What do you do?

Most people, I think, would finagle a ticket on the next ship back to Philadelphia. Not Franklin. I don't know if he knew the word *chutzpah*, or if it even existed back then, but that's what he displayed. He talked his way into not one but two printing jobs. He met some of London's most eminent thinkers, such as the writer and philosopher Bernard Mandeville. And he managed to leverage his status as an "exotic" colonist.

The New World was the crypto of the eighteenth century. Virginian tobacco. Jamaican rum. Antiguan sugar. It was all new and therefore good. Everyone wanted a piece of the action. Was it risky? Sure, but investors didn't ask too many questions. The potential payoff was too tempting. Curiosities from the New World were also in demand. No one knew this better than a young printer from Philadelphia with outsized confidence and at least one exotic goodie tucked in his luggage. But, first, he needed to navigate a colossal and unforgiving city, alone and destitute.

EIGHT

RESILIENT BEN

I cross the Thames by foot, marveling at the endless construction sprouting from either side of the river like runaway shrubbery. London has always been a city in a hurry. As I navigate the currents of pedestrians, I try to imagine young Ben here, in the "great and monstrous thing" that was, and still is, London.

I hop on the Tube, a mode of transport Franklin would surely like, offering, as it does, the twin appeals of both speed and equality. Anyone can ride the Tube. I arrive at my destination where I navigate a long pedestrian tunnel. I pass a busker playing the violin. He's not bad, I think, but where is his hat or violin case? How does he make money? Then I spot it: a card reader. The tunnel musician takes credit cards, and Apple Pay too. I can see Franklin smiling at this incongruity. He was always dreaming up new forms of currency. In Pennsylvania, he promoted the use of paper money, a novel concept at the time, and invented ways to print bills designed to thwart counterfeiters.

I exit the station and slalom through a gaggle of schoolkids, led by a mother duck of a teacher. As I approach London's Natural History Museum, I see a sign that reads, "Our Broken Planet. How We Got Here and How to Fix It." Good topics. Franklin would be more concerned with the latter one. He was less interested in the causes of problems than in finding novel solutions. I am the opposite. I'd rather chew on a problem than cough up a solution. This approach has its advantages; by not finding solutions to problems, I needn't worry about my solutions flopping. There are downsides too. Squabbles with my wife, for instance. Whenever I present her with a problem I'm facing, she has the audacity—the gall!—to offer a solution. Sometimes, and this is the truly warped part, she suggests *multiple* solutions. What she fails to realize is that I'm not looking for solutions to my problem. I'm looking for someone to mull it over with, a chewing partner.

I step into the vast Victorian-era building that is London's Natural History Museum. A giant blue whale named Hope hangs from the ceiling. I smile and wonder if giant dangling whales are a requirement for all natural history museums. I head for the minerals exhibit, a cavernous hall. It takes me a while, but I find it, encased behind an antiquated wooden display cabinet that looks like something Charles Darwin owned. The label reads: "Sloane Artifacts."

Hans Sloane was a wealthy physician and collector of curiosities. Beginning in the late seventeenth century, he traveled the world searching for them. Nothing was too obscure or bizarre for Sloane. His collection, the *Guardian* newspaper recounts, included "gnats' blood, Inuit sun visors, a stick to put down your throat to make yourself sick, a cyclops pig, a silver penis protector and a bit of coral that looked just like someone's hand." By the time he died in 1753, Sloane had amassed some 71,000 objects, which the government acquired and used to found the British Museum and its offshoots, like the one I'm in now.

Sloane's curios displayed here include an amber brush holder from China and an amethyst snuff box from Germany, but my eyes are drawn elsewhere—to a tangle of spindly white strands that look like a hairy squid. "Asbestos Purse," the label informs me. It is no longer recognizable as a purse, but that doesn't matter. It once belonged to Benjamin Franklin.

Franklin knew enough to bring the purse with him from Philadelphia and that a man like Hans Sloane would be interested in acquiring it. So he wrote to him. First, he played up the exotic nature of the purse. "Having lately been in the northern parts of America, I have brought from thence a purse made of the stone asbestos . . . call'd by the inhabitants, Salamander Cotton." Then Franklin pivoted to flattery—"As you are noted to be a lover of curiosities . . ."—before deploying the soft sell: "If you have any inclination to purchase them, or see 'em, let me know your pleasure." He ended his letter with a postscript: "I expect to be out of town in 2 or 3 days, and therefore beg an immediate answer."

This was a lie. Franklin wasn't going anywhere. It was the classic *hurry, limited time offer!* ploy used by salespeople everywhere. It worked. Hans Sloane invited Franklin to his elegant home in Bloomsbury Square, where he purchased the purse for a handsome sum. Franklin doesn't mention what he did with this money. Did he use it to buy books, or did he indulge in the "amusements" London offered? A little of both, I suspect.

I spot a sign for the "Contemplation Room" and am intrigued. I could use some contemplation. I enter a sparsely decorated room that is part yoga studio, part mosque. On the floor are a beanbag chair and half a dozen Muslim prayer rugs. A sign on the wall informs me of the rules. No eating or drinking or using mobile phones—all sound prohibitions—but also a warning to "refrain from using scented products." That strikes me as going a bit too far. Who doesn't like a good scented product?

The room is blissfully quiet. I collapse onto the beanbag chair and contemplate. Questions abound. What was this young Ben Franklin like? And where did he get the moxie to meet bigwigs like Hans Sloane and Bernard Mandeville? Was it merely the heedless confidence of the young, or was Franklin already exuding greatness? Was he, I wonder, displaying nascent signs of the extreme usefulness that would define his life? There were indications. In London, he taught one friend how to swim and lent another money. It was not the methodical benevolence that would characterize his later projects, but it was a start.

It must have been a heady—and terrifying—experience for Franklin to visit London for the first time. London was unlike any city he'd ever seen, with a population fifty times larger than Boston's or Philadelphia's. It was also a giant mess, still recovering from the Great Fire of 1666 and the Great Storm of 1703, not to mention an economic downturn.

The buildings were in various states of disrepair, looking "like skeletons of buildings, like what in truth they were, heaps of ruins," writes Jerry White in his encyclopedic history of eighteenth-century London. The streets were treacherous, pitted with troughs that could crack an axle or a bone. The street names told you everything you needed to know about them. There were Foul Lane and Dirty Lane and Rotten Row and, my favorite, Pissing Alley ("a very proper name for it," one contemporary observed). The air was so foul that in the summer, the royal family decamped from St. James's Palace to Hampton Court Palace. Others were not so fortunate.

London was dirty and dangerous, but also enticing. The smell of progress was in the air, as pungent and irresistible as the smoke and dust. The Enlightenment was in full swing; sparks were flying everywhere. The Royal Society, home to Isaac Newton and other natural philosophers, as scientists were known at the time, was blossoming. Writers like Jonathan Swift and Addison Steele were breaking new ground. And with the publication of Daniel Defoe's *Robinson Crusoe* in 1709, the modern English novel was born.

Many of these new and exciting ideas were birthed not in the lecture halls or laboratories but in coffeehouses. They were the petri dishes of intellectual fermentation, places where ideas flowed as freely as "the bitter black drink called coffee." You could read the latest newspapers splayed across tables or pick up the freshest gossip. You could educate yourself by listening to lectures on philosophy or the arts or sciences at these "penny universities," as coffeehouses were known.

Each had a different specialty. Some were all business, places where merchants and bankers would meet over coffee and strike deals. Lloyd's and Christie's and Sotheby's all got their start in coffeehouses. One, Don Saltero's, housed a vast collection of curiosities from around the world, a museum that served coffee. Another required all customers to converse only in Latin. (It was short-lived.)

I can see why Franklin loved London's coffeehouses. They were cheap, one of the few places he could afford to visit. They were highly social, and

Franklin was a social animal. They were useful and egalitarian, or as egalitarian as eighteenth-century England permitted, where men (and, with few exceptions, only men) of different social strata could mingle over a penny cup of coffee and see what new ideas emerged.

Franklin had his favorites. He frequented the Pennsylvania Coffee House, of course, where he read the latest news from Philadelphia. Then there was the New England Coffee House and his go-to, the Golden Fan, conveniently located near the cheap room he rented in a neighborhood called Little Britain.

Today, Little Britain is dotted with shiny new condominiums, gleaming office towers, and pubs with names like The Lamb and Trotter and The Hand and Shear. Turn a corner, and you come upon Christopher Wren's masterpiece, St. Paul's Cathedral. It's a view young Ben Franklin would have seen often. The cathedral was destroyed in the Great Fire of 1666. It took decades to rebuild and wasn't completed until 1711, only thirteen years before Franklin arrived.

In Franklin's time, traffic in Little Britain consisted of hackney carriages, oxcarts, and nervous pedestrians. Today traffic consists of Range Rovers, Teslas, and nervous pedestrians. I pass a hospital, shiny and new on one side, old and yellowing on the other, effortlessly straddling the centuries in a way American buildings do not. For us, something is either new or it is old. Rarely is it both.

I close my eyes and picture eighteen-year-old Ben walking these streets. He was young and ambitious—a bit cocky, no doubt, but with enough self-awareness to know he didn't know what he didn't know. He frequented a secondhand bookshop called the Green Dragon, owned by a kind man, John Wilcox. Franklin couldn't afford to buy books, so Wilcox allowed the young printer to borrow a few titles overnight "on certain reasonable terms."

Not everyone was so welcoming. Franklin was an American, and thus a country bumpkin by default. For the ordinary Briton, America was like a dentist's office: a somewhat mysterious, possibly painful place you might visit if you were desperate enough but not otherwise. America was an untamed land filled with wild beasts and primitive "savages." Many Britons believed Americans could not speak English, which strikes me as odd considering so many of them came from . . . England. Said the contemporary writer Samuel Johnson: "[Americans] are a race of convicts and ought to be thankful for anything we allow short of hanging." Those are fighting words, but belligerence was many decades away. Benjamin Franklin, like nearly all Americans of the time, saw himself as a proud and loyal British subject.

He was not a happy one, though. He knew he needed to change course; no, he needed to *set* a course. Until now he was like one of those hot-air balloons he would later witness soaring over Paris, drifting here and there, whichever way the wind took it.

I walk a bit farther and spot a bistro with a sign that reads: "Today's Inspirational Quote: Don't be an arsehole." Solid advice. Benjamin Franklin followed it. Mostly. When his friend James Ralph was out of town, Franklin visited his girlfriend and "attempted familiarities." Later in life, he was largely an absentee husband and father. So, yes, Franklin could be an arsehole. He was no saint.

The Priory Church of St. Bartholomew the Great, or Great St. Bart's for short, is the oldest surviving church in London. It is also where Ben Franklin, not exactly a regular churchgoer, found work.

I traverse a small courtyard, populated by workers on smoke breaks, then walk through a narrow passageway and into the main sanctuary, where I spot a young, plump priest.

"I'm looking for Marcus," I say to the priest.

"I am Marcus," the priest says.

Marcus is garrulous and proud of the church's Franklin connection. Founded as a monastery in 1123, the church is old "even by English standards," says Marcus, subtly boasting the way the English do, suggesting, in a covertly condescending way, that their country is really *really* old and, by extension, America is but an infant.

Great St. Bart's, like nearly all medieval churches, had a smaller separate chapel devoted to the Virgin Mary and known as the Lady Chapel. During the Reformation, "the Virgin Mary fell off a cliff," explains Marcus, and for the rest of our conversation I can't dislodge the image of a free-falling mother of Christ from my mind.

Saddled with extra floor space, the custodians of Great St. Bart's did what any landlord would do: find a new tenant. In this case, it was a printer named Samuel Palmer. It must have been quite the scene, parishioners worshipping in the church while, a few yards away, Palmer and his printing presses made an unholy racket. When I ask Marcus about this incongruity, he replies philosophically.

"Such were the times."

Franklin found work at Palmer's as a compositor. He was "pretty diligent" on the job, he recalled, but spent much of his earnings hanging out with his friend James Ralph, a flighty poet from New Jersey, "going to plays and other places of amusement." Franklin doesn't say what sort of places of amusement he means, but they were probably located across the Thames in Southwark, London's seedy alter ego, where circuses and bear baiting were common, not to mention numerous opportunities to engage in "intrigues with low women."

Today, Palmer's Printing House, long gone, is commemorated with a plaque. "The Lady Chapel: Where Benjamin Franklin Learned His Trade." The plaque notes this is where Franklin wrote his first and only work of moral philosophy: *A Dissertation on Liberty and Necessity, Pleasure and Pain.*

It is a strange and disturbing little piece. In it, Franklin argues that, in so many words, nothing matters. Virtue and vice? No difference. Pleasure and pain? Same. Ditto good and evil. There is more to it than that, but not much more. Flirting with atheism, the paper made the case for deism, the belief that while there is a supreme being that created the universe, such a being does not control events or interact with humans in any way. Deism, also called Natural Religion, was popular in some circles at the time, but it remained a heretical idea.

Franklin's paper was scandalous and would have landed him in trouble with the authorities had anyone read it. Fortunately, hardly anyone did. He immediately regretted writing his "London pamphlet" and scrambled to retrieve and burn the one hundred copies he had printed.

The paper marked the beginning and end of Franklin's career as a meta-physician; such speculation now "disgusted" him, he said. Searching for absolute truth is pointless, a distraction. People can't agree on the visible world. How do you expect them to agree on the invisible one? He would continue to philosophize but by other means. His life became his message. His was a philosophy based on deeds, not words. A philosophy of the useful.

Franklin, the young man in a hurry, soon grew restless at Palmer's and moved to a larger, more prestigious printing house, owned by one John Watts. This time Franklin worked the presses, a much more physically demanding job but one he craved, for he "felt a want of the bodily exercise I had been us'd to in America."

Whenever I pictured Benjamin Franklin, the same image came to mind: a squat, rotund man whose idea of exercise was lifting pints of beer to his mouth. Not true, at least in Franklin's youth. At five foot ten, he was tall for the time. He was toned and muscular, with brown eyes and thick brown hair. Benjamin Franklin, the founding grandfather, was ripped. Throughout his life, he regularly walked, rowed, swam, and lifted weights at a time when few others did. As a boy, he was a skilled boxer who could deck an opponent with a mean uppercut to the jaw. Sadly, we have no portraits of this buff Franklin. He wasn't famous yet.

As for beer, Franklin drank it only occasionally (he preferred Madeira) and, unlike his colleagues at Watts Printing House, abstained in the morning. He drank water instead, earning him the nickname "The Water American."

The moniker was apt, and in more ways than his beer-guzzling cowork-ers knew. His aquatic skills had crossed the Atlantic with him and distin-guished him in London. Few people at the time knew how to swim. Even bathing was frowned on. Immersing yourself in water was considered un-couth and medically unsound. Body odors were thought to form a protective cocoon and act as a sexual stimulant. I'd feel right at home in the eighteenth century—not because of the body odor but my aversion to swimming.

One day, at the urging of friends, Franklin stripped and dove into the Thames, easily traversing the river from Chelsea to Blackfriars, "performing on the way many feats of activity both upon and under water." Everyone was impressed. A wealthy nobleman learned of Franklin's prowess and offered to pay him to teach his children to swim. Franklin was tempted but turned down the offer. It was a different proposition that won him over: a Quaker merchant named Thomas Denham proposed paying Franklin's fare to Philadelphia if he would work for him as a clerk, with the prospect of becoming a partner. Franklin, ready to go home, accepted. He spent his final days in London the way I spend my days before every trip, no matter how short: packing, repacking, running errands, and purchasing supplies, needed or not.

Before boarding the ship, Franklin reflected on his time in London. He had gained valuable printing experience, read voraciously, and "pick'd up some very ingenious acquaintance[s]." He developed healthy habits, drinking water in the morning instead of beer, swimming regularly, and going for long walks. Overall, though, he was disappointed. He was leaving the way he arrived: broke. (His friend James Ralph owed him twenty-seven pounds, a considerable sum, but was unlikely to repay it given Franklin's attempted seduction of his girlfriend.) He had written a misguided and potentially dangerous dissertation. He had borne the brunt of rabid anti-Americanism. He had not made his mark. He had not been useful. How could he be when he was such an impoverished, directionless mess of a man?

It was time to go home, and so on July 21, 1726, Franklin boarded the *Berkshire*, bound for Philadelphia. It was a journey that should have taken five or six weeks. It took nearly thirteen. Yet it was aboard this ship, floundering in a windless Atlantic, that Franklin became Franklin.

NINE

HOMEWARD BEN

Some journeys change us on a molecular level. We depart one person and arrive another. I'd like to say it is magical, but that is not right. Something else is going on. The act of travel, of movement, doesn't change us so much as solidify us. On the road, free from expectations, others and our own, pieces of ourselves, previously scattered fragments, click into place, and we are whole. This is what happened to Charles Darwin in the Galapagos, Mahatma Gandhi in South Africa, George Harrison on the banks of the Ganges. They all experienced what author Robert Grudin calls "the beauty of sudden seeing."

Benjamin Franklin took such a journey. Only twenty years old, he traveled from London to Philadelphia. He departed one person and arrived another. He left London a punk, engaging in "intrigues with low women," making moves on his best friend's girl, cozying up to aristocrats, writing a scandalous and largely inane dissertation, and in general acting like a typical guy. Thirteen weeks later, he arrived in Philadelphia a man.

I gingerly step aboard a bullet of a boat called the Red Jet and find a seat up front. Soon we're rocketing across the English Channel, powered, the brochure informs me, by "high-speed MTU diesel engines with waterjet propulsion." I have no idea what that means, yet I marvel at the smoothness and effortlessness of it all, so different from Franklin's time. Speed seduces. It lures you with flagrant flattery and enticing promises. *Hey, you, yeah you,* Speed whispers, *you seem like a person going places. Come with me and you'll go to more places, see more,* live *more.* Who can resist?

The boat is sleek and airline-like, with seats seemingly designed not for comfort or safety but to amplify the sense of speed and, by extension, of progress. Is it a sham? Franklin wouldn't think so. He cared a lot about appearances, not as a substitute for authenticity but as an augmentation. When Franklin was a young apprentice-printer, freshly arrived in Philadelphia, he made a point of noisily carting his wheelbarrow through the city's cobblestone streets. "Thus being esteem'd an industrious thriving young man, and paying duly for what I bought . . . I went on swimmingly." Franklin *was* industrious. He just wanted to make sure everyone knew it.

We're zipping along, subduing nature, conquering time. This, too, Franklin would appreciate. His lifelong mission, one of them anyway, was to defang nature, a commitment epitomized by his most famous invention, the lightning rod—or, as it was known in his day, the "Franklin Rod."

The captain cuts the engine. We glide like an airliner on final approach. Directly ahead lie the Isle of Wight and the harbor town of Cowes, with its hodgepodge of buildings clinging to the shoreline and, atop a hill, what looks like a castle. To my side is the harbor, specked with tiny sailboats and the occasional yacht.

I've arrived nearly three hundred years to the day since twenty-year-old Benjamin Franklin did. It took Franklin's ship more than a week to reach here from London. I made the journey, by rail and sea, in a few hours. I didn't worry about fickle winds or changing currents or mutinous crews or scurvy or the sundry other perils that tormented seagoers of the eighteenth century. This too represents progress, I know, but I can't help but wonder about the cost. By "conquering" nature, have we jettisoned vital aspects of our humanity?

This is not a question Franklin spent much time fretting over. He was a consequentialist. What mattered was not the perceived morality of any given action but its outcome. If it was helpful, *useful*, then it was good. If not, it was bad. I am not that way. I am an inconsequentialist. My mind is easily derailed by the theoretical. I am more comfortable in the world of ideas than in the world of, well, just about everything else. I've been called "Esoteric Eric." I'd like to think it was meant as a compliment, but I know it wasn't.

As I disembark the Red Jet, clutching Franklin's account of his three-hundred-year-old journey, a thought occurs to me: *This is like stepping back in time.* I immediately regret that thought. Such a cliché! Such nonsense. Stepping back in time is a lie that tour guides and high school teachers tell us. Sure, we can visit museums, read history books, watch reenactments, wear funny hats, and even close our eyes and picture centuries past, but these are crude facsimiles of time travel. We are forever prisoners of the present. As for the past, the best we can hope for is the occasional conjugal visit. It is, I suppose, better than nothing. As Franklin would no doubt advise: Work with what you have.

Franklin walked the four miles from Cowes to Newport, the island's largest town. I take a double-decker bus, sitting up front and upper deck, entranced like a wide-eyed eight-year-old. If Franklin was right and travel lengthens life, then I want to have a front-row seat to this elongated life.

Fussy Franklin liked Newport. "The houses are beautifully intermixed with trees, and a tall old-fashioned steeple rises in the midst of the town," he notes in his journal. I like it too. Everything feels old, not musty old but heritage old. Good old. The yoga studio, the barbershops, the Comic Coffee café, and the supermarket ("Morrisons: Since 1899") all exude comforting continuity. Even the McDonald's looks old. I find a park bench and ponder.

Why are we so drawn to old buildings? It is about appreciating—and decoding—works of art written in an architectural language at once familiar and foreign. It is also about connecting to the past and locating ourselves on this vast temporal continuum. But it is more than that. Old buildings make us feel better about the present too. No longer is it free-floating, severed from what came before and what will come after but, rather, just another link in a long chain. The more fluid and unpredictable life in the present is, the greater the need for this continuity with the past. Nothing is more comforting than a building that has seen more than you ever will.

"Old buildings are like memories you can touch," says architect Mary DeNadai. I like that. It explains why people still travel in the age of Google Street View. It explains why I am here now, on this small island in the English Channel when every bit of information I might gather, every data point, is available online. Yet it is not the same. I need to touch memories, Franklin's three-hundred-year-old memories, to be precise.

I walk, the latest version of Apple Maps in one hand and Franklin's journal in the other. I turn a corner and pass an old man shuffling down the street, deploying his metal cane as both walking aid and percussive instrument, a *clink-clink* reverberating with each step. Reflexively, I avert my eyes. Why does the man's aged visage offend me? It's not only me. Most people find old places desirable but not old people. We showcase the former—charge admission prices, open gift shops—and warehouse the latter. We avoid the elderly not because they are different but because they are familiar. We catch a glimpse of our future selves in them, and we don't like what we see.

I walk a bit farther then stop, pocket my phone, and read Franklin. The journal, chronicling his journey home to Philadelphia, is a rarity. Franklin seldom kept a journal. This annoys me, to be honest, but I can't blame Ben. He was too busy being a traveler to write about travel just as "he found it more pleasant to be a philosopher than to write philosophy," as Carl Van Doren, the renowned Franklin biographer, notes.

On this journey, though, he had the gift of time. Like most true gifts, it wasn't recognized as one at first. Far from it. This ocean crossing was Ben Franklin's Terrible Horrible No Good Very Bad Journey. It was plagued from the moment the *Berkshire* sailed from London. The winds blew infrequently or, when they did, from the wrong direction. Progress was stunningly, painfully slow. At one point, the ship traveled backward. Nearly everyone on board (except Franklin) got seasick. A shark circled the ship, forcing Ben to skip his daily swim. Onboard, a card cheat was uncovered, as well as a careless cook.

There was one significant upside. Ben had time on his hands, and he used it. He mused about the sciences—natural history, navigation, mathematics—and also psychology and morality, matters of the heart. He got personal, too. The journal provides a rare window into the mind and heart of a private man who rarely revealed his interior life. It's no coincidence Ben opened up on the open seas, sailing in slow motion. Speed may be seductive, but it is during life's slower moments, its intermissions, when genuine breakthroughs become possible.

I turn off the main road and onto a footpath. I like that very English term, *footpath*, and prefer it to *trail* or *walkway*. To my ears, it sounds softer, friendlier. A woman on a bike tinkles her bell and apologizes profusely—"sorry, sorry"—as she's about to pass and then thanks me just as profusely—"thank you, thank you"—once she has done so. It seems a bit "extra," as my teenage daughter would say.

Was the woman on the bike really sorry? Was she really grateful? Frank, an American friend who has lived in London for years, assured me that no, she was not. The Brits are polite, yes, but they don't mean it, he told me. Does this alleged lack of sincerity matter? Franklin, I bet, would answer no, it does not. Sincere or not, the British are polite, and politeness serves a social function. It is the lubricant that keeps society's wheels turning. Writing years later, he describes politeness as a universal value. "Perhaps if we could examine the manners of different nations with impartiality, we should find no people so rude as to be without rules of politeness." For Ben, politeness is useful and therefore good.

The footpath wends through the countryside. I spot something around the bend but at first can't identify it. Then I realize it's the old church Franklin mentioned in his journal. Three hundred years later, there it is, just as he said it was. I know it's silly, but matching Franklin's journal to what I am seeing—not on my iPhone but in real life—makes me feel closer to Ben.

I arrive first at the churchyard cemetery. Tombstones lean every which way, yet for centuries they haven't fallen. I try to read the inscriptions, but they are too weathered to make out, some so pockmarked and faded it's hard to believe anything was ever inscribed on them. Yet there was. Someone is buried here. Someone lived here. Like me, Franklin was unable to read the inscriptions; they were too faded even then. Three hundred years is a very long time, and no time at all.

I approach the church's front door. A sign informs me that it is "open daily for private prayer and reflection." Franklin would like that. For him, prayer was a private matter, always. Inside, it is cool and quiet. Two microphones hang from the ceiling. Otherwise, the church is unchanged since Franklin's time. It is still "an elegant building," as he noted, and still "looks very venerable in its ruins." Everywhere I look I see wood rafters and stone and, on the walls, plaques commemorating the dead. This time they are legible. The ages range from nine to eighty. Death was closer during Franklin's time than it is now, and even more capricious.

I resume my walk, paralleling the stream Franklin mentions. I feel as though he is guiding me and doing a better job than Apple Maps, which is flummoxed by the English countryside. The path steepens, just as Ben said it would. I am huffing and puffing. Ben, some forty years younger than me, did not strain a bit. Whippersnapper.

I walk under a canopy of trees, then open sky. The path is paved, then not, then paved again. All is flux, Franklin would say. He was a fluid thinker whose life revolved around flow in its sundry forms. Cash flow. The flow of printer's ink, and of blood pumping through veins. The river under the Atlantic, the Gulf Stream. The flow of water under his body as he swam the Thames. The flow of coffee at St. Paul's Coffee House in London or Café Procope in Paris, and of Madeira everywhere. The rising air that lifts a balloon aloft. Most of all, the unceasing, turbulent flow of history.

During Franklin's time, people thought a lot about motion and change—not any particular change but about the idea itself. One product of the eighteenth century, the century of progress, was the belief in perpetual progress. The present is better than the past and the future will be better than the present. Today, such a progression, at least when it comes to science and technology, strikes us as self-evident, but it is a relatively new idea, born in the coffeehouses of London and the salons of Paris three centuries ago.

It was a difficult birth. There were dissenting voices. The loudest of these belonged to the philosopher Jean-Jacques Rousseau. "There is no real advance in human reason, for what we gain in one direction, we lose in another," he said. We think we're swimming across the English Channel but maybe we're doing laps in a pool, exerting much energy but getting nowhere.

I enter dense woods, and the footpath turns cooler and steeper. The quaint village of Carisbrooke lies below, a miniature collage of black roofs resting atop red-bricked houses. What a beautiful scene, I think, unmarred by the passage of time, when a tour bus roars by, jerking me back to the twenty-first century.

I walk downhill, catch a double-decker bus, and soon I am back at the harbor town of Cowes. I have some time to kill before catching the Red Jet, so I grab a flat-white coffee and stop to listen to a street musician, playing the guitar and singing. "*Where you gonna sleep tonight . . .*" He's no spring chicken, I note, but he's good. I stop myself. Why the "but"? Why do I assume abilities diminish with age? They didn't with Franklin, at least not the abilities that matter.

Age reveals character, good and bad. That was Ben's conclusion after learning of one Joseph Dudley, a former governor of the Isle of Wight. Not a nice man, he was universally despised. Dudley tried to conceal his nastiness, as nasty people do, but to no avail, prompting Franklin to latch onto a truism that stuck with him the rest of his life and, thanks to his snappy formulation, with us too: "Honesty is the best policy."

> I believe it is impossible for a man, though he has all the cunning of a devil, to live and die a villain, and yet conceal it so well as to carry the name of an honest fellow to the grave with him, but someone by some accident or other shall discover him. Truth and sincerity have a certain distinguishing native lustre about them which cannot be perfectly counterfeited; they are like fire and flame that cannot be painted.

Franklin left Cowes, much as I do: reflective. I'm thinking about the specter of—I'll just say it—old age. It frightens me. Death frightens me too, but old age frightens me more. Death—dying, to be more precise—is a finite experience. Nature ensures it won't take long (even if it feels interminable). Old age is another story. It can last a long time and, unlike dying, the rules are less clear. The dying are supposed to die. The old are supposed to ... what? Get older? Pretend they are young? I don't know what the correct answer is. I'm not sure anybody does.

The *Berkshire* finally broke free of the English Channel and was now in open ocean, sailing for Philadelphia. It was doing so slowly. The winds remained uncooperative. Days passed with hardly a breeze. Franklin's journal entries toggle between the loquacious and the staccato, depending on the wind. Here is his complete entry for Monday, August 8: "Fine weather, but no wind worth mentioning, all this day; in the afternoon saw the lizard."

He spent a lot of time observing marine life: porpoises, flying fish, oysters, dolphins, sharks and a tiny crab "about as big as the head of a ten-penny nail, and of a yellowish colour." A few days later, he placed a crab in a vial filled with saltwater, hoping to preserve it for future study. Franklin the Possibilian at work.

The flying fish were of particular interest. They leaped out of the sea, soaring gracefully but unable to turn midflight. This lack of directional control, notes Franklin, made the fish easy prey for the dolphins. I can't help but wonder if he was talking about more than flying fish. Franklin always needed to turn, to pivot at a moment's notice, as he did when Governor Keith duped him. He needed options. That way, he avoided the dolphins and the sharks.

Franklin also observed the social life aboard the *Berkshire*. People's moods swayed with the winds. When they blew strongly and from the East, spirits soared. "Every one puts on a clean shirt and a cheerful countenance, and we begin to be very good company," he notes in his journal. But when the winds flagged or turned contrary, the mood onboard soured. From his journal entry on September 11: "The long continuance of these contrary winds has made us so dull, that scarce three words have passed between us."

With supplies running low, the captain was forced to ration bread; each passenger was allowed two and a half biscuits per day. The cook, suspected

of "making an extravagant use of flour in the puddings," was whipped. I read
that and cringe. Whipped for using excess flour? Life on the *Berkshire* makes
The Great British Bake Off look like a cakewalk.

One day, a Dutchman spotted a fellow passenger marking a deck of
cards. This was a serious accusation. A "court of justice" was convened, and
the passenger was found guilty. The accused man maintained his innocence
and refused to pay the fine levied. The "court" then devised an especially
cruel punishment: the man was excommunicated. No other passenger would
dine, drink, play, or converse with him until he paid his fine. This continued
for several days until the convicted passenger could no longer bear the isola-
tion. He paid his fine and rejoined his shipmates.

The episode prompted Franklin to ponder the nature of solitude. He
acknowledges it can serve as a tonic, "an agreeable refreshment to a busy
mind," but on balance, he found solitude disagreeable, even a form of tor-
ture. "Man is a sociable being, and it is for aught I know one of the worst of
punishments to be excluded from society." He recalled hearing about a man
sentenced to seven years' solitary confinement at the Bastille prison in Paris.
He was "a thinking man" and, were it not for the inventive ways he occupied
his mind with scraps of paper, would have gone insane.

I'm not so sure, Ben. Don't get me wrong. I like people (most anyway),
but I like them the way I like exercise: intermittently, in small doses, and with
plenty of recovery time afterward. Solitude is underrated.

Adrift in the Atlantic, Ben pondered other big questions, his mind
churning in the still, summer air. He began to question his earlier convic-
tions—about everything. He started with his London pamphlet. Virtue and
vice are different, he decided, and they matter. A lot. He vowed to lead a virtuous, useful life. For him, the two were inseparable. Virtues such as sincerity
and industry are the personal tools that enable you to achieve social goods.
He also began to question the philosophy of deism. Years later, recalling this
shift in thinking, he wrote, "I began to suspect that this doctrine tho' it might
be true, was not very useful."

When I first read that sentence, it flummoxed me. Isn't something that
is true also, by definition, useful? Two plus two equals four. That is true and

useful when it comes to tasks like, oh, counting and making it past elementary school.

Sure, Franklin would say, but the connection between truth and usefulness grows murkier when it comes to ethical and religious matters. He was less interested in lofty truths and more interested in what the philosopher John Dewey would later call "instrumentalism." For Franklin, the ultimate test of any moral proposition was not its truth but its utility. Okay, something is "true." *That's nice*, says Franklin. *But what are the consequences of acting on it? If they are not good, not beneficial either on a personal or societal level, discard it and find another, more useful truth.*

Franklin valued truth, of course, just not at all costs and not blindly. There are many truths out there, and it is our job as intelligent and caring humans to separate the useful truths from the useless ones. Or, as the philosopher and psychologist William James would say more than a century later, "Truth is what works." James helped construct a philosophy, pragmatism, to describe the way Franklin lived.

Journeys, the good ones, never really end. They stay with us long after our bags are unpacked and we've returned to "the world of dust," as the Chinese call our everyday existence. So it was with Franklin. His Great London Adventure had begun with a ruse and ended with a revelation.

He was still at sea but no longer adrift. He had devised a "Plan of Conduct" and vowed that "henceforth, I may live in all respects like a rational creature." His plan consisted of four simple rules. He would be frugal and pay off his debts. He would aim for sincerity "in every word and action." He would practice patience and focus on the business at hand, not allowing himself to be distracted by "any foolish project of growing suddenly rich." And he would not speak ill of anyone and instead excuse their faults.

It is a simple plan, deceptively so. I like it. It identifies the basics needed to become better, more useful humans. Pay what you owe. Say what you mean. Focus on what matters. Treat people kindly.

But a problem remained. Franklin couldn't implement his plan while bobbing aimlessly in the Atlantic. Would the *Berkshire* ever reach its destination? Franklin and his fellow passengers began to doubt it. He won-dered, only half-jokingly, if America had sunk under the sea, or perhaps the entire world had been swept away in a tremendous flood and the *Berkshire*'s passengers and crew were now "the only surviving remnant of the human race."

One day, Ben noticed the water had changed color, as it often does near land, and his mood lifted. But he soon realized it was just his imagination. "We are very apt to believe what we wish to be true," he writes. This quirk of human nature—the rational mind's tendency to trick itself—is something Franklin would remain wary of throughout his life. He was a rational man, the Age of Reason embodied, but he also recognized the limits of reason.

Finally, after thirteen long weeks at sea, came the sound Franklin had longed to hear. "Land! Land!" cried the lookout. Passengers scrambled to the deck. Soon, most could discern the outline of the mid-Atlantic coast, "appearing like tufts of trees." It took Franklin a while longer to see this. There was nothing wrong with his vision. "My eyes were dimmed with the suffusion of two small drops of joy," he said.

Ben Franklin, home at last, was right. Travel does lengthen life. What he failed to note is that sometimes, when the winds are fickle and the seas rough, when speed takes a holiday and everything that can go wrong does, travel deepens life too.

TEN

FLUID BEN

For Ben Franklin, freshly returned to his "dear Philadelphia" after his Great London Adventure, life got worse before it got better. He had been working for the kindly Quaker merchant Thomas Denham for only a short while when both men fell seriously ill, Franklin with pleurisy, a dangerous disease of the lungs. Denham eventually succumbed to his disease. Franklin nearly did too. He was only twenty-one years old.

In his memoir, Franklin reveals little about this dark period, but he does sound a pessimistic note in what is an otherwise stubbornly hopeful work. "I suffered a good deal, gave up the point in my own mind, and was rather disappointed when I found my self recovering; regretting in some degree that I must now some time or other have all that disagreeable work to do over again."

What to make of Franklin's tumble into the slough of despond? Not too much, I think. He was human and, like most of us, occasionally felt the black dog of depression nip at his heels. There is nothing remarkable about that. What is remarkable is that if you read Franklin's voluminous writings, you find so little darkness and so much light. His outlook, I think, is best summed up in an exchange with his sister Jane.

Ben, older now and back in London, was enduring another rough spell.

This time it wasn't his health but his political opponents, haughty British parliamentarians slinging copious amounts of mud in his direction. His sister asked, in so many words, *Doesn't this upset you?*

Not really, Franklin replied. "These are the operations of nature. It sometimes is cloudy, it rains, it hails; again 'tis clear and pleasant, and the sun shines on us. Take one thing with another, and the world is a pretty good sort of a world; and 'tis our duty to make the best of it and be thankful."

I read those words and feel small. Franklin lived in a time before antibiotics and airplanes, before air-conditioning and modern dentistry. A time before free two-day shipping. Life was a crapshoot. Any number of ailments and accidents could cut you down; that is, if the redcoats didn't get you, yet Franklin declares it, on balance, "a pretty good sort of a world."

I'm beginning to suspect it's not the world that is the problem but my perception, my vision. Consider one of Franklin's best-known inventions: bifocals. They enable you to see both near and far, and all in one handy pair of spectacles. Franklin possessed that ability naturally. He could see the horrors of the world, near as they were, but he never lost the distant, brighter view. He was no Pollyanna. He knew what evil men (and it was almost always men) were capable of. But he never let that truth blind him to more useful truths.

In the depth of his illness, at age twenty-one, Franklin composed his own epitaph. He deployed the language of his craft, printing, and in typical Franklin style, a stiff dose of humor. As usual, the humor masked a serious point. Ben compares his body to an old book, its pages ripped out, its cover stripped of lettering. The man, like the book, will reappear, though, "in a new & more perfect edition, corrected and amended by the author."

Every first edition of a book contains errors. Trust me. I was giving a talk about one of my books at the Rochester Public Library when someone asked, "I assume you know about the typo on page 247?"

"Oh, uh, yes, that typo, of course," I improvised before scrambling to find page 247 where there was indeed a misprint. Publishers correct these errors, called errata, in future editions, creating, as Franklin notes, more perfect though never flawless versions. This process of fault finding and correcting is never ending.

So, Franklin thought, why not apply this printer's method to life? We all make mistakes. We all commit errata. His Puritan brethren called these errata "sins," with all the guilt and hair-shirting that word entails. Not Franklin. For him, errata were simply mistakes. They happen and they are correctable. In the next life, yes, but—and this is crucial—in *this life* too. Our lives are written in pencil, not pen.

Franklin's friend, the preacher George Whitefield, read his epitaph and lost no time trying, not for the first time, to convert Ben. "I have seen your epitaph. Believe [in] Jesus, and get a feeling... of God in your heart and you cannot possibly be disappointed of your expected second edition, finely corrected, and infinitely amended."

Franklin surely chuckled, but he wasn't buying what Whitefield was selling. He didn't believe correcting our errata required any outside editorial assistance. Nor did he subscribe to the beliefs of the early Romantics, such as his contemporary, Rousseau. In his memoir, *The Confessions*, Rousseau mines his troubled childhood for the source of his chronic melancholy. More than a century later, Freud would posit essentially the same idea, albeit more scientifically. We are wounded at a young age and spend the rest of our lives trying to unwound ourselves. Ben didn't see it that way.

Franklin's notion of errata implies a fluid and fixable world. Nothing is broken beyond repair. Our childhood need not scar us for life. We are not the sum of our wounds. Every errata is correctable. You just need a good printer. Better yet, print thyself. The writer corrects future editions. In the end, we are the authors of our own lives, and we all self-publish.

Franklin lists five errata in his autobiography. They range from the financial (spending money that was not his) to the intellectual (writing his ill-conceived dissertation on virtue) to the personal (attempting to seduce his friend's lover in London). Most of these transgressions were interpersonal. They represented a tear in the social fabric, and for Franklin, the most social of animals, there was nothing more regrettable. He made a point of correcting each of these errata, even if it was decades later.

Mistakes are made. Mistakes are corrected. More perfect editions are released. If this all sounds a bit too tidy, that's because it is. Not all of Franklin's mistakes made his list of errata, and not all could be corrected.

A few years after his brush with death, Franklin married Deborah Reed, and they had a son, a "fine boy" named Francis, or Franky, as he was known. He was the Franklins' only child after six years of marriage and was deeply loved. One day, four-year-old Franky developed a fever and the telltale pustules of smallpox. He soon died. Deborah and Ben were devastated. Did they do all they could? A crude but effective smallpox inoculation existed at the time, but Franklin did not have his son immunized. A vocal proponent of the procedure, he had intended to do so, he said, as soon as his son recovered from "the flux," an unrelated stomach ailment.

Franklin would regret this lapse for the rest of his life. Writing to his sister Jane, some four decades later, he said he still could not think of Franky "without a sigh." Some errata cannot be corrected in future editions. They can only be accepted. This painful truth is something Franklin struggled to come to terms with. Just as I do. Just as we all do.

Thomas Denham's death came as a blow to Franklin. He had lost a man who "counsell'd me as a father," he recalled. "I respected and lov'd him: and we might have gone on together very happily."

Franklin couldn't afford to freeze, unable to maneuver like the flying fish he had seen over the Atlantic. He needed to pivot midflight. So he did. He got his old job back with that "odd fish," Samuel Keimer. As expected, they squabbled. Franklin was an excellent worker, but Keimer wanted to cut his pay. In the end, it was a "trifle" that severed their relationship. Franklin heard a commotion one day and, always curious, poked his head out the window. Keimer scolded him loudly and profanely and, worse, did so in earshot of the neighbors. He had publicly humiliated Franklin, and for Ben there was nothing worse. Ben Franklin walked out of Keimer's print shop, never to return.

Again, Franklin was broke and unemployed. His "Plan of Conduct," so resolutely conceived aboard the *Berkshire*, had stalled. He needed a miracle. He knew it would not come from either heaven or himself. For Franklin, miracles always arrived in the form of other people.

ELEVEN

SOCIAL BEN

Ben Franklin's long and useful life spanned nearly all of the eighteenth century, coinciding with the Enlightenment. The period of scientific and philosophical progress yielded a harvest so rich and varied we are still partaking of it today. Every time you visit a doctor or contribute money to Amnesty International or turn on the lights or drink a cup of coffee, you have Enlightenment thinkers like Franklin to thank.

Bountiful harvests don't just happen, of course. They require diligent farmers and healthy seeds as well as plentiful sunlight and, perhaps most of all, good soil. The soil of the Enlightenment was the word, in written and spoken form.

The Age of Enlightenment was also the Age of Conversation. These gabfests took place in the coffeehouses of London and the salons of Paris, in the learned company of the Royal Society, and in the rough-and-tumble dockyards of Glasgow, where Adam Smith developed many of his economic theories.

A good conversationalist doesn't necessarily make a good public speaker. Awkward and faltering, Benjamin Franklin was not a gifted public speaker, and he knew it. In larger groups or among strangers, he hardly uttered a word.

But Franklin was a superb conversationalist. On this point, everyone agreed. Chatting with Ben "was always a feast to me," recalled James Madison, who was young enough to be Franklin's grandson. "I never passed half an hour in his company without some observation or anecdote worth remembering." No frivolous anecdotes, either. Franklin's stories and jokes were intended not only to entertain but to illuminate.

While still in his twenties, Franklin wrote a brief essay about the art of conversation. I've read it and reread it and every time I marvel at how relevant and contemporary it feels. Franklin was writing at a time before telegraphs and telephones, Facetime and Zoom, Slack and Snapchat. Yet his observations about the art of conversation are just as applicable as when he wrote them nearly three hundred years ago—a reminder that despite our many technological advances, conversation still amounts to one person talking to another, hoping to connect.

Most people believe they excel in conversation, he said, but they deceive themselves (just as today most people claim to be above-average drivers, a statistical impossibility). In conversation, people tend to go to extremes, either focusing exclusively (and annoyingly) on themselves or mercilessly probing their hapless conversant for some dirt. Some people wrangle and dispute incessantly; "thus every trifle becomes a serious business." Some people dwell on one topic too long, while others "leap from one thing to another with so much rapidity . . . that what they say is a mere chaos of noise and nonsense."

The biggest mistake people make, Franklin thought, was "*talking overmuch*, and robbing others of their share of the discourse." I love that phrase, *talking overmuch*, and plan to use it the next time I find myself straining to get a word in with an overtalker. A good conversationalist is a good listener. "Observe, the precept is *hear much*, not *speak much*," he declared, from behind his Poor Richard mask. The mask was no act, though. Franklin was genuinely interested in people, and that's not something that can be faked, not even by the Old Conjurer. No matter how busy, he always had time to talk, recalled Pierre Cabanis, a medical student who knew Franklin during his stay in France. "Whenever one found him, he was available . . . he always had an hour to devote to you."

Franklin knew Westerners had no monopoly on good conversation hygiene. He expressed admiration for the "profound silence" observed by Native Americans when someone else was speaking. Compare that, he said, to the raucous British House of Commons or the so-called polite company of Europe, "where if you do not deliver your sentence with great rapidity, you are cut off in the middle of it."

A good conversationalist doesn't simply master a bundle of clever techniques. He possesses a generosity of spirit, a genuine willingness to better, not best, the person at the other end of the table. This demands a "readiness to overlook or excuse their foibles," Franklin said. Overlooking is different from not seeing. You see and hear your interlocutor's flaws, but choose to move past them, for now, so the conversation is freed to elevate both of you.

Being a good conversationalist doesn't mean swallowing your opinions and beliefs. Franklin had many but never used them as a cudgel. They arrived Bubble-Wrapped. If asked what he thought about a subject, Franklin typically replied by asking a question or raising a doubt, engaging his interlocutor rather than alienating him. You could surmise where he stood, but he never allowed opinions, even strong ones, to come between people. Preserving a friendship was more important than scoring points, a useful truth that argumentative people fail to grasp. "They get victory sometimes," he said, "but they never get goodwill, which would be of more use to them." For Ben, the relationship was always more important than the problem.

But where to find good conversation in Philadelphia, a colonial backwater without a decent newspaper or bookstore? Philadelphia did have a few social clubs, but none dedicated to meaningful conversation and certainly none accessible to a leather-apron man like Franklin. So Ben created it.

That sounds awfully Silicon Valley, I realize. You sense a need for something but this something doesn't exist, so you invent it. Too often, though, the need is imagined and the invention silly. Franklin's start-ups mattered. They made a real difference in people's lives. He founded (or cofounded) a library, a fire department, an insurance company, a militia, a scientific organization, a hospital, and more. I don't think he saw these as "start-ups" or himself as a "founder." It was more reflexive than that. He was, in that wonderfully antiquated Britishism (still used in India), "doing the needful." When he invented the lightning rod, he was doing the needful. When he invented a flexible catheter or a stove that burned cleaner and more efficiently, he wasn't doing it for the money or the followers. He wasn't getting all Elon Musky. He was doing the needful.

And so, one autumn day in 1727, Franklin, only twenty-one years old, unemployed and still recovering from that serious bout of pleurisy, sat down and did the needful. Perhaps it was along the banks of the Schuylkill, or maybe on a barstool at the Indian Head Tavern. Either way, I can see him with notebook and quill, devising a plan.

First, he needed a name. Franklin knew you can indeed judge a book by its cover, which is why as a printer, he went to such great lengths to design beautiful ones. How about the "Leather Apron Club"? It made sense. He would draw the club's membership from tradesmen, working-class slobs like himself. I suspect he found the name too limiting, though, so he searched for something else. How about "the Junto"? Derived from the Latin *juncta*, or "joining together," the name underscored Franklin's unshakable belief in the power of the group. Yes, the Junto it was.

Next, he needed members. There was no shortage of young men (the club was not open to women; Franklin's inclusiveness went only so far) like himself in Philadelphia. He recruited three colleagues from his former print shop, as well as a smattering of others: a clerk, a surveyor, a shoemaker, a mechanic. They belonged to various political parties and Christian denominations but shared a love of reading and poetry and ideas. They were not the sort of people with trust funds or private libraries or access to the creamy layer of Philadelphia society. Franklin wanted to ensure the club remained small and intimate, so he capped membership at twelve.

Next, he needed a venue. The Indian Head Tavern seemed as good a place as any. The food would be a draw, and the ale would lubricate conversation. It was settled. The Junto would meet at the Indian Head every Friday evening.

Finally, saving the hardest part for last, Franklin turned to the club's raison d'être. He knew it wasn't simply a place for a bunch of young working-class men to fling off their leather aprons, down pints of ale, and gab about sports or town gossip. Franklin aimed higher. His Junto was part Rotary Club, part book club, part fitness club, part group therapy, part incubator, and part confessional. It was Franklin's Harvard, "the best school of philosophy, morals, and politics that existed in the province," he said. The Junto was also Franklin's church, its members his congregation. There was an initiation ceremony. Each new member had to stand and affirm his love of truth, and for all people, regardless of religion or occupation.

The Junto didn't coddle its members. It made demands of them. Each week, the young men had to supply questions "on any point of morals, politics, or natural philosophy," to be discussed by the group, and every three months they presented an essay on a subject of their choosing.

Let's pause and consider how demanding this must have been. Life in colonial Philadelphia was hard, especially for this group of working-class men, who put in six days' work each week. They had precious little leisure time. Yet they chose to spend a good chunk of it conversing about weighty subjects, writing queries and essays. Homework. What does this say, I wonder, about them—and about us? Why do we fritter away our leisure time? Perhaps it's because, ironically, we don't take it seriously. "Leisure is time for doing something useful," Franklin said. He wasn't being a killjoy. For Franklin, usefulness was fun. I understand that intellectually, but to understand something only intellectually is not to understand it at all.

The Junto's methods were secular, but the group's animating question mirrored Reverend Cotton Mather's: "What good may I do in the world?" Franklin first floated his many ideas for civic improvement at these meetings. The fire department, insurance company, Pennsylvania militia, and the Philadelphia Academy (later to become the University of Pennsylvania) were all first aired at the Junto. It was Franklin's sandbox.

At the heart of each Junto meeting was a list of twenty-four standing queries drafted by Franklin. Members were to meditate on these each Friday morning ahead of their weekly meeting. These were big, weighty questions. One example: "Do you think of any thing at present, in which the Junto may

be serviceable to *mankind*? to their country, to their friends, or to themselves?"

Note the order. The highest priority is helping humanity, then country,
then friends and, finally, yourself. The phrase that drove these discussions,
one that Franklin and many of his fellow founders used often, was "public
felicity." In the eighteenth century, happiness was not merely a personal as-
piration. It was a communal imperative and thus demanded a group effort.
Either everyone was happy or no one was.

Questions at the Junto meetings ranged from the scientific (How does
dew form on a tankard containing cold water?) to the philosophical ("Is it
justifiable to put private men to death for the sake of public safety or tranquility?") to the political ("Have you lately observed any encroachment on
the just liberties of the people?").

Lest you think the Junto was a joyless club, hold your ale. This was no
sober debating society. There was plenty of levity. A standing query was, in
essence, *Have you heard any good jokes or stories lately?* One member played
the flute at meetings. These gatherings were infused with as much heart as
head. Writing to a fellow Junto member years later, Franklin said, "We loved
and still love one another, we are grown grey together and yet it is [too] early
to part."

The conversation was freewheeling but not a free-for-all. Franklin
erected guardrails. Members were not permitted to interrupt one another or
ridicule another member's manner of speaking. They must converse in a col-
legial manner "without fondness for dispute, or desire of victory." Members
took these rules seriously. Those who violated them were fined.

The Junto was not entirely altruistic. Members looked out for one another. Consider one standing query: "Hath anybody attacked your reputation lately? And what can the Junto do towards securing it?" They clearly
had each other's backs—and wallets. The Junto was also a networking club.
Early LinkedIn. Members steered business toward each other. Franklin,
soon to start his own print shop, landed his first major account thanks to
a fellow Junto member. Despite the Franklin myth, he didn't pull his boot-
straps alone. He enlisted the help of friends, patrons, benefactors, and other

bootstrap pullers. Does this diminish his accomplishments? I don't think so. Success is always a group effort, whether acknowledged or not.

At one point, Franklin suggested members pool their books so all could benefit. It was a good idea, but it flopped. These book lovers weren't about to part with their precious tomes. Franklin, as usual, pivoted, drawing on a larger pool of participants and founding the Library Company of Philadelphia, America's first successful lending library.

For many decades the Junto went on swimmingly, to use a favorite Franklinism, even after Ben had decamped again to London. What made the Junto such an enduring success? Trust explains a lot. The people of the eighteenth century were inundated with new information, some of it credible, much of it not. (Sound familiar?) They needed a reliable means with which to filter this flood of information, help make sense of it. The Junto provided that means. It was useful.

As usual, Franklin didn't hoard his success. He shared it. Though the word didn't exist yet (and wouldn't until 1924), "sustainability" was his goal. He encouraged Junto members to start their own clubs, mini-Juntos. He was planting seeds.

TWELVE

HABITUAL BEN

The Age of Reason was also the Age of Uncertainty, a time when people experienced a "crisis in narrative," as Vaclav Havel called unsettled and unsettling eras. Old ideas washed away; new ones had yet to come ashore. Strong currents tugged in competing directions. Ben didn't fight these currents or surrender to them. He surfed them. As any surfer knows, you don't stand on the board; you *plant* yourself on it. Habits were the glue that enabled Ben to do this.

For Franklin, habit was a powerful force, right up there with electricity. Habit explained why good people did good deeds and why bad people did the opposite. "Men don't become very good or very bad in an instant," he said, "both vicious and virtuous habits being acquired by length of time and repeated acts."

Ben was obsessed with the power of habits from his early years as a habitual reader in Boston. In Philadelphia, that interest accelerated, peaking in 1731 when Franklin, aged twenty-five, entered one of his periodic I-need-to-get-my-act-together phases.

I am familiar with these phases. Mine occur often, usually at the start of a new year, but they can crop up anytime. (I feel one coming on now, in fact.) These cloudbursts of self-improvement are like the weather: always unpredictable, often messy, never conclusive.

Paper is involved. Lots of it. I've tried apps and other digital doodads but keep coming back to paper. Beginning in January and often extending well into spring, a steady parade of planners and organizers lands on my doorstep. They come in various sizes, colors, and configurations, but each contains the implicit promise of redemption. If I can just find the perfect planner, I tell myself, the many moving parts of my life will click into place.

Whenever a new planner arrives, my hopes soar. *This is the one*, I tell myself. And it is—for a while. But after a few weeks (sometimes only days), I discover something wrong with my perfect planner. The margins are too wide or too narrow, the timeline too vertical or too horizontal, the to-do section too large or too skimpy, the paper too thick or too thin, the cover too stiff or too flexible, the pen loop (pen loops are important) too tight or too loose. I worry I spend more time arranging my life than living it. Surely Ben was more disciplined.

I am pleasantly surprised to learn he was not. Like me, he also wrestled with order throughout his life. Like me, he was prone to distraction and absentmindedness. Like me, he loved a good planner. Like me, he possessed a strong and persistent drive to improve. Unlike me, Ben converted that drive into an actual plan and—this is where we truly part ways—*implemented that plan.*

First, he subdued his daily schedule. For Franklin, as for all us self-employed, unstructured time was the enemy. As a young printer in Phila-delphia, he methodically vanquished it. He assigned tasks for each hour of the day. He woke at 5 a.m., then washed, and said a prayer, addressing not God per se but *Powerful Goodness* before plotting his day's business. He then studied for two hours, ate breakfast, and worked at his print shop from 8 a.m. until noon. He had lunch, studied for another hour or two and worked until 6 p.m. He set aside 6 p.m. to 10 p.m. for dinner, music, and "diversion."

It sounds like a remarkably twenty-first-century day, only without time allotted for catching up on emails or binge watching. There's another significant difference: Ben bracketed his day with two questions. In the morning, he'd ask, "What good shall I do this day?" and in the evening, "What good have I done today?" These are simple questions, yet few of us bother asking them. I know I don't. Several of my planners prompt me to note my productivity or what I'm grateful for or my "wins." They say nothing about doing good, about being useful. Clearly, I have yet to find the perfect planner.

Ben emphasized actions, not motives. Not what good thoughts or feelings did he have today but what good did he *do*? Results, not intentions, mattered to him. He had no desire to get in touch with his inner child, or his inner anything, to be honest. While ours is largely an inside-out approach to self-improvement, Franklin's was outside-in, a philosophy later articulated by the twentieth-century psychologist B. F. Skinner: "The problem is to induce people not to be good but to behave well."

The first person Ben needed to induce to behave well was . . . Ben. As he explains in his autobiography, he decided to embark on a "bold and arduous project of arriving at moral perfection." His goal was nothing less than to live "without committing any fault at any time."

I sigh. I have just collided with Ambitious Ben. Ambitious Ben annoys me. We have nothing to say to one another, Ambitious Ben and I. A bold and arduous plan for moral perfection? Really, Ben? I have no such aim. Sure, I have been known to launch bold and arduous plans to lose fifteen pounds or to clean out that desk drawer, the one that has possibly become home to a family of small rodents. I once vowed to prep the coffee maker *the night before*. These are my bold and arduous plans. But moral perfection? Never.

As a budding possibilian, I regroup and read on. Ben called his plan "The Art of Virtue." His choice of that term was no accident (little is accidental when it comes to Ben Franklin). He believed virtuous behavior could be learned just like any art or skill. "If a man would become a painter, navigator, or architect, it is not enough that he is *advised* to be one . . . he must also be taught the principles of the art, be shown all the methods of working, and how to acquire the *habits* of using properly all the instruments; and thus regularly and gradually, he arrives by practice at some perfection in the art."

I can see that, but why the fixation on virtue? To my twenty-first-century ears, the word smacks of smug self-satisfaction. Virtuous people are better than me, or at least they think they are, and they trumpet their alleged superiority. Striving for moral perfection sounds noble, I suppose. It does not sound like much fun.

None of this was true during Franklin's time. Virtues were seen as character traits that consistently yielded goodness. Character meant a lot to Ben. He used the word frequently in his autobiography. *Character* comes from the Greek *charassein*, meaning "to sharpen or engrave." Originally, it referred to the molding and stamping of coins, but soon expanded to the molding of humans. We are not born with character. It is stamped on us. How? Through the grace of God, said the Puritans. Through self-discipline, said Ben.

Virtue was not a nicety or a signal (of anything) during Franklin's day. It was the key to happiness. "Happiness is the aim of life, but virtue is the foundation of happiness," said Thomas Jefferson. Franklin, as usual, expressed the same idea more succinctly: "Virtue and happiness are mother and daughter."

The virtuous life was not a luxury accessible to only a few, he said. It should interest anyone "who wish'd to be happy even in this world." Even a rascal would act virtuously if he knew a jackpot of happiness awaited him. Recent studies bear this idea out. People who regularly engage in altruistic activity report higher levels of happiness, life satisfaction, and meaningfulness. Yet virtue has fallen out of favor. The twentieth century saw a sharp decline in the use of words related to virtue and moral character, such as "perseverance, kindness, gratitude, courage and honesty," one recent study found.

One of Franklin's more quixotic ideas was to found a United Party of Virtue, open to virtuous people everywhere. It sounds risible today, but it was no joke. Virtue held the key not only to happiness, Franklin believed, but to progress as well. *"There was never yet a truly great man that was not at the same time truly virtuous."* Virtue, and by extension happiness, were necessary for a truly free and democratic society. "Only a virtuous people are capable of freedom," Ben told a friend.

Any attempt at leading a more virtuous life immediately encounters a speed bump: Just what counts as a virtue? That question has been asked for millennia. Aristotle had his list, the Christians theirs. Working from these and other sources, Franklin drew up his own list of Thirteen Virtues:

1. TEMPERANCE. Eat not to dullness. Drink not to elevation.

2. SILENCE. Speak not but what may benefit others or yourself. Avoid trifling conversation.

3. ORDER. Let all your things have their places. Let each part of your business have its time.

4. RESOLUTION. Resolve to perform what you ought. Perform without fail what you resolve.

5. FRUGALITY. Make no expense but to do good to others or yourself: i.e. Waste nothing.

6. INDUSTRY. Lose no time. Be always employ'd in something useful. Cut off all unnecessary actions.

7. SINCERITY. Use no hurtful deceit. Think innocently and justly; and, if you speak, speak accordingly.

8. JUSTICE. Wrong none, by doing injuries or omitting the benefits that are your duty.

9. MODERATION. Avoid extremes. Forbear resenting injuries so much as you think they deserve.

10. CLEANLINESS. Tolerate no uncleanness in body, clothes or habitation.

11. TRANQUILITY. Be not disturbed at trifles, or at accidents common or unavoidable.

12. CHASTITY. Rarely use venery but for health or offspring; Never to dullness, weakness, or the injury of your own or another's peace or reputation.

13. HUMILITY. Imitate Jesus and Socrates.

One virtue missing from Ben's list is charity. I don't think it was an oversight. For Ben, benevolence was a given, the natural consequence of a virtuous life.

Why thirteen? Why not the four cardinal virtues of the ancient Greeks:

prudence, justice, courage, and temperance? Ben did value simplicity after all. Yes, but he wanted to slice those larger virtues into smaller bite-sized ones, figuring they'd be easier to master. Another reason for thirteen was strictly mathematical. His plan called for devoting four weeks to each of the thirteen, a routine that would take one year to complete.

The order of the virtues mattered too. One led to the next. Temperance came first because, he figured, without "coolness and clearness of head" he could never tackle the other twelve virtues. Silence came next, since knowledge was obtained "rather by the use of the ears than of the tongue." And so on. Ben added the final virtue, humility, after a Quaker friend suggested he could be "overbearing and rather insolent."

One quality all of Ben's Thirteen Virtues have in common is that I cannot in good conscience claim a single one. Does this make me a moral failure? Or, worse, a sinner? Ben wouldn't think so. I am simply a craftsman who has not yet mastered his craft. More specifically, I have yet to harness the power of habit. We are fluid beings. Our habits and customs, even our beliefs, are malleable. That is good, Franklin thought, for what can be molded can be molded into something beautiful—and useful. What prevents us from acting virtuously is not an evil heart but simply bad habits. Thus, Lieutenant Governor Keith, who dispatched young Ben on a fool's errand to London, was not a bad man. His tendency to overpromise didn't stem from evil intent—quite the opposite; he wanted to please everyone. "It was a habit he had acquired," Franklin concludes, not a character flaw.

The key is constancy. Too many people, Ben said, "wander perpetually from one thing to another." A habit applied only once is no habit at all. What distinguishes a true virtue from a false one is not its purity but its consistency. Acting courageously once may be admirable, but it does not mean you possess the virtue of courage. The inconsistent person, Franklin said, is like the captain of a ship who steers toward one port and then another, never getting anywhere. Just as we learn to build by building or to be a musician by playing music, "we become just by doing just acts; temperate by doing temperate acts, brave by doing brave acts," Aristotle said. At first, we may perform these virtuous acts because our parents insist or because we think it will boost our standing in the community, but through regular practice, they become internalized. It's the fake-it-until-you-make-it school of self-improvement.

Ben's plan for moral perfection worked this way. First, he needed to find the right notebook (notebooks, like pen loops and planners, are important). Allotting a page for each virtue, he then marked one column for each day of the week, then crossed those columns with thirteen red lines, one for each virtue. He pocketed the little book and went about his day. Every time he'd stray from a virtue—by drinking too much ale or telling a hurtful lie, for example—he'd put a small black mark in the corresponding square. He focused on one virtue per week.

Ben's plan strikes me as overly methodical. But that was the point. Everyone knows what virtue is, Ben thought. We just don't know how to achieve it. Self-control is the key. It's the "master virtue," the one that unlocks all the others. Sadly, self-control is the character strength that today people across all fifty states and in fifty-four nations say they possess the least.

Franklin's plan was methodical but not cold-blooded. He never saw habit formation as self-denial. His aim was to internalize these habits, rendering them second nature. He wanted to make these exercises in self-discipline not only tolerable but pleasurable, fun even. One way was by deploying his notebook and pen to aim for a high score. His bold and arduous plan for moral perfection was also a game.

That doesn't make Ben frivolous or unserious. We can take games seriously, as any Red Sox or Manchester United fan can attest. The difference is that in a game, as opposed to, say, a war, the stakes are not as high. We always get another roll of the dice, another move on the chess board, another shot at moral perfection. Should your notebook fill up with black marks, buy another one and start again. You can always start again.

Franklin didn't think it would come to that. He thought his plan for moral perfection would be relatively easy. "As I knew, or thought I knew, what was right and wrong, I did not see why I might not *always* do the one and avoid the other." But Franklin soon discovered he wasn't nearly as virtuous as he thought. "I was surpriz'd to find myself so much fuller of faults than I imagined." Virtue demanded constant vigilance, like weeding a garden. When focused on eliminating one fault, others cropped up—so many faults that his little book was soon riddled with holes due to all those black marks (a different kind of holy book, he punned). He switched to a more durable ivory paper and a gentler lead pencil, "which marks I could easily wipe out with a wet sponge."

Ben struggled with two virtues in particular: order and, especially, humility. "I cannot boast of much success in acquiring the *reality* of this virtue; but I had a good deal with regard to the *appearance* of it," he said.

Moral perfection. Such an odd, almost laughable, term. We seek perfection in so many aspects of life—technology, SAT scores, bowling—yet not when it comes to something as important as morality. Try telling friends you're aiming for moral perfection and see their response. Franklin did not achieve moral perfection, but that was not the point. He emerged from the experiment "a better and a happier man." He compares himself to scribes who strive for perfect calligraphy by imitating the masters. They may not achieve the desired excellence but "their hand is mended by the endeavour." Better to miss a faraway target than hit a nearby one.

Ben stuck to his plan diligently for the first few years, less diligently afterward, but he always carried his little book with him wherever he went. So do I. Back home in Maryland, I order it online from a website called The Art of Manliness. Such a wonderfully retrograde name! I feel my testosterone levels spike when I click on the "complete your order" button.

A few days later, a brown leather notebook with a nice pen loop arrives. The cover reads, "Ben Franklin's Virtues. Daily Record & Journal." Inside is a faithful replica of Franklin's virtues book, complete with lined pages for tracking your habits, as well as space to meditate on the question, "What good should I do this day?" I like it and bump it up to the top of my planner lineup.

I decide to tackle just one virtue, the one I struggle with the most: silence. I am that rare introvert who talks too much. Silence makes me squirm. I shuddered when I heard a friend was embarking on a ten-day silent retreat.

Ten days! I once went ten *hours* without talking. Then I woke up. But that was the old me. The new me is better than that. For the next week, I vow to take my Franklin journal with me wherever I go and record any lapses from the virtue of silence.

I would like to report that the experiment went swimmingly and I achieved a prolonged and profound silence of Dalai Lama proportions. Alas, I did not. So defaced was my journal with black marks, I had to abort the project after a few days. I. Could. Not. Stop. Talking. My daughter felt vindicated by the results. My wife was more blunt. "You are constitutionally incapable of shutting the fuck up," she said.

She may be right, but I don't think the exercise was a failure. I had discovered the extent of my verbosity—not only how much I talked but when. Without fail, the words began to fly whenever I was nervous. The greater my anxiety, the higher my word count. My *talking overmuch*, as Ben would put it, is a coping mechanism. An imperfect one, yes, but it serves a purpose. Talking reduces my anxiety. Vices can be useful too.

Like the ambitious scribes, I had progressed, even if I failed to achieve perfection. I was mended by the endeavor. I realized just how far I had to go before mastering the virtue of silence, and that matters. The next time I annoy the heck out of someone with my incessant and inane verbiage, I will know why. And knowing why you do something annoying is the first step toward undoing it.

THIRTEEN

TEXTUAL BEN

Benjamin Franklin loved words. He loved how they felt in his printer's composing tray and how they looked on the printed page and how they sounded on the lips of great orators like the preacher George Whitefield. He loved the musicality of words. "Here Skugg lies snug as a bug in a rug," he wrote to young Georgiana Shipley when her pet squirrel, Mungo, a gift from Ben, met an untimely demise. He invented words, too, mostly electrical terms but also everyday ones like *mileage* and *fellow-man*, and *magical circle*, and *power of attorney*. He also loved the money that words yielded. Franklin, unlike most wealthy people of his time, owed his small fortune not to gold or tobacco or land speculation but to words.

From a young age, Ben wore the printer title proudly and continued to do so even once he had become internationally renowned, occasionally signing documents simply "B. Franklin, Printer." He began printing at age twelve and continued well into his seventies when, as US representative to France, he set up a small press at his residence in the village of Passy. There he printed everything from quirky bagatelles to the first US passports to a copy of the peace treaty he helped negotiate with Britain.

For Franklin, printing was more than a profession or business. It was an art, a calling, and a force for good in the world. It was a way of seeing the world too. Franklin, like all printers, had to compose the type backward and upside down. He grew accustomed to altered perspectives.

The year is 1728. Franklin has just opened his own print shop on Philadelphia's Market Street. At first, he subsisted on "job printing": blank forms, legal documents, ledgers. It was dull but lucrative work. Franklin was printing money. Literally. He landed contracts to print the currencies of Pennsylvania, the Three Lower Counties (now Delaware), and New Jersey. He developed innovative ways to thwart counterfeiters by using complex variations of spelling and type, as well as "nature printing," inserting images of leaves and other foliage that were extremely difficult to mimic.

Life was good but not good enough. Franklin, still in his twenties, was itching to expand into newspapers and book publishing. His bête noire, Samuel Keimer, had launched Pennsylvania's second newspaper, a dull rag with a name to match: *The Universal Instructor in All Arts & Sciences and Pennsylvania Gazette*.

Keimer was as lazy a publisher as he was a printer. He filled space by reprinting excerpts from a popular encyclopedia, working his way through the alphabet. He didn't get far. When he reached "Ab," he published a short article on abortion, as sensitive a topic then as it is now.

Franklin saw an opening and donned his mask. Two masks, in fact: Martha Careful and Caelia Shortface. The "ladies" were outraged to see an article on such a private topic in a family newspaper. Writing in the *American Weekly Mercury*, a rival newspaper, they warned Keimer that "if thou proceed any further in that *scandalous manner*, we intend very soon to have thy right ear for it." Franklin-in-drag concluded his letter with some advice: "If thou [cannot] make no better use of thy dictionary, sell it . . . and if thou hath nothing else to put in thy *Gazette*, lay it down."

That is what happened. Keimer sold his newspaper to Franklin, for a pittance. Ben renamed it the *Pennsylvania Gazette*. The first edition under new management was published on Christmas Eve 1728. It no longer featured excerpts from the drab encyclopedia but, instead, passages from Xenophon's

Memorable Things of Socrates and *The Morals of Confucius*, among other imaginative sources. Franklin added more local and colonial news and published more frequently. The new *Pennsylvania Gazette* was livelier, timelier, and, of course, funnier than Keimer's. It was, like Franklin himself, at once highbrow and lowbrow.

Franklin crowdsourced the *Gazette*. He solicited help from readers well versed in geography, history, and international customs. "Men thus accomplish'd are very rare in this remote part of the world; and it would be well if the writer of these papers could make up among his friends what is wanting in himself." Classic Franklin. Never hesitate to tap into collective wisdom. Soon, he would establish a network of printers from Boston to Antigua—an early Internet.

Ben was a discerning editor. He valued writing that was "*smooth, clear, and short*." Some confused this simplicity of expression with shallow thinking. If a simple Pennsylvania farmer could understand these ideas, how profound could they be? But Franklin, like Einstein, believed the ability to express complex ideas simply was the true mark of genius. Baroque prose risks offending "the ear, the understanding, or the patience," whereas simplicity represents "the highest happiness."

Good writing must be, above all else, useful. It must, he said, "*benefit the reader, either by improving his virtue or his knowledge*." Today, such useful books are relegated to the self-help sections of bookstores where they are taken less seriously than "literary" works, though they do sell well. Franklin would be confused by this disparity. What is more serious than the truly useful?

A half century before the First Amendment, Franklin championed freedom of the press. In response to charges that he was publishing scandalous material, he wrote a spirited defense of printers everywhere: "The opinions of men are almost as various as their faces," he said. If printers vowed not to print anything that offended someone, "there would be very little printed."

I am at the Library Company of Philadelphia, America's first lending library. Of all the institutions Franklin founded, this was his favorite: "The Mother of all the [North] American Subscription Libraries," he called it. It is here where he taught himself several languages. Before long, he was reading Machiavelli in Italian and Cervantes in Spanish.

Today, the library building is new and boring, but the books are old and fascinating. One in particular catches my eye, a 1744 edition of *Cato Major*, Cicero's meditation on old age. "Franklin's most beautifully printed book," the sign reads. And it is. Exquisitely bound and printed on large sheets of creamy white Genoese paper, it is an object of art. I want to touch it but can't. It is encased in glass.

Franklin published the book partly as a business venture but mostly as a gift to his friend and mentor, James Logan. Logan's eyesight was failing, so Franklin printed the book, which Logan had translated, in large type and with wide margins. It was an extravagant production, and even Logan tried to dissuade Franklin from going through with it. "I advised him against it as I think he must surely lose by it."

Ben did lose money, but as a publisher, he knew taking risks was crucial to success. He published Samuel Richardson's *Pamela*, among the first English novels. He published military books and dictionaries and guides to courtship and marriage and medical treatises, including one with the catchy title *Essays on the West-India Dry-Gripes*.

Some of his publishing projects succeeded. Others failed spectacularly. His two German-language newspapers folded after only a few editions, as did his general interest magazine. Other projects didn't even get that far. He wanted to write a book called *The Art of Virtue* but never did, nor did he launch a support group called the Society of the Free and Easy, which is a shame because, well, sign me up.

The truth is Franklin failed often. He never folded, though. When confronted with a setback, he didn't abandon the idea. He retooled it and tried again. Franklin never let failure discourage him from taking new risks, including his biggest gamble of all: jumping from British Loyalist to American rebel, and at age sixty-nine. For Franklin, failure was a down payment on success.

•   •   •

Three years after revamping the *Gazette*, Franklin launched his most famous, and profitable, publication, *Poor Richard's Almanack*. The man behind this new almanac, Franklin would have us believe, was a humble, cash-strapped, hard-of-hearing astrologer named Richard Saunders. It was great parody, but would it sell? Ben and Richard were up against a tough crowd. The dominant group in Pennsylvania, the Quakers, were known for many things. Humor was not one of them.

The first edition of the annual *Poor Richard's Almanack* took aim at the competition. Titan Leeds, a Quaker from Philadelphia, published the bland and predictable *American Almanack*. Poor Richard (aka Franklin) brazenly predicted Leeds's imminent demise, and with great specificity. Leeds would die on October 17, 1733, at precisely 3:29 p.m. at the very instant of the conjunction of the sun and Mercury. There was no denying this. It was written in the stars.

As you can imagine, Titan Leeds was not happy to hear this news. Very much alive and writing in his own 1734 almanac, Leeds had some choice words for Poor Richard (and, by extension, Franklin), calling him "a fool and a liar." Ben was ready with a parry. Surely this outburst proved Leeds was indeed dead and an imposter was now publishing in his name. The real Titan Leeds would never treat anyone "so indecently and so scurrilously." Titan Leeds never recovered from the dustup. His almanac soon folded.

A few years later, in 1738, Titan Leeds died. Franklin had predicted correctly. He was just off by a few years.

Leeds's demise left the field wide open for Poor Richard, the simple yet wise astrologer mistreated by both his overbearing wife, Bridget, who had expensive taste, and his printer, B. Franklin, who "runs away with the greatest part of the profit." It was all great fun and wildly successful. *Poor Richard* became the best-selling almanac in the colonies. The first one thousand copies sold out in two days. In most Pennsylvania homes, you would find two, and only two, books: the Bible and *Poor Richard's Almanack*.

Franklin's almanac, like others at the time, contained crop forecasts, high and low tides, the times of sunrise and sunset, court dates, distances between towns, recipes, astrological predictions, instructions for making

herbal remedies, and other bits of useful information. Franklin also peppered the pages with "the wisdom of many ages and nations," pithy proverbs,
some original, most borrowed and revised. What others said, Franklin said
better—and funnier. He converted an Italian proverb, "The man who lives
by hope will die by hunger," into "He that lives upon hope, dies farting." He
took a sixteenth-century saying, "Fish and guests in three days are stale," and
rendered it as "fish and visitors stink in 3 days." It is Franklin's version we
remember today.

Poor Richard is forever pleading with his readers to cut him some
slack. Sure, he sometimes makes mistakes, but he always gets the day of the
month right. As for his wayward weather predictions, he requested "the
favourable allowance of *a day or two before* and *a day or two after the* precise
day against which the weather is set." He begged forgiveness for failing to
include eclipses of the moon one year, but "the truth is, I do not find they
do you any good."

Franklin's almanac was amusing, but it was more than that. It was useful, "a proper vehicle for conveying instruction among the common people, who bought scarce any other books," he said. Franklin knew people
hate to take advice, even good advice, and "would never read beyond the
first line of my lectures, if they were usually fill'd with nothing but whole-
some precepts and advice." So he peppered his proverbs—"scraps from the
table of wisdom," he called them—with whimsy. Franklin's follies lured
readers inside the circus tent, where they "will perhaps meet with a serious
reflection . . . [and] may ever after be the better for." The Old Conjurer at it
again, tricking people into becoming better versions of themselves.

Ironically, it was the character named Poor Richard who made Ben
Franklin's rich and varied life possible. The success of his almanac, along
with his newspaper and print shop, enabled him to retire from business at
age forty-two and turn his attention to "philosophical amusements."

But with Ben Franklin, nothing was ever so straightforward. His retirement turned out to be short-lived and his amusements considerably more
than that.

FOURTEEN

CURIOUS BEN

I walk right by it, oblivious. The red brick building looks identical to the other red brick buildings lining Philadelphia's Fifth Street—vaguely colonial but otherwise unremarkable. There is no obvious indication this is home to America's oldest scholarly organization.

"Scholarly" doesn't tell the whole story. Franklin founded the American Philosophical Society in 1743 with the aim of "promoting useful knowledge." Of course. Never knowledge for its own sake, always useful knowledge.

Franklin is again looking down at me, this time from the top of the unremarkable red brick building, the small bust mocking anyone who tries to unmask him. *Good luck,* he says, before adding, from behind his Poor Richard guise, "Men and melons are hard to know."

They sure are, Ben. I feel like a shopper adrift in the produce department, trying to commune with a melon and attracting disapproving looks from other shoppers.

Undaunted, I cross the street to a small museum run by the society. I'll take a small museum over a large one any day. Small museums are intimate and digestible. They're less likely to overwhelm or induce spasms of

107

guilt for overlooking some LIFE-CHANGING exhibit. *What? You visited the Met and didn't see the ancient Egyptian paint-by-numbers exhibit? Cretin!* Small museums, like small books or small portions, make you feel better, not worse, about yourself.

The current exhibit here is titled "Dr. Franklin: Citizen Scientist." I smile, knowing the "Dr." title is partly subterfuge, but I let it slide. I am focused on the "citizen scientist" part. It's an intriguing combination. We don't normally associate the two. Citizen soldier? Yes. Citizen Kane? Sure. But citizen scientist? The term, coined only in 1998, refers to crowdsourced research. Another term for citizen scientist is "free labor."

I once spent a week as a citizen scientist. I was on an Earthwatch expedition in Brazil's Atlantic rainforest. Half a dozen citizen scientists and I helped actual Brazilian scientists plant trees and track the health of the rodent population in the rainforest, all in hopes of helping to stem climate change. It was difficult, dirty work. I molded table-tennis-sized balls of rodent bait, a mealy mush of bananas, peanut butter, and rancid meat that felt and smelled exactly how you'd expect it to feel and smell. I collected seeds, planted seeds, replanted seeds, watered seeds, and did other things to seeds that I now cannot recall but at the time felt meaningful. I sweated more than I had ever sweated in my life even though I showered more than I've ever showered. I weighed and measured and photographed numerous mammals, including Rodents of Unusual Size. I set animal traps and expunged slimy, encrusted lizard scat from them.

I had worked—*with my hands.* Not just any work but demanding, dirt-under-your-fingernails, tropical-sun-on-your-head, mosquitos-up-your-nose work. I was not paid for this work but had—and I realize this sounds crazy—*paid* for the privilege of doing it. I had (and this is the truly insane part) *enjoyed* the work, for I knew that in some minuscule yet undeniable way, I had made the world a better place: a slightly greener, cooler, healthier planet.

Ben would approve, I'm sure, of my spate as a citizen scientist. Technically speaking, though, he was neither. For the bulk of his long and useful life, he was a proud subject of the British Empire. As for "scientist," the word didn't exist in the eighteenth century. Franklin was a natural philosopher, a term that encompassed what today we call science. The two disciplines had yet to divorce, though the marriage was in trouble.

The difference between a scientist and a natural philosopher is more than nominative. The natural philosopher was not consigned to any one discipline. He (and it was almost always a he) pivoted effortlessly from chemistry to botany, from botany to ethics. All human knowledge was of a piece.

I step inside the small museum and find books from Franklin's sprawling library: sturdy, leather-bound volumes that look like they will last forever. They just might. Books printed in the eighteenth century are far more durable than those printed later, owing to the type of paper used and the overall attention to quality—a sign, I think, that progress moves in more than one direction.

I notice one book in particular: *The Philosophy of Earthquakes* by William Stukeley. At first, the title strikes me as odd. Do earthquakes have philosophies? In a way, they do. Earthquakes were much on people's minds. In 1755, a massive temblor struck Lisbon, leveling the city and killing more than 50,000 people. The natural disaster presented a major challenge to the sunny optimism of the Enlightenment. Was the earthquake divine punishment for people's misdeeds? Or was it a result of natural laws? If so, what kind of God would establish such cruel laws? "Evil stalks the land," warned the French philosopher Voltaire in a poem about the quake, "its secret principle unknown to us."

Unknown *so far*, Voltaire implied. Nature was revealing its secrets, thanks to the work of natural philosophers like Franklin, but that only increased the urgency of the era's animating question: Was nature humanity's friend or foe? It was into this supercharged atmosphere that Franklin's electrical discoveries would soon arrive like a thunderclap.

Several examples of Franklin's handwriting are on display in the museum. The pen strokes are confident and distinctive—not quite John Hancockian but close. I want to touch it, but I can't. The papers, yellowing but intact, are behind glass. Not for the first or last time, I lament that we are permitted to see the past but not touch it.

I nearly collide with Isabel Miller. She is a docent. It is one of my favorite words. I always smile when I hear it. It sounds like a composite of *doer* and *decent*. Isabel has been docenting here for the past two decades, a long time, yes, but only a small portion of her eighty-four years.

"Oh," I blurt out, when she tells me her age. "You're the same age as Franklin when he died."

"Yes," she says, giving me a look that I would see again several times during our conversation. No words, just that look, an incongruous combination of crushing disdain and utter indifference. Like Franklin, Isabel knows that silence stings.

I like Isabel. There is something Franklinesque about her, and not just her age. Perhaps it's the way she's so comfortable in her own skin, or how she deflects delicate questions with a joke or a story. She is sharp and opinionated and, at times, saucy and provoking, just like Ben. When I ask her what most visitors to the museum know about Franklin, she doesn't hesitate.

"Two things," she says, "the kite experiment and the women."

I decide to start with the women. Franklin has a reputation, then and now, as a Lothario, the founding flirt. Was he?

Yes, says Isabel, but not in the way I'm thinking. "Franklin knew that the way to a woman's heart is through her brains. He recognized that women were more than bodies. They had brains." Franklin was content to know their brains, and only their brains, she believes, dismissing rumors of his serial philandering. "He flirted with a lot of women but he never bedded them," she says. Historians are not so sure. There is no evidence Franklin was ever unfaithful to his wife, Deborah, during their long separations but, as the good doctor himself would agree, absence of evidence is not evidence of absence. The rumors persist to this day.

No wonder. Ben fueled them himself through his occasionally risqué writing. Most famous, or infamous, is his "Advice to a Friend Choosing a Mistress" (also known as the "Old Mistress's Apologue"), in which he enumerates the many advantages of older women (reason number eight: "They are *so grateful!!*"). But I think we are also to blame for sustaining bawdy Ben. We like this image of Franklin as the naughty founder. It makes him more real. It makes him one of us.

I trail Isabel as she greets tour groups, large and small, deploying her Franklinian knowledge fluently and humbly. I'm sure she's delivered her spiel a thousand times before, but it sounds like the first.

"I'm a colonial gossip," she tells a couple from Florida, eliciting a laugh.

"The average person, learned person, back then, in the eighteenth century, owned eleven books," she tells a family from India. "Books were precious." They nod knowingly.

Now she is talking about how Franklin was "addicted to chess" (true) and how he was "not so kind to the women in his life" (also true, up to a point). She points to a portrait of Deborah and explains how she ran the business and post office while Franklin was away for years at a time yet gets no credit. "Anyway, that's Deborah," concludes Isabel, keeping the mood light. "We're good friends."

One tourist, a fit young guy wearing a baseball cap, says, "He was a womanizer, right?"

"No, he was more of a woman user," Isabel parries. That silences him.

"He had nice handwriting," someone else says.

"Yes, he did," Isabel says.

Later, when we're alone again, I ask her: "If you could transport yourself to colonial America, who would you want to have lunch with?"

Not Franklin, she replies: "He is too self-centered for me." I notice she speaks of him, and all these other historical figures, in the present tense. "No, I'd probably have lunch with his sister, Jane. As a woman, she was stuck. If she were a man, she would have been another Ben Franklin." This is quite possible, as Jane herself acknowledged toward the end of her long life. "Thousand[s] of Boyles, Clarks and Newtons have probably been lost to the world, and lived and died in ignorance and meanness, merely for want of being placed in favourable situations, and enjoying proper advantages." There are dozens of portraits of Ben Franklin but not a single one of Jane. The women and enslaved persons in Franklin's life, his invisible helpers, remain largely out of sight.

Or, says Isabel, she might lunch with one of Philadelphia's other Benjamins: Rush or Lay, early abolitionists both. And, yes, the New Englander

John Adams may have been "prim and proper," as she generously puts it, but unlike Franklin, he never enslaved anyone. She has a point. Franklin would change his mind about slavery, but it took him a long while.

I'm not sure why, but I feel the need to defend Ben. "This is all true," I say feebly, "but he could be quite witty and charming."

"Sometimes charm and wit cover a great hole in your character," she counters, before moving in for the kill. "No, he is just a fat old fart."

Ouch. How would Ben respond? He'd laugh, I'm sure, and probably agree. For much of his life, he *was* fat ("Dr. Fatsides," he called himself). And he was old, outliving nearly all his contemporaries. As for flatulence, he wrote an entire essay extolling its virtues. Yes, he was a fat old fart but a self-aware fat old fart.

We are all born with an innate sense of wonder and curiosity. Somewhere between birth and adolescence, this quality is beaten out of us. It happens so gradually we're not even aware of it. One moment we're staring for hours at the rainwater sluicing across the road and glowing alternately green and red from the light cast by a nearby traffic signal, and the next moment we're sleepwalking by the same scene, oblivious to its beauty.

Franklin never lost his sense of wonder. He was curious about everything. He was curious about how rain falls, the nature of sunspots, the Gulf Stream, nor'easters, dust devils, recipes for cheese (parmesan in particular), how windmills are built in Poland, the electric shocks delivered by the torpedo fish, the biochemistry of flatulence, the causes of the common cold. Peering through a microscope for the first time, he marveled at how it "opened to us . . . a world utterly unknown to the ancients," noting that the spleen of a single codfish contained ten times more living organisms "than the inhabitants of Europe, Asia, Africa, and America." I have never seen the spleen of a codfish under a microscope, but I doubt I would have the same reaction as Franklin. This worries me: I'm beginning to wonder about my sense of wonder. Has it been beaten out of me? Worse, have I beaten it out of myself?

The full range of Ben's curiosity is on display here at the American Philosophical Society's small museum: a detailed map he drew of the Gulf

Stream, a portable chess set, illustrations of waterspouts. What I see as an impressive variety Isabel diagnoses as an inability to focus. Early ADHD. "He was a dabbler," she says.

Yes, he was, but is that so terrible? Another word for dabbling is experimenting. How do we know which flavor of ice cream we like best if we don't sample many? Besides, everyone was a dabbler back then. The Age of Enlightenment was also the Age of the Amateur. Many of the era's greatest scientific breakthroughs were made by rank amateurs with no special training. An English clergyman named Joseph Priestley discovered oxygen. A German composer named William Herschel discovered a new planet, Uranus. And a Philadelphia printer with two years of formal education pioneered a new science.

Today, Franklin, he of the electrified kite, is so coupled with electricity we assume it could not have been any other way. Electricity, though, was not an obvious choice. Other fields, such as chemistry and botany, were far riper for exploration. Electricity was a scientific cul-de-sac, "a strikingly useless commodity." So why did Franklin, the King of Usefulness, choose to focus his not insignificant intellectual powers on such a "useless" discipline? Was it merely, as he said, a "philosophical amusement"? No, he had a hunch that electricity would prove fruitful, a hunch driven partly by his love of adventure and partly pure chance. *Distrust not providence.*

He happened to be visiting his hometown of Boston in 1743 when he attended the electrical demonstration by Archibald Spencer. What he saw "surprised and pleased" him. Franklin relished surprise, cultivated it. To be surprised was to be invited to play a game, and for Franklin, there was nothing better than a good game.

Spencer was one of the era's itinerant "electricians," as those who studied electricity were known. They held public lectures that were partly educational but mostly entertainment. A popular demonstration, which Franklin witnessed in Boston, was called the Dangling Boy. An eight-year-old boy was suspended above the floor. The electrician then touched a charged glass tube to his bare feet. The boy, now electrified, could attract metal shavings as if by magic, while sparks flew from his face and hands.

Some electrical demonstrations had erotic overtones. In the eighteenth century, electricity and sex were linked. Electric eels inspired erotic poems. Some people believed the sexual act was, literally, electrified. No wonder an audience pleaser was the "Venus electrificata," or electric kiss. The electrician asked a woman volunteer to sit on an insulated stool. He then connected her to a conductor and charged her with static electricity. When a man from the audience attempted to kiss her, sparks flew from her lips, and he received an electric shock.

Meanwhile in France, the electrician Jean-Antoine Nollet asked that age-old question: Does this nonsense scale? He gathered two hundred monks in a circle, connecting them with iron wires. He then delivered an electric shock to one monk and all two hundred recoiled, demonstrating both the profound speed of an electrical charge and the profound credulity of French monks. Thus was the state of electricity when Franklin found it, more parlor trick than science.

On display at this blissfully small museum is an original copy of the book that cemented Franklin's reputation: *Experiments and Observations on Electricity*. The subtitle is key: *Made at Philadelphia in America*. The Philadelphia Experiments, as Franklin's research became known, both impressed and perplexed Europeans—impressed because it represented a giant leap in humanity's understanding of a previously mysterious force, perplexed because of where it happened, not in London or Paris, or even Edinburgh, but in far-flung "Filthy-dirty." How could this be?

American researchers such as Franklin were working at a disadvantage. Scientific instruments were scarce. A telescope was a rare treasure. There wasn't a single laboratory in the colonies. For his experiments, Franklin used simple materials from his house: cork spheres, metal bodkins or pins, silk thread, thimbles, a cake of wax, a pump handle, the gold leaf on a book binding.

But distance is a blessing as well as a curse. From where he sat, Franklin possessed bifocal vision; he could see both near and far. He had the space to think differently, to pursue hunches without the scientific establishment peering over his shoulder. He looked at what the European scientists looked at and saw something different. As William James would later say, "Genius, in truth, means little more than the faculty of perceiving in an unhabitual way."

Franklin may have been working far afield, but he remained tethered to the mother ship, thanks to help from friends. Peter Collinson, an English botanist from London, was the conduit that made Franklin, Franklin. He may not be a household name, but without Mr. Collinson, there would be no Dr. Franklin. Collinson sent Franklin experimental apparatus and the latest literature on electricity. He corresponded with Franklin throughout his electric days, then compiled those letters into the extraordinary book I am looking at now.

Franklin also had help in Philadelphia from an unlikely assortment of friends: a silversmith named Philip Syng, a lawyer named Thomas Hopkinson, and an unemployed Baptist minister named Ebenezer Kinnersley. Syng and Hopkinson were also members of the Junto, underscoring how Franklin's social ties overlapped and complemented each other. One connection led to another, like an unbroken electrical circuit.

Isabel points out a collection of glass jars on display, each about the size of a milk bottle, arranged in neat rows and housed in a chunky wooden case. The jars are crude electrical capacitors connected by wires. The gangly contraption made it possible for the first time to store electrical charges. I am looking at the world's first battery. Invented in 1745, just as Franklin was embarking on his electrical experiments, it was the handiwork of a Dutch scientist named Pieter van Musschenbroek. It was called the Leyden jar, named after the town where it was invented (presumably easier to pronounce than "Musschenbroek").

The Leyden jar represented a giant leap forward. The only problem was no one knew in which direction they had just leaped or where to leap next. Electricians had no idea why or how the jar worked. It was one of the great scientific puzzles of the eighteenth century. Even Musschenbroek was baffled by his own invention: "I've found out so much about electricity that I've reached the point where I understand nothing and can explain nothing," he said.

The Leyden jar wasn't only mysterious. It was also dangerous. Muss-chenbroek was handling one when "my right hand was struck with such force that my whole body quivered just like someone hit by lightning. . . . I thought I was done for." He would not want to experience such an electrical shock again, he said, even if offered the kingdom of France.

Musschenbroek's close call underscores the visceral nature of electric-ity. It was a physical science in the truest sense. Crafting the glass tubes and other equipment needed for the experiments demanded manual dexterity, as did the experiments themselves. They were tactile. Nothing separated the experimenter from the phenomenon he was studying. The scientist's body was no different from the Leyden jar or conducting wires, another tool in the service of knowledge.

The downside of this physicality was the inconvenient possibility of grave injury or even death. On the bright side, it made for an intimate sci-ence, which suited Franklin's temperament, not to mention his fleshly and fluid body. In no other scientific discipline were intellect and intuition so closely linked. "To know was to feel, and to feel was to know," as one histo-rian put it.

One day, Franklin was attempting to electrocute a turkey (it supposedly tasted better that way) when something went wrong. Handling two large Leyden jars, he inadvertently touched an electrified wire connecting them. There was a bright flash and "a crack as loud as a pistol." Franklin only knew this from friends who were present. He had blacked out. When he regained consciousness, "part of my hand and fingers which held the chain was left white as tho' the blood had been driven out, and remained so 8 or 10 min-utes after, feeling like dead flesh, and I had a numbness in my arms and the back of my neck, which continued till the next morning." Franklin was lucky. At about the same time, a Russian electrician named Georg Richmann was killed while conducting an experiment.

Franklin trusted knowledge gained by experience more than that ac-quired by reading. Such experiential knowledge is immediate and irrefut-able. "If any one should doubt, whether the electrical matter passes thro' the substance of bodies . . . a shock from an electrified large glass jar, taken thro' his own body, will probably convince him," he said. He also deployed reason, of course, but always in tandem with experience, head and hand working together.

Franklin was no dispassionate observer. He had skin in the game, as well as bone and soft tissue, and was clearly in awe of this invisible yet powerful force. Writing about the "doctrine of points"—how pointed objects attract more electricity than rounded ones—he said, "The doctrine of *points* is very curious, and the effects of them truly wonderful." Here he is describing the properties of a Leyden jar. "So wonderfully are these two states of electricity, the *plus* and *minus* combined and balanced in this miraculous bottle! situated and related to each other in a manner that I can by no means comprehend!"

I've never seen so many exclamation marks in a scientific paper. Question marks? Sure. Semicolons? Absolutely. But not exclamations. Some of my scientist friends possess an almost childlike sense of wonder, but most, as far as I can tell, seem to suppress any signs of wide-eyed enthusiasm, suspect as it is among today's scientists. This is a shame. Natural philosophers didn't merely study the wonders of the world. They stood in awe of them.

I was once like that too. I remember my first airline flight at age ten, wearing my first suit, a powder blue polyester abomination with matching clip-on tie. I gazed out the window from takeoff to landing, soaking it all up. Now I choose an aisle seat for easy lavatory access. This must stop. The heart is a more vital organ than the bladder.

Almost as remarkable as Ben's curiosity is his scientific writing. It is simple and clear and inspiring. He was the Carl Sagan of his time. He devised an entire electrical vocabulary, one still used today: *electrical battery*; *positive and negative*; *plus and minus*; *conductor*; *condenser*; *charging*; *discharge*. These are Franklin's terms.

How we talk about something matters. Scientists, no matter the field, need a shared and nuanced vocabulary. How we frame a subject determines not only how we see but what we see. Words matter. Embedded in each is not only a literal meaning but a suggestion, and often an expectation. When my wife tells me that she is "simply saying" (her favorite term) that when I have a chance I might want to possibly if it's not too much trouble perhaps consider taking out the trash before it rains, I know exactly what she is saying and exactly what I need to do.

Through a series of cleverly designed experiments, Franklin demonstrated that electrical charges arise not from the creation of any new substance but, rather, from redistribution of electrical "currents" (another Franklin term). He showed that electricity isn't created by friction. It is always present in all matter. At the time, researchers believed there were two types of electrical fluid, *vitreous* and *resinous*. One attracts and the other repels. Franklin disproved this. What appeared to be two separate entities was actually one.

Franklin soon landed on his greatest theoretical finding: the law of conservation of charge. Electricity is never really destroyed; it is only dispersed. What appeared to be differing amounts of electrical charge was an illusion. "There is really no more electrical fire in the [vial] after . . . *charging* than before; nor less after it's *discharging* . . . the equality [of charge] is never destroyed, the fire only circulating."

How did Franklin see what others did not? By deploying analogous thinking. He borrowed concepts from one field to understand and explain phenomena in another. The personal and the scientific intersected and complemented one another. His electrical experiments may have lasted only a few years, but they reflected a lifetime's contemplation. The concepts he used to describe electrical phenomena—equal and opposite budget, natural capacity, free circulation, ultimate restoration—appear in his writing two decades before he adapted them to describe electricity.

Ben valued equilibrium. He sought balance in his relationships and in his statesmanship. So he brought that mindset to his makeshift laboratory in Philadelphia, that cluttered collection of Leyden jars, wax cakes, silk threads, and nervous turkeys. When he saw that nature also valued equilibrium, he recognized it instantly. Electricity, like all other fluids, seeks a state of equilibrium. Any imbalances are temporary. "When by any operation of art or nature, there happens to be a greater proportion of this fluid in one body than in another, the body which has most, will communicate to that which has least, till the proportion becomes equal." He's describing electrical currents, but the face of American capitalism also appears to anticipate the words of Karl Marx: "From each according to his ability, to each according to his needs." Natural philosophers of the eighteenth century explored connections between the laws of nature and the laws of the moral universe in ways we no longer do.

Franklin was also obsessed with flow and circulation. Whirlwinds, waterspouts, and tornadoes fascinated him. He once followed a dust devil for miles, on horseback. He charted the Gulf Stream, studied the body's circulatory system, and observed the ebbs and flows of history. So naturally he believed electricity could best be understood in terms of fluid dynamics. Electricity, "the electrical fluid," moved like a current. Motion is how it reveals itself to us. "The electrical fire is never visible but when in motion, and leaping from body to body," he observed. "It is through connection that we can see the full force." Motion is not the exception. It is the rule, and a good rule too. Life is fluid. Only death is static.

Franklin explored the how of electricity, not the why. It is enough to know the natural laws themselves. You need not grasp the intricacies of Newton's law of universal gravitation to know that if you drop a plate of fine china, it will break. "'Tis a Pleasure indeed to know them, but we can preserve our china without it," he said.

Franklin gripped his china tightly but his conclusions lightly. He was always open to revising or even discarding them. He did not suffer from a lack of self-confidence, but he approached his experiments with "a winning modesty," as one contemporary put it. He knew what he didn't know and never muzzled his ignorance, for it supplied the path to knowledge. As he told Peter Collinson in 1747 after several electrical false starts, "If there is no other use discover'd of electricity, this, however, is something considerable, that it may *help to make a vain man humble.*"

Franklin was that rare person who didn't merely talk about the weather. He did something about it. For centuries, thunder and lightning—"that great artillery of God Almighty"—terrified humans. Many church bells bore a Latin inscription, *Vivos voco, mortuos plango, Deum laudo fulgura frango.* "I

summon the living, I mourn the dead, I praise God, I shatter the lightning."
Left unsaid was that lightning tends to strike church steeples, especially
when the bells are ringing. Newspapers, including Franklin's *Pennsylvania
Gazette*, regularly carried reports of people killed by lightning strikes.

Franklin couldn't have invented the lightning rod had his analogous
mind not linked observations made in the lab with phenomena in the "real
world." Franklin's great discovery was that they were the same. The electricity in his lab was the same electricity found in lightning. Franklin was not
the first person to speculate about this connection, but he was the first to
design an experiment meant to prove it. There was only one problem: the
experiment required a tall structure, and at the time Philadelphia had none.
So he pivoted.

It was June 1752. His son William, twenty-four years old, accompanied
him. He swore William to secrecy, lest the experiment fail and they face ridicule. He constructed a special kite, tied at the four ends to a thin silk hand-
kerchief. To the top of the kite he attached a foot-long wire that extended
to the middle, where he attached a hemp string and a key. Father and son
waited for a thunderstorm. Franklin biographer Leo Lemay describes what
happened next.

> William raised the kite, and then Franklin, standing in a shed, held the
> hempen string by the silk ribbon, which would not, when dry, conduct
> electricity. . . . With the kite raised and Franklin waiting, one dark cloud
> passed, and nothing happened. Franklin must have been glad no one but
> William was watching. Perhaps his hypothesis was wrong. Then, as a sec-
> ond cloud drew near, the threads of the hempen string stood erect and
> avoided one another. The string was electrified! He put his knuckle near
> the key and drew a spark. Again, another spark. Again, another.

Today, Franklin's kite experiment seems almost quaint, an endearing
episode from colonial history. The reality is that it was dangerous. Had lightning struck the kite, Franklin could have been killed. Science took guts. As
the German philosopher Immanuel Kant said, *Super Aude!* "Dare to know!"

Franklin wasn't looking for practical applications of his electrical experiments but, ever the possibilian, was receptive when one landed on his lap. Later in life, witnessing the launch of a manned balloon over the Champ de Mars in Paris, Franklin heard a bystander mutter, "What good is that?" Franklin turned and replied, "What good is a newborn baby?"

It was only once he linked electricity in the lab and electricity in the sky that he made the leap from the theoretical to the practical. It began with a thoughtlet articulated in a section of his pamphlet called *Opinions and Conjectures.* "What if we erected pointed rods on our houses and churches and ships? Would not these pointed rods probably draw the electrical fire silently out of a cloud before it came nigh enough to strike, and thereby secure us from that most sudden and terrible mischief!"

The lightning rod fit Ben's temperament. A lightning rod doesn't combat electricity. It doesn't vanquish it. It diverts it, draws it away, using misdirection and sleight of hand, just like the Old Conjurer.

Franklin believed everything should circulate freely: air, water, blood, money—and information. To hoard information was to kill it. So he published instructions for constructing a lightning rod in the 1753 edition of *Poor Richard's Almanack.* Was it a bit premature? Probably, but it saved lives, possibly including that of Thomas Jefferson, who erected a Franklin Rod at Monticello. "If it hadn't been for that Franklin the whole house would have gone," Jefferson was heard saying. The lightning rod on the tower of the old Pennsylvania State House (now known as Independence Hall) was most likely the first Franklin Rod attached to a building. It protected the historic structure for more than two hundred years, with only one recorded instance of lightning damage.

Franklin's invention and electrical experiments earned him worldwide fame. Europeans in particular were enthralled. Immanuel Kant called him a "modern Prometheus," the gutsy Greek who stole fire from the gods. The French statesman Turgot went a step further, proclaiming that Franklin had "snatched the lightning from the skies, the scepter from tyrants." Comments like that incensed John Adams, who griped that it "is universally believed in

France, England and all Europe, that [Franklin's] electric wand has accomplished all this revolution."

Sorry, John, but in a way, it did. As tensions between Britain and her colonies spiked, Franklin's electrical theories became an apt metaphor and rallying cry for the American cause. It was a metaphor deployed by friend and foe alike. The British solicitor general publicly chastised Franklin, calling him the "prime conductor" of the troubles between Britain and its colonies. He meant to diminish Franklin, but his comments had the opposite effect. It reminded those in attendance just how much Franklin of Philadelphia had accomplished.

Franklin's electrical career was relatively short. After six years, he moved on, never to return full time to his electrical experiments. Historians find this puzzling. Was he bored? Did he, as Isabel suggested, suffer from ADHD? I don't think so. The themes raised by the new science of electricity—unity, fluidity, conservation—continued to occupy his fertile mind for many years to come. Their usefulness shifted fields, from science to public service.

As much as Franklin loved his laboratory and his experiments, he recognized a higher calling. When his friend Cadwallader Colden said he was considering retiring so he too could dabble in natural philosophy, Franklin advised him to reconsider and not to forsake his other obligations. Had Isaac Newton abandoned the helm of a ship during an hour of danger, that lapse would erase all the good accrued by his scientific discoveries. Given a choice between science and public service, it was, as far as Benjamin Franklin was concerned, no contest.

Electricity, long feared, was also thought to have therapeutic benefits. The ancient Romans used electric rays to treat people suffering from paralysis, epilepsy, and other ailments. In the Middle Ages, Avicenna, a Persian physician, used electric fish to treat headaches, vertigo, and even melancholy. So it wasn't surprising that when word of Franklin's electrical discoveries spread, people hoped they could cure what ailed them. People suffering from partial paralysis and other ailments approached Franklin, asking to be shocked. He obliged but remained skeptical. Patients did show some signs of improvement, but this lasted only a few days. Franklin suspected any therapeutic benefit was due to the power of suggestion.

There was one exception. A twenty-four-year-old woman known as C.B. had suffered from severe convulsions for ten years, apparently due to a condition known at the time as "hysterical paralysis." She asked Franklin if he could help. He agreed, administering four electrical shocks each morning and evening. Franklin then gave her a Leyden jar so she could treat herself at home. Her symptoms gradually decreased "'til at length they entirely left me," she said. She went on to live a long and useful life, dying at age seventy-nine. It would be many years later, in the 1780s, when Franklin proposed using electric shocks to treat severely depressed patients.

Fast-forward 240 years to my Philadelphia hotel room around the corner from Franklin Court. It is morning. I make my coffee before doing anything else. Once sufficiently caffeinated, I reach into my backpack and remove a small device, about the size of a deck of playing cards. I attach four tiny cotton pads to a set of electrodes, then pour an aqua green liquid onto the pads. I clip the electrodes to my ears and push a button on the device. A surge of electricity—not nearly enough to kill a turkey, let alone a man—seeps into my brain. It is followed by lightheadedness, a not unpleasant sensation of vertigo, and, incredibly, a sense of equilibrium, a peace of mind, that otherwise eludes me.

The device is called an Alpha-Stim. I use it to treat my stubborn depression. I mainly like it for what it is not. It is not a pill. I've had enough of those. It is not a therapist. I've had enough of those as well. And it works. It keeps the black dog at bay just long enough for me to make it through another day. I don't know how it works and, to be honest, my doctor doesn't either. That's okay. Truth is what works. The device is useful, and it wouldn't exist had a curious forty-two-year-old printer with an analogous mind not embarked on a series of daring experiments in Philadelphia a long time ago. As I unclip the electrodes from my ears, my twenty-minute session complete, I say softly, "Thank you, Ben."

•   •   •

A beam of light dances across the museum floor. Isabel is wielding a flashlight, shining it here and there, searching for her lost hearing aid, a Franklinian invention if ever there were one. She's frustrated but not defeated and, in true Ben fashion, has retained her sense of humor. "That's what I get for saying nasty things about Franklin," she says.

I feel the urge to help, to be useful. I ask myself, *What would Ben do?* He'd organize a search party or start a volunteer organization devoted to solving such crises, a sort of fire department for lost things. He might even invent a hearing aid locator. I do not do any of this, but I do help search. I get down on all fours and shine my phone's flashlight under Franklin's portable chess set, in between the Leyden jars, behind *The Philosophy of Earthquakes*.

Others help too. Someone suggests a kid took it, not knowing what it was. That strikes me as the kind of blame game Franklin wouldn't play. He was more interested in lending a hand than pointing fingers.

Isabel is upset but resigned to the loss, which, she points out, in the hierarchy of losses, ranks quite low. That strikes me as a healthy, useful mindset.

I've been loitering in this museum for hours now. It is time to leave. I say farewell to Isabel, still searching for her lost hearing aid, then walk down the short flight of stairs to Fifth Street and a sunny eighty-degree day. It is late October. That's odd, I think, then drop the thought. Franklin wouldn't drop it. He would turn it over in his mind. He would engage in analogous thinking. He would investigate, and wouldn't stop until he found an answer.

FIFTEEN

FUNNY BEN

Undeterred by the unseasonably warm October weather, I saunter to the nearby Franklin Museum, another Philadelphian ode to Ben. It is not a small museum but it's not massive. I like it. I like the signs that read "Please Touch." I like the Franklinian whimsy: the friendly squirrel named Skuggs who directs you to various exhibits; the animated videos, colorful and campy, like something from a Monty Python skit.

I am rounding a corner when I hear a distinctive moaning sound. That's Ben, I think, and worry that the moans, growing louder, are the sounds of him mid-ecstasy during one of the dalliances he may or may not have had. I am relieved to discover it is the soundtrack from one of Ben's amusing but G-rated bagatelles. Called "Dialogue between the Gout and Mr. Franklin," it opens with Franklin confronted by his own gout, a debilitating form of arthritis that plagued him for years:

> FRANKLIN. Eh! oh! eh! What have I done to merit these cruel sufferings?
> GOUT. Many things; you have ate and drank too freely, and too much
> indulged those legs of yours in their indolence.

FRANKLIN. Who is it that accuses me?

GOUT. It is I, even I, the Gout.

The Gout scolds Franklin for his gluttony and sedentary lifestyle until, finally, Franklin agrees to eat less and exercise more.

I don't have gout, not yet, but I find the dialogue relatable. I'm considering conversing with my IBS (irritable bowel syndrome), a condition I'm convinced is brought on by stress and, like Franklin in his later years, insufficient exercise. It would be a one-sided conversation, with my IBS doing all the talking and me listening and nodding in chastened agreement.

Franklin's humor often swerved toward the bawdy and scatological: "The greatest monarch on the proudest throne is oblig'd to sit upon his own arse." And this doozy: "He that is conscious of a stink in his breeches, is jealous of every wrinkle in another's nose."

Flatulence appears surprisingly often in his writing, sometimes as an aside and at least once as the main subject. One year, the Royal Academy of Brussels put out a call for scientific papers on some esoteric topic. This annoyed Franklin. Why not solicit practical solutions to real problems—like the "fetid smell" of flatulence? Forcibly restraining this natural impulse was neither possible nor healthy, Dr. Franklin said. What the world needed was a drug that, when mixed with food, "shall render the natural discharges, of wind from our bodies, not only inoffensive, but as agreeable as perfumes."

It's not so far-fetched. After all, Franklin explained, some foods, such as asparagus, alter the odor of our bodily discharges. Why not do the same with our wind? Such a breakthrough would contribute much to human happiness and restore natural philosophy to its rightful, practical place. Converting farts into perfume would mark a milestone in scientific achievement and render the discoveries made by the likes of Aristotle and Newton, "scarcely worth a FART-HING." Is the essay brilliant or sophomoric? Yes. And should such a miracle flatulence formula be invented, I'd be first in line to buy it.

When the delegates at the Second Continental Congress were casting about for someone to draft the Declaration of Independence, they considered

Benjamin Franklin. It made sense. Franklin by that time was an accomplished writer and a highly respected statesman and philosopher. He had won several election campaigns (to the Pennsylvania Assembly) and knew how to sway public opinion. But the delegates nixed the idea. They were afraid he would insert a joke.

The story is almost surely apocryphal, but it gained traction because it sounded plausible. Inserting a joke into America's founding document is just the sort of thing Franklin *would* do—not out of disrespect, but to lighten a perilous historic moment and to encourage ordinary Americans to read the document. Humor makes us pay attention.

We don't take humor as seriously as we should. It is not taught in our schools or celebrated in our academies. There is no Nobel Prize for humor and, with few exceptions (Art Buchwald, Dave Barry), humorists don't win Pulitzer Prizes—ironic, given that Franklin's visage appears on the medallion Pulitzer recipients receive.

As usual, the ancient Greeks are to blame. They were suspicious of laughter and humor. Humor hijacked reason, Plato said, and easily veered toward malice. In his ideal republic, humor would be tightly controlled and "left to slaves and hired aliens." Aristotle was a bit less uptight, but not much. Wit was an important part of good conversation, he conceded, but laughter was to be avoided. "Most people enjoy amusement and jesting more than they should . . . a jest is a kind of mockery."

Ben Franklin thought otherwise. He cherished humor. He used it as a billboard, an entrée, a shield, a diversion, a balm, and a weapon. He used humor to conceal his shyness. He used humor to make a point without offending and to air serious differences without losing a friend. He used humor to expose harsh truths, and perhaps most of all, to relieve unbearable tension. It's impossible to laugh without exhaling. For Franklin, humor was a means to an end, not an end in itself—in other words, useful.

Ben's humor ripened during his fertile Philadelphia years, but the seeds were planted much earlier in the Boston of his youth. While still a teenager, he laid out his philosophy of funny in an open letter to readers of the *New England Courant,* his brother's newspaper. In it, he bestows humor with an almost divine power to calm agitated minds and soothe troubled souls. "Pieces of pleasancy and mirth have a secret charm in them to allay the heats and tumors of our spirits, and to make a man forget his restless resentments," he writes. "They have a strange power to tune the harsh disorders of the soul, and reduce us to a serene and placid state of mind."

That is an astute observation for a sixteen-year-old. It also represents a rare instance where Franklin openly acknowledges life's dark side. Who did he have in mind when he wrote of "tumors of the spirits" and "harsh disorders of the soul"? Was he writing about himself, a passing storm of adolescent angst, perhaps—or something more? Maybe this model of perfect sanity was a bit less perfect and a bit less sane than I'd been led to believe. I hope so. Perfect sanity is as annoying as perfect teeth. Both conceal the genuine person behind the blinding smile. I am drawn to people who, like me, possess neither perfect teeth nor perfect sanity.

Franklin didn't force his humor. It was reflexive, "as natural and involuntary as his breathing," observed one contemporary. While composing type for his newspaper, he'd occasionally add a quip or joke. Compiling a dispatch from Boston on the death of a famed lion—"the King of Beasts who had traveled all over North America by sea and land"—Franklin added, "Like other kings, his death was often reported, long before it happened."

Franklin possessed what one contemporary, a lawyer from New York, called "a great share of inoffensive wit." *Inoffensive* is key. Franklin always punched up, never down. The target of his upward jabs included pompous British ministers, overzealous preachers, and, in his later years, defenders of slavery.

Satire is asymmetrical warfare. The satirist strikes his target with a glancing blow that seems to come out of nowhere. Stunned and disoriented, his victim is immobilized, unable to retaliate. Best of all, the satirist's bite leaves no teeth marks. There is always plausible deniability. It was just a joke. It doesn't mean what you think it means.

"Rattlesnakes for Felons" is a good example of Franklinian satire. The British were sending convicted criminals to the American colonies. Not surprisingly, crime rates in places like Philadelphia spiked. Franklin, writing under the pseudonym "Americanus," suggested the colonists show their gratitude by sending hundreds of rattlesnakes—"felons-convict from the beginning of the world"—to Britain. "Rattle-snakes *seem the most suitable returns* for the human serpents sent us by our *Mother* Country." It's no problem at all, Franklin continued; Americans would happily send thousands of rattlers and generously distribute them among the gardens of London's nobility and even the homes of ministers and members of Parliament. It's the least we can do, Ben said.

"Rattlesnakes for Felons" was the most vicious anti-British satire to date and was reprinted in several colonial newspapers. Afterward, these newspapers changed how they reported on crime, noting when an alleged criminal was an ex-convict dispatched from Britain.

Franklin's satire was always biting but never cruel or capricious. Like his lightning rod, it always had a point and used misdirection to diffuse powerful forces. Humor, at its best, is disruptive but not destructive. One of Franklin's favorite targets was . . . Franklin. He poked fun at himself. He poked fun at his weight ("Dr. Fatsides"), at his sartorial choices, at his French grammar. He also poked fun at his editorial blunders.

In a 1729 edition of his newspaper, the *Pennsylvania Gazette*, he fessed up to an embarrassing error. He had reported that a royal governor, Jonathan Belcher, had "died elegantly" at a popular London tavern. "The word *died* should doubtless have been *dined*," Franklin noted wryly. He then used the mistake as an opportunity to publish a collection of infamous printers' errors, such as the Bible that omitted the word *not* from the Seventh Commandment, leading the faithful to wonder why God Almighty would command *"Thou shalt commit adultery."* Franklin's readers no doubt chuckled at that blunder and forgave the one he had made. Humor diverts.

Franklin's contemporaries marveled at his ability to deploy the perfect joke or anecdote at precisely the right moment. He "had wit at will," conceded John Adams. From behind his Poor Richard mask, Franklin took aim at gossips ("Three may keep a secret, if two of them are dead") and doctors ("There's more old drunkards than old doctors") and lawyers ("A country-man between two lawyers, is like a fish between two cats").

Franklin's biggest target was the British. He relayed a story about a lone Irish soldier who captured five British troops by surrounding them. His 1775 satirical song, "The King's Own Regulars," also mocked the cowardice and incompetence of British soldiers: "For fifteen miles they follow'd and pelted us, we scarce had time to pull/a trigger/But did you ever know a retreat perform'd with more vigour?" Not only did the song deflate British morale, it also accomplished a feat many thought impossible: it made George Washington laugh.

Humor, like electricity, is a powerful force, and must be deployed judiciously. A little is good, but too much is harmful, like oversalting a meal. Ben worried about getting the proportions right. When, as a young man, he embarked on his self-improvement plan, he did so, in part, "wishing to break a habit I was getting into of prattling, punning and joking." Humor can heal. Humor can also harm. Misused, it "inflicts a wound that rankles in the heart and is never to be forgiven."

I hear you, Ben. I know the power of humor, and I know I sometimes misuse it. I regret the times I have rankled hearts. Whenever I find myself in an uncomfortable social setting—in other words, *any* social setting—I resort to humor. It is my default mode. Sometimes this is useful. Sometimes it backfires. I intend no harm, but Franklin wouldn't want to hear excuses. He cared about results, not intentions.

My teenage daughter often calls me out on this. "It's not funny, Dad," she says whenever I make light of a subject. Rather than heeding her words, I double down and perform a monologue, a one-man show when there are two of us in the room. I ramble rapid-fire, doubling down on a lame routine. I repeat the same joke, waiting, hoping, for a reaction. I am, as comedians say, dying out there, but even death can't stop me.

Why do I dig myself into such an unfunny hole and, despite the flashing red lights and alarm bells, continue to dig? I'm not sure, but I think it has to do with my fear of silence. I rush to fill the void with something, anything, and a joke seems like the best filler. Humor is my way of relieving unbearable tension. Humor is how I bond with people. It is my love language. At least I thought it was. I'm beginning to suspect it is the opposite: a language I speak to avoid intimacy.

What would Ben do? He'd remind me I have a choice. Humor may be like breathing, but breathing is one of the few bodily functions that is both involuntary *and* voluntary. We can't control whether we breathe, but we can control how. Do we take long, deep breaths or frantic, staccato ones? Do we breathe mindfully or mindlessly? Ben would also remind me that usefulness is relative. What works in one situation doesn't necessarily work in another. I need to look and listen. See the world through the eyes of others. Wear a mask if necessary.

He'd also suggest I lighten up. My over-joking has done no permanent harm. It is just another erratum. I can correct it and release a new, better edition of myself—perhaps in paperback, with a nice Franklinesque cover.

SIXTEEN

BUDDHA BEN

I reach for a pair of scissors. I am about to unbox. I have unboxed before. I have unboxed watches, and I have unboxed leather planners. I have unboxed shoes, wallets, handheld massagers, coffee makers, and more bags than I care to admit. But this is different.

The blades sever the packing tape easily. I unhinge the cardboard flaps and reach inside. Slowly, ever so slowly, I lift the contents and place it on my desk. I remove the paper packaging and stare at my purchase.

It stands, or rather sits, only six inches tall. It is a gold statue of a man, seated in the lotus position: legs crossed, eyes closed, hands resting on his lap. He appears to be deep in meditation. The crown of the man's head is bald, but long strands of hair unfurl along the sides, settling on his shoulders.

The resemblance is not obvious—it takes me a few seconds—but it is undeniable. The man is Benjamin Franklin. Buddha Ben. I reach for the card that accompanied the package. It begins with a Ben quote: "He that can have patience can have what he will." Then, this: "We hope this Buddha helps you find patience. Be free, Steffi & Austin."

I discovered my Buddha Ben the way all great discoveries are made: on eBay. I had grown obsessed about the connection between Franklin and Buddhism. The more I investigated, the more I became convinced of the Buddha nature of Benjamin Franklin. I searched library shelves and bookstores and the deepest recesses of the Internet when—WHAM!—up popped Buddha Ben. And for only $14.95. A bargain Franklin would like, I'm sure.

My Buddha Ben obsession began innocuously enough. At first, I noticed the physical resemblance. Ben—older, rotund Ben—looked an awful lot like the laughing Buddha found everywhere from upmarket spas to ratty college dorm rooms. The same corpulent belly. The same cherubic yet vaguely mischievous smile.

Then I saw the philosophical similarities. Like the Buddha, Ben had no patience for metaphysical puzzles. As he said, "Many a long dispute among divines may be thus abridged: It is so; It is not so. It is so; it is not so." Ben, like the Buddha, focused his considerable energies on the practical, the here and now. Like the Buddha, Ben valued silence. Both were empiricists; experience, not dogma, guided their actions. Both Ben and the Buddha believed in the power of habit to shape our characters and thus our destinies. Both avoided going to extremes, steering a middle path through life. Both worked hard to transform anger into something less toxic, more productive.

Both developed detailed plans for overcoming suffering: the Buddha had his Noble Eightfold Path and Ben had his Thirteen Virtues. Ben, like the Buddha, soared above the turbulence of life, maintaining an ironic distance from the updrafts and downdrafts. He was disinterested but not uninterested. Both men were pseudo-doctors. Ben had his honorary doctorates. The Buddha and later teachers saw themselves as physicians of the mind dispensing good medicine, the dharma. As the eighth-century Buddhist monk Shantideva said: "May I be the doctor, the medicine/And may I be the nurse/For all sick beings in the world/Until everyone is healed."

Both the Buddha and Ben recognized the inherent impermanence of all beings. The Buddha illustrated this essential fact with a number of parables, Ben with a charming bagatelle about a species of fly whose life span is but a single day. Writing toward the end of his long and useful life, Franklin connected the fly's fate with his own: "What will fame be to an ephemera who no longer exists?" And with his serial masking, Ben seems to intuitively recognize the Buddhist notion of a fluid, impermanent self. That's why he could be a middle-aged widow one day and an Algerian emir the next.

Everywhere I look, I see more signs of Buddha Ben. Am I onto something big, or have I deluded myself bigly? Have I fallen prey to confirmation bias, like the person with a hammer who sees nails everywhere? Franklin was keenly aware of these sorts of traps. "It's the easiest thing in the world for a man to deceive himself," he said.

I'm not sure if it's by coincidence or design, but across the street from Franklin Court, Ben's old home, is the Philadelphia Museum of Illusions. I visited one day. Ben greeted me at the door. A modernist portrait constructed from sundry geometric shapes—trapezoids, rhombuses, octagons—and with bright blue eyes (his eyes were brown) staring into the distance and looking quite insane. Scary Ben.

Inside, I couldn't believe what I saw. Or could I? So many mind tricks. There I am standing on the ceiling or hanging bat-like from a wall or grown to ten feet tall and then shrunk to a few inches. At one point, my head departs my body and rests on a platter. All is *maya*, illusion. Our senses are unreliable. Our powers of reason too. We can rationalize anything. Franklin recognized this quirk of human nature at an early age. He was sailing from Boston to New York and was, at the time, still a vegetarian. He stuck with this diet for several days on the ship, but then the winds absconded, and the ship slowed to a standstill. Provisions ran low, so people fished and soon were hauling huge amounts of cod aboard and frying them in a pan. It smelled "admirably well," Franklin recalled.

He had taken a vegetarian vow, believing that "taking every fish is a kind of unprovok'd murder." But then he noticed smaller fish inside the larger one's stomachs. If the fish could eat each other, Ben reasoned, why couldn't he eat them? "So convenient a thing it is to be a *reasonable creature*, since it enables one to find or make a reason for everything one has a mind to do."

Have I done something similar—rationalized my belief in Buddha Ben?

I'm not sure. *It is so; it is not so.* I'm going in circles, the sort of metaphysical machinations that Ben avoided.

I email Mitch Kramer, a Franklin interpreter (never call him an "impersonator," I learned) who looks and acts and sounds an awful lot like Ben. He knows the man the way few do, from the inside out. What does he think of my Buddha Ben theory? Mitch replies a few hours later. He had also made the connection—aha!—but (there's always a *but*) it's not so simple, he says:

> Franklin seems driven by the quest for personal and societal betterment. He trained himself to be intensely observant, especially when it came to the natural world. Do these seem like attitudes common in Buddhism? Some of them. But they are also comparable to other seekers. His views on scholarship and ethics have been related to Judaism. His embrace of certain Christian ideas is only matched by his disdain for their orthodoxy. He was familiar with Islam and offered positive remarks regarding his contact. Overall, I think he was most driven by what he would call reason.

Sigh. So, Buddha Ben was also Jewish Ben and Muslim Ben? Same hammer, different nails. I'm determined not to give up on my Buddha Ben theory. At first, my library and Internet search unearths nothing, so I redouble my efforts. Then I find it: an obscure academic paper titled "Dharma of the Founders." The paper's author, Ryan Aponte, makes a compelling case that several of America's founders articulated ideas remarkably similar to those found in Buddhism, especially the Mahāyāna school practiced in Tibet and elsewhere in Asia. *Yes,* I think; *I am not crazy.* Or at least I am not the only crazy one.

Ben was a Buddhist but not the way the Dalai Lama or Californians are Buddhist. He never read the Dhammapada, the classic collection of sayings of the Buddha. They had yet to be translated into any Western language. He did not meditate. He did not join a *sangha*, a Buddhist community, for there were none in Philadelphia or London. He did not say things like "That's very Buddhist of you." No, Ben was a purely accidental Buddhist. He didn't study Buddhism, but he thought and acted like a Buddhist.

I am the opposite. I study Buddhism but don't act or think like a Buddhist. My bookshelves overflow with works by monks, lamas, rinpoches, and various other enlightened beings. As I type these words, I hear a distinct clinking sound as the *mala*, or prayer beads, I'm wearing brush against the keyboard. When I look up, I see at least four tiny Buddhas gazing at me.

I travel to Buddhist lands like Thailand and the Himalayan nation of Bhutan. I can spin a prayer wheel with more force than Rafael Nadal's forehand. I can talk *maya* and karma and *dukkha* with real Buddhists, and for a good fifteen minutes, sometimes longer, pass as one of them. I can do Buddhist math. I know my Four Noble truths and my Noble Eightfold path. I meditate, though sporadically and only while heavily caffeinated. I am Buddhist adjacent. Being Buddhist adjacent, though, is like being lottery ticket adjacent. Either you've got the winning number or you don't.

I'm not sure why I'm incapable of making the leap from theory to practice. It is a short distance, I know, yet it feels as wide as the Grand Canyon. Sometimes it's the smallest jumps that are the hardest. The truth is that I'm more comfortable in the world of words and ideas than I am in the world of experience. Over the years, this disposition has protected me, made me feel safe, but has it helped me? I used to think so. Now I'm not so sure.

Ben wasn't just any kind of accidental Buddhist. He was a bodhisattva, an enlightened being who defers entering Nirvana to help their fellow sentient beings. The bodhisattva does not sit in a monastery meditating, at least not just that. They get out into the world and help others advance in their journey toward enlightenment. Every bit helps. As Shantideva said in his classic text, *A Guide to the Bodhisattva's Way of Life*, even relieving someone of a headache is "a beneficial intention endowed with infinite goodness."

All this bolsters my Buddha Ben theory, but there is one pesky problem: money. The Buddha advocated a simple life, free of excess desire. Ben's face is plastered on the hundred-dollar bill, an image news outlets unfurl to illustrate a report on inflation or a banking crisis or any other dollars-and-cents story. One-Hundred-Dollar Ben has permeated our culture, infiltrated our online lives. I noticed that since I started researching Franklin, I see targeted ads on my social media feeds from companies like the Penny Hoarder.

We've got Franklin all wrong. Yes, he believed in capitalism and free trade and, yes, he thought amassing some wealth was good. "It is hard for an empty sack to stand upright," he said. But nowhere does he say the sack must be full or, worse, overflowing. He never argued for unbridled capitalism—quite the opposite. He saw money as a means to an end, never an end in itself. "The use of money is all the advantage there is in having money," he said. Reading *Poor Richard's Almanack*, I'm surprised how many of the proverbs strike a similar, Buddhist theme. Here are just three examples:

Enjoyment is not to be found by excess in any sensual gratification.

Nothing brings more pain than too much pleasure.

Avarice and happiness never saw each other. How then should they become acquainted?

Franklin never patented any of his many inventions, forsaking a small fortune. His was a pay-it-forward philosophy: "That as we enjoy great advantages from the inventions of others, we should be glad of an opportunity to serve others by any invention of ours, and this we should do freely and generously." Franklin retired at the peak of his business career, aged forty-two, to devote himself to his electrical experiments and then public service. He gave to causes in which he believed: supplying wagons to the ill-fated Braddock Expedition during the French and Indian War and donating his $1,000 per year salary as US postmaster general to help care for soldiers wounded during the Revolutionary War. During an outbreak of smallpox in Philadelphia, he printed and distributed, at his own expense, 1,500 copies of a pamphlet describing how to administer inoculations.

He opposed the unchecked amassing of private property, sounding more like a socialist than an apologist for American capitalism. "I imagine that what we have above what we can use, is not properly *ours*, tho' we possess it," he said. And he liked to tell friends this story:

One day, a Quaker man invited him to see a house he had just built. Franklin was struck by the grandeur of the place, especially since the man lived alone and rarely entertained.

"Why do you need such huge rooms?" Franklin asked the man. "You live here alone."

"It's nothing," the man replied. "I can afford it."

When Franklin saw a vast dining room with a beautiful mahogany table easily capable of seating twenty-five people, he asked, "Why do you need such a grand table?"

Again, the man replied, "It's nothing. I can afford it."

This time Franklin shot back: "Why don't you have a hat that size? You can afford it."

That sure doesn't sound like a cheerleader for unbridled materialism. How did we get Franklin so wrong?

Blame it on Poor Richard. With the hapless astrologer, Franklin had created his best mask yet—a perfectly believable character. Maybe a little *too* believable. Over the years, people began to confuse the mask and the man. Like any other well-drawn character, Poor Richard took on a life of his own.

In 1758, Franklin published his last almanac. Donning a new mask, that of one Father Abraham, he uncorked his most mercenary maxims: "He that goes a borrowing goes a sorrowing" and *"Nothing but money is sweeter than honey"* and the classic "Early to bed, and early to rise, makes a man healthy, wealthy, and wise." Publishers smelled gold and reissued Franklin's essay as a pamphlet called *The Way to Wealth*. The title wasn't Franklin's, but that didn't matter. *The Way to Wealth* cemented his reputation as the avuncular face of capitalism. It was only a matter of time before his face landed on the hundred-dollar bill.

I'm feeling good about my Buddha Ben theory, but something is missing, some irrefutable piece of evidence. One day I find it, hiding in plain sight at the corner of Spruce and Ninth Streets in Philadelphia.

•   •   •

I don't like hospitals. No one does, I know, but I like them even less than most people do. I trace my hospital-phobia to the fact that my father was a doctor, an oncologist. His idea of quality father-son time was dragging me along while he did his rounds. He'd park me in the cafeteria of one hospital after another, often for hours at a time. I can still see the doctors, exhausted and numb, and the families, exhausted and worried. If I close my eyes, I can smell the burnt coffee and the fear.

As I enter the grounds of the Pennsylvania Hospital, threading a brick-lined archway ("Ben's Den," a sign reads) into a pleasant outdoor café and garden replete with flowers and soft spring air, I think, *Yes, finally a hospital I like.* The grounds feel more like those of a college campus. I spot a plaque that reads: "The Nation's First Hospital. Founded 1751."

Nearby is more signage. I learn that the archway was the old carriage entrance. A guard closed it at midnight. If you needed medical attention later than that, you rang a large bell that roused him and he opened the gate. Today the hospital is in the center of Philadelphia, but at the time, it was stranded on the outskirts, a lone building amid a vast field, reachable only by rough, unpaved road.

I descend a small set of stairs and see the hospital cornerstone, the words written by Franklin more than 250 years ago: "The Building by the Bounty of the Government, and of many Private Persons, was Piously Founded for the Relief of the Sick and Miserable." Technically accurate, but there is more to the story—much more.

I order a coffee, not burnt, and find a seat among the doctors and nurses on break. I exhale. I've noticed how a sense of peace adheres to locales associated with Benjamin Franklin. The mulberry tree casting shade over Franklin Court, the Boston waterfront, the snow-dusted cemetery where Ben's parents are buried. Maybe my impression is real. Maybe it is just another illusion, my mind seeing what it wants to see. Maybe it doesn't matter. Peace is peace.

The idea for the Pennsylvania Hospital was not Franklin's. That honor goes to Thomas Bond, a Philadelphia physician who ran a private practice and served as port inspector for infectious diseases. Bond was a good doctor but a hopeless fundraiser, so he turned to Franklin for help. The two men were friends, both members of the library Ben had founded.

Franklin liked the idea. There was no public hospital in the colonies or a medical school. Of the 3,500 Americans practicing medicine (key word: *practicing*), only 10 percent had a college degree, let alone a medical one. William Douglass, a Scottish doctor visiting Boston, summed up the state of medical care in North America. "Frequently there is more danger from the practitioner than the distemper," he said, before adding dryly, "but sometimes nature gets the better of the doctor and the patient recovers."

Dr. Franklin may not have been a real doctor, but he was keenly interested in medicine. He theorized (correctly) about lead poisoning and developed a new (and, again, correct) theory of the common cold. He promoted smallpox immunization and experimented with electrical and music therapies. He espoused the benefits of air circulation and regular exercise long before it was popular to do so.

At first, Franklin didn't have much more luck than Thomas Bond in raising funds for the hospital. Donor fatigue is not a twenty-first-century phenomenon. He decided to approach the Pennsylvania Assembly for help. The meeting did not go well. Some legislators objected to the cost. The salaries for physicians alone would "eat up the whole of any fund," they fretted. Others, from rural areas, questioned why they should fund a hospital that would mainly benefit residents of Philadelphia.

Franklin pivoted. What if, he asked Isaac Norris, the speaker of the assembly, he raised two thousand pounds through private donations? Would the assembly then match that amount with another two thousand?

Sure, Norris said, barely concealing his incredulity. There's no way Franklin could raise that kind of money, he thought. "Utterly impossible." Norris and his fellow legislators promised to match Franklin's fundraising effort because they thought it wouldn't cost them a penny. As Franklin put it, they enjoyed "the credit of being charitable without the expense." Or so they thought.

Ben got to work. He wrote an anonymous article laying out the case for a hospital. He reached into his bag of masks and pulled out a minister's disguise, or at least the Church's vocabulary. Ben was not the least bit religious, but he was no atheist, and possessed what one friend called "the religion of the heart." For Franklin, religion may or may not be true, but it was useful. Religion, at its best, was a means to an end, and that end was good deeds.

He began his appeal with a saying in Latin. *Pos obitum benefacta manent.* "Good deeds survive one's death." It sounds ancient and wise, but Franklin invented it. He deplored Latin as much as he deplored organized religion but gladly deployed both when useful to do so. He then quoted from the Book of Matthew: "I was sick, and ye visited me." Then, in his own words, he reminded readers of their interdependence. "We are in this world mutual hosts to each other," he wrote, and must not "*harden our hearts* against the distresses of our fellow creatures."

Building a hospital isn't only charitable, Franklin continued. It is also practical. The young who train there will share their knowledge with others. It's economically sound as well. It costs less to treat a patient in a hospital than in a private home. The pièce de résistance is his reminder that "the circumstances and fortunes of men and families are continually changing." The rich become poor; the healthy become sick. No one is immune from the vagaries of fate. Who knows, dear reader; you might one day be the one in need of a hospital.

Bravo, I think. I had just witnessed a master class in convincing people to part with their money for a good cause. Franklin appealed to both heart and head, other and self. Building the hospital is the right thing to do, and the financially prudent one as well. It will help others, and it just might help you too. By the time I'm done reading, I'm ready to open my own wallet.

People gave generously not only because Franklin had made such a compelling case but because their contribution was amplified, thanks to the pledge by the assembly. In effect, Franklin said, "every man's donation would be doubled." He had just invented the matching grant, now a staple among foundations and nonprofits everywhere.

Franklin and Bond met, and then surpassed, their goal, raising more than

2,700 pounds. I would love to have seen the look on the face of Isaac Norris, speaker of the assembly, when Franklin broke the news. Norris hemmed and hawed but soon relented and cut a check for the new hospital. There were more obstacles—the land Pennsylvania proprietor Thomas Penn had "generously" bequeathed for the hospital was swampy and fetid ("More fit for a burying place")—but these hurdles were overcome and on February 11, 1752, the Pennsylvania Hospital admitted its first patient.

Franklin was delighted. "I do not remember any of my political maneuvers, the success of which gave me more pleasure," he recalled years later. His plan, Franklin acknowledged, entailed "some use of cunning." He had once again tricked people—in this case, a group of self-serving legislators— into being more generous versions of themselves. He believed people were capable of acting selflessly, but they need a little nudging, and even a dash or two of deception.

How to square this flexible view of the truth with Franklin's famous aphorism that "honesty is the best policy" or his father's lesson that "nothing was useful which was not honest"? I don't have the answer, but the Buddha does. It's called *upaya-kausalya*, or "skillful means." A Buddhist teacher employing skillful means tailors his lessons to the student, meeting them where they are. This approach might mean speaking in the vernacular rather than scholarly language. Or it might entail less conventional methods, like telling jokes or wearing masks or, in the case of one Zen priest, concluding a lesson by slamming shut a door on his disciple's leg, supposedly leading to a profound insight, in addition to the compound fracture. Skillful means can also involve deception. Consider a classic Buddhist parable, the "Burning House."

A wealthy man lived with his children in a large, rambling house that had only a single door. One day, the man smells smoke and discovers the house on fire. He urges his children to flee, but they are engrossed in their games and don't budge. The man considers wrapping them in blankets and carrying them to safety, but the one door is narrow and the flames are spreading quickly.

Then he decides to lure them outside with some much-coveted toys.

"The kind of playthings you like are rare and hard to find," he tells them. "If you do not take them when you can, you will surely regret it later." This stratagem works. The children scamper out of the house unharmed.

The man had dissembled. He had no such toys (though he did later buy them each "a large bejeweled carriage drawn by a pure white ox"). Upon hearing this story, one of the Buddha's disciples asked if the man was guilty of a falsehood.

No, replied the Buddha. He was not. He had acted wisely, employing skillful means.

The parable could be renamed the "Pennsylvania Hospital." The burning house was the sorry state of medical care in colonial Pennsylvania. The children were the tight-fisted legislators. The toy was the lure of appearing charitable in the eyes of others. The wise father was Franklin. Both stories have happy endings.

Franklin had stumbled on a big and unsettling idea. We're told democracy rests on free and frank speech. Honesty. Franklin suggests a different set of ideals: "flexibility, compromise, negotiation, and a measured dose of hypocrisy," notes scholar Alan Houston.

I'm not sure how I feel about this. Skillful means are well and good in the hands of a benevolent being like Franklin, but what happens when they're deployed by a more malign leader?

Ben's writings offer some clues. Franklin doesn't prohibit all deceit. He prohibits "hurtful deceit." There is a difference. Helpful deceit is telling your spouse that no, they have not gained an ounce of weight. Hurtful deceit is spiking their low-carb, keto meals with boatloads of sugar. By nudging the Pennsylvania legislators into acting generously, Franklin hurt no one. Everyone benefited. The people of Pennsylvania got a much-needed hospital. And the legislators tapped into a generous spirit they didn't know they possessed. Drawing the line between helpful and hurtful deceit is tricky, of course. One person's "measured dose of hypocrisy" is another's cruel gaslighting. It is, I imagine, like pornography. You know it when you see it.

•   •   •

I gaze at my golden Buddha Ben, looking so serene in his Buddhahood, and his Benhood too. "Were you really a Buddhist?" I ask this aloud, which is kind of weird, I realize.

I hear only silence in return. The "noble silence" of the Buddha and the coy silence of the Ben. *It is so; it is not so.*

I sigh. Then a thought bubbles up: What difference does it make? Maybe, I think, it doesn't matter whether my Buddha Ben theory is true. Maybe that's the wrong question. Asking if my theory is true is like asking if a pair of eyeglasses are true. Do they improve your vision? If so, great; they are true. If not, they are false, and you need to get another pair. My Buddha Ben theory helps me see Franklin and the ideas he espoused, the life he led, more clearly. My theory is useful, and therefore it is true.

SEVENTEEN

NAKED BEN

I am standing in a three-hundred-year-old London townhouse, alone, eyes closed, trying to picture Benjamin Franklin naked. Not naked anywhere but naked here, in his old first-floor study with its bare wooden floors, mint green walls, and sash windows facing Craven Street, a small lane nestled between Charing Cross and the Thames.

If there's any place where I have a chance of communing with Ben, it is in this Georgian row house, the only one of Franklin's many homes still standing. That it still stands is a miracle, one abetted by fortuitous twists and turns—*distrust not providence*—as well as a hearty band of Franklinistas who rescued it from likely extinction.

I am not thinking about any of that now, though. I am picturing, *trying* to picture, Benjamin Franklin, scientist and statesman, inventor and founder, nude as a newborn. I have my reasons. Nudity played an important supporting role in this act of Ben's life.

The image of Ben in the buff does not come easily, but I persist and, sure enough, it materializes, like the old photographs I used to develop in my home darkroom. Yes, there he is, Naked Ben, fleshly and fluid. Dr. Fatsides in all his corpulent glory.

•   •   •

Naked Ben was in London on a mission that was supposed to last six months. He ended up staying more than fifteen years, a sizable chunk of his long and useful life. (Between 1757 and 1785, he lived only three years on American soil.) Three decades had passed since he was last here. London was a different city, and Franklin, now fifty-one years old, a different man. Both had matured and gained new prominence. Both were more self-assured and less indulgent. Ben tempered his drinking. London authorities cracked down on the cheap gin joints that had proliferated. Ben's waistline had expanded, and so had London's population, ballooning to 750,000 thanks, in part, to an influx of immigrants from places like Ireland. Londoners had grown more clothes conscious. Hoop petticoats as wide as five feet were all the rage, though of no interest to Naked Ben. New roads were built and bridges erected. The city had a new museum too, the British Museum, an institution built on Hans Sloane's vast collection of curios, including the asbestos purse Franklin had sold him more than thirty years earlier.

Franklin's London chapter, part two, was a love story in reverse, a slow-motion divorce. As with all divorces, the final break was not inevitable—until it was. When he sailed from Philadelphia in 1757, he told friends he was "going home to England." Franklin, like many Americans of the time, was a proud and loyal British subject. He even considered staying and becoming "a Londoner for the rest of my days." It was the superior city in the superior nation, he said. Every English neighborhood is home to "more sensible, virtuous and elegant minds, than we can collect in ranging 100 leagues of our vast forests." The prospect of the colonies uniting and rising up against their motherland "is not merely improbable," he said, "it is impossible."

Seventeen years later, Franklin left—fled, really—disenchanted, humiliated, and a wanted man. The divorce was finalized and implausibly, incredibly, a rebel was born at age sixty-nine.

It was a home birth. Number Seven Craven Street, to be precise. When Franklin first saw the house one July day in 1757, he knew he had found his London home. It was perfect: large yet cozy, quiet yet centrally located, in the shadow of Charing Cross where, as Samuel Johnson said, you could

witness "the full tide of human existence." It was a short walk from White-
hall, the center of British government, as well as the Houses of Parliament.
A few yards uphill was the Strand, the popular shopping street anchored by
Hungerford Market, with its array of fresh produce and meats. In the opposite direction was the Thames, and the promise of swimming. There were
plenty of pubs and clubs nearby, as well as the Drury Lane Theatre, where
Ben could catch a performance by David Garrick, the renowned actor.

Franklin soon moved into Number Seven Craven Street. His wife,
Deborah, had stayed in Philadelphia, where she managed the family store
and other business interests. She was afraid to travel by sea, a not unrea-
sonable fear at the time; she wouldn't even cross the Delaware, let alone
the Atlantic. That is the official story, at least. I can't help but wonder if the
long-distance arrangement suited Ben. He was forever promising Deborah
he would return home soon, but "soon" grew later and later. Eventually he
stopped promising.

Ben's twenty-seven-year-old son William accompanied him, as did two
enslaved persons, Peter and King. Ben hardly mentions the two men, except
in passing. "Peter behaves very well to me in general," he relays to Deborah
in 1758. "My shirts are always well air'd as you directed."

Franklin wrote to Deborah often, at least in the early years. One of his
first dispatches describes his new lodging: four furnished rooms on the first
floor of the Craven Street house, and "every thing about us pretty genteel."
Ben needed all the gentility he could get. His mission to London was not
only difficult but, in hindsight, impossible.

His remit was to win over the haughty heirs of Pennsylvania's founder,
William Penn. The two brothers, Richard and Thomas Penn, lived in a pa-
latial home in London's Spring Garden neighborhood while collecting tax-
free revenue from their vast holdings in Pennsylvania. They were absentee
landlords, with the ethical standards that implies. Pennsylvania was their
private piggy bank. They insisted their huge tracts of land and the revenue
they produced were exempt from taxes. The Pennsylvania Assembly disagreed and dispatched Franklin, the most famous American, to London to
change the Penns' minds.

If this sounds like a minor, intramural dispute, that's because it was. But tax disputes are never just about taxes, and this one was no exception. Scratch beneath the antiquated tax codes and legalese and you find the dry kindling that would ignite a revolution. Listen to the words the Pennsylvania Assembly used in describing the Penns' recalcitrance and you hear whispers of rebellion. The Penns' behavior was "injurious to the interests of the Crown, and tyrannical with regard to the people." The T word had been uttered.

Ben was slow to embrace it. During his many years in London, he worked to prevent a break between Britain and its American colonies in hopes of preserving that "fine and noble china vase," the British Empire. He knew that "once broken, the separate parts could not retain even their share of the strength or value that existed in the whole." Thus, the second aim of Franklin's London mission was wresting control of Pennsylvania from the odious Penn brothers and waltzing into the supposedly friendlier embrace of George III. Franklin was aiming not for American independence but the opposite: a *closer* relationship to the British sovereign.

This is not what I learned in high school. My history teacher portrayed the founding fathers as single-minded men on a singular mission and traced a straight line from subjugation to freedom. As Franklin's experience shows, the reality was much messier. The road to independence was long and winding, replete with switchbacks, detours, and even U-turns.

Such roads are not easily traversed. They demand skill, patience, and, perhaps most of all, a reliable and reassuring routine. Ben had his. He'd wake early and peel off his sleepwear: calico bedgown and footed flannel trousers. Then he'd open a few more windows (he slept with at least one open) and spend the next hour or so reading and writing and letting it all hang out. "Air baths," he called them. After an hour or so of air bathing, he'd get dressed and begin his day. Sometimes, though, he'd return to bed and experience "one or two hours of the most pleasing sleep that can be imagined."

Ben Franklin was comfortable in his own naked skin. He was born naked but, unlike the rest of us, remained naked his entire life—sometimes metaphorically, often literally. He had no interest in haute couture. Clothing binds and constricts, and in direct proportion to cost. The fancier the attire, the greater the amount of toxic envy it arouses. *"The eyes of other people* are the eyes that ruin us," he said. If everyone but him were blind, he'd have no need for fine clothing, or any clothes at all.

Was Ben a nudist? In a sense, yes. To be naked is to be open to experience, and Franklin remained wide open even as he aged, *especially* as he aged. As the years ticked by, he continued to change his mind about vital issues, democracy and slavery to name just two, yet another trait that set him apart. Most of us become less, not more, open to experience as we age.

To be naked is also to be vulnerable. At first blush, this doesn't seem to fit Franklin. He was cautious ("the most cautious man I have ever seen," said one Pennsylvanian visiting London). In large gatherings or among strangers he could be "cold and reserved," acknowledged his friend Joseph Priestley, "but where he was intimate, no man indulged more to pleasantry and good-humour." Franklin did get naked, just not with anyone.

Writing to a physician friend, possibly in the nude, he gushed about the joys of air bathing. "This practice is not in the least painful, but on the contrary, agreeable." I suspect Ben's neighbors found the practice a bit less agreeable. Air baths soon became a habit that he stuck with for the rest of his years. Even as he grew older, his skin flabby and wrinkled and flaked with a disease he called the "scurf" (psoriasis, most likely), he continued to air-bathe unabashedly. In France, well into his seventies, he swam in the Seine, naked.

Franklin, a son of Puritan Boston, seemed immune to even a twinge of shame about his naked, imperfect body. I, a son of Jewish Baltimore, do feel such shame, and more than a twinge. When it comes to nudity, I'm with *M*A*S*H*'s Radar O'Reilly. "Nudidity [*sic*] makes me breathe funny."

I never sleep naked. I've never been to a nude beach. I do shower naked, but quickly, as if I'm being timed, then dress immediately afterward. I dread doctor visits, unless it's a waist-up doctor. Those are okay. Ophthalmologists are my favorite.

What about emotional nakedness? On one level, I am, like Ben, open to experience. I've traveled the world, eaten rotten shark in Iceland and fried insects in Thailand. Those who meet me find me outgoing and gregarious. They mistake me for an extrovert. Sure, I can imitate one for a while, but it is an act, one I find thoroughly exhausting.

Emotionally, I am the opposite of naked. I am swaddled in layers of protective outerwear that come in various sizes and styles. Humor is one of my favorites. So tight fitting is that garment that only the most attentive souls, like my teenage daughter, see through it and call me out. All this clothing constricts, limiting my range of motion. Beneath all those layers, people can barely see me, let alone touch me.

Maybe this is why I travel. On the road, alone among strangers, it's easy to disrobe. Foreigners are less likely to judge my Ben-sized belly or surgical scars or my many other somatic imperfections. Ditto my emotional ones. And should they do so, who cares? I'm just passing through.

Franklin didn't always endorse the therapeutic benefits of fresh air. Like many people at the time, he suffered from "aerophobia," as he called it, diligently closing every crevice in every room. As usual, direct experience changed his mind. He noticed he was healthier when exposed to regular doses of fresh air. "I now look upon fresh air as my friend," he said. He embraced his new friend with open, naked arms. He began sleeping with windows open; no outside air—not even London's smokiest—could possibly be as unhealthy as the fetid atmosphere found inside a closed room.

Franklin's theory about the benefits of fresh air, if not air baths, caught on. During the Revolutionary War, many physicians ensured that their patients had access to fresh air. Ebenezer Beardsley noticed that troops quartered in "putrid atmospheres" were much more likely to contract dysentery than those housed in airier venues. Franklin's friend, the physician Benjamin Rush, suggested treating patients in rural areas rather than overcrowded urban hospitals.

One person who did not accept Franklin's advice was the mulish John Adams. In one of the more amusing episodes of American colonial history,

Adams and Franklin had to share a room at an overbooked inn in Brunswick, New Jersey, in 1776. The windows were open. Adams, an aerophobe, jumped up and shut them.

"Oh," said Franklin, "don't shut the window, we shall be suffocated."

No, we won't, replied Adams, explaining his concerns about the cold outside air.

Wrong, retorted Franklin. "The air within this chamber will soon be, and indeed is now, worse than that without doors. Come! Open the windows and come to bed."

Franklin sprang to his feet, opened the windows, and delivered a long lecture about his theory of head colds and the benefits of fresh air. Adams, exhausted and scientifically outgunned, absorbed little but, he recalled, "I was so much amused that I soon fell asleep, and left him and his philosophy together."

I love this story. Here are two giants of the American Revolution, the most fatherly of the founders, bickering like two siblings forced to share a room. Open the window! No, close it. Adams doesn't say whether Franklin tried to convert him into an air bather, but I suspect Ben didn't bother. Some mountains are too daunting to summit, even for a possibilian.

Ben's London house wasn't easy to find. After crossing the Thames on foot, I circled Charing Cross in search of Craven Street. It's more lane than street, only a block long, but it packs in more history than many US cities. Not only did Franklin live here, but so did Aaron Burr and, later, Herman Melville and the German poet Heinrich Heine. John Quincy Adams had an office on Craven Street.

Ben would still recognize the Georgian architecture, red-bricked and sturdy, and his trusty Thames, narrower and more polluted than in his day but otherwise unchanged. The sushi takeaway joints and CCTV cameras would befuddle him, but he'd smile at the sight of a Tesla Model S parked near his house, the chassis concealing its 7,000 batteries. His terms, his science, at their most useful. He'd surely approve of the neatly arranged phalanx of Boris Bikes. The bike rental scheme, launched by Boris Johnson when he was mayor of London, is a combination of the civic-mindedness and entrepreneurial spirit Franklin appreciated. He'd also appreciate the College of Optometrists, adjacent to his old house and with a mockup of the bifocals he invented displayed in the window.

I like old Number Seven (since renumbered thirty-six) Craven Street. I like the simple, quotidian feel, so less intimidating than Monticello or Mount Vernon. I like how the hallways are lit by candles, just as they were in Ben's day. I like how the floors list in random directions and creak when you walk on them. I like how, despite these peculiarities, the Franklin house "shows no signs of being haunted," according to operations manager Michael Hall. (He can't say the same about other historic houses he's managed.) I like how the staff don't take Ben any more seriously than he took himself. During Christmas season, they place a red Santa hat on a marble bust of Ben. It fits.

Ben's house is now a small museum. The Franklinistas who run it let me come and go as I please. One afternoon, after the tourists have left, I am alone. Just me and Ben. I climb the stairs—the very stairs he climbed, sometimes just for exercise. I step into his old study. This is the room where Ben spent most of his time. It is an ordinary room, not too large or small or special in any way, yet it is its ordinariness that makes it so extraordinary—just like the man who lived here.

The walls are painted the same pale shade of green as in Ben's day. The curators couldn't find any contemporary drawings of the interior so rather than guess how it was furnished, they left the rooms bare. Naked. I respect that decision. It means I can fill in Ben's study with my imagination. I imagine him here, sitting at his desk, quill in hand, firing off a letter to his friend Peter Collinson or maybe to Deborah in Philadelphia, telling her about his latest shopping expedition, rushing to finish his missive before the packet ship departed. I can picture him playing the glass armonica, the musical instrument he invented here. I can picture him pacing the room, worried about the political storm clouds gathering outside, a tempest so explosive even his mighty Franklin Rod couldn't defuse it.

Given its age, the Craven Street house feels surprisingly robust. Yes, it's had some work done, but you would too if you were nearly three hundred years old and endured flooding, fire, and a World War II bombing. The house has good bones. Several are on display here: femurs and tibias and clavicles, all arranged in a glass display case. Another Franklin surprise.

When workers were excavating the house in 1998, converting it into a museum, they found a human thigh bone. Then another bone, and another. Eventually they discovered 1,200 bones, the remains of more than fifteen bodies. Some of the bones bore saw marks while others were cut clean through. The skulls had been trepanned. People began to wonder: Was Ben Franklin a mass murderer?

He was not. It turns out a physician named William Hewson also lived at Number Seven Craven Street at the same time as Franklin. Hewson ran an anatomy school from the house. He needed cadavers, but they were hard to come by, given the moral prohibition against dissections at the time. So Hewson hired "resurrection men" skilled at digging up bodies in the middle of the night. After the dissections, Hewson disposed of the cadavers in the garden at the rear of the house. Franklin was probably aware of the dissections and may have participated in a few.

It's a good story, but I can't help but wonder if the same rumors would have surfaced had workers found bones at Monticello or Mount Vernon. I don't think so. There is something about sly Ben that says, *I could be a genius. Or I could be a mass murderer. You decide.* Wink, wink.

Bones and all, this house was more than a place to hang his bifocals. It was home. He may or may not have been sexually promiscuous, but there's no doubt he was emotionally promiscuous. He was forever inventing new homes with new families. So it was at the house on Craven Street. The landlady, Margaret Stevenson, and her teenage daughter, Mary (or Polly, as everyone called her), soon became Franklin's second family. Polly adored Franklin, and Franklin adored her. My "dear good girl," he called her, or "my dear philosopher." Ben had his share of stormy relationships, but with Polly, he said, it was "all clear sunshine."

He made himself at home, converting one room into an improvised laboratory and buying his own coach so he could make a good impression on those he visited. Franklin knew appearances mattered. He made new friends, generous ones with large country estates at Ben's disposal. He was so much in demand that "I seldom dine at home in winter, and could spend the whole summer in the country-houses of inviting friends, if I chose it." He and William attended the coronation of George III ("the best King any nation was ever blessed with") and dined with another monarch, the king of Denmark. Franklin even sketched the seating arrangement and sent it to his sister Jane in Boston.

Franklin, a social creature, was in his element. In the daytime, he frequented coffeehouses like Waghorn's or the Jamaican or the Pennsylvania Coffeehouse on Birchin Lane, where he could catch up on the news from home. In the evenings, it was taverns and club meetings. Mondays he dined at the George and Vulture with a group of fellow scientists and explorers, sometimes including Captain James Cook. Thursdays it was the Club of Honest Whigs, where he dined on Welsh rarebit and apple puffs with a group of physicians, dissenting clergy, and other freethinkers. He'd visit friends' homes and play cribbage and chess. Each summer, he traveled— to Ireland, France, the Netherlands, and, his favorite destination, Scotland, where he experienced the "densest happiness" of his life.

Life was good. Yet in his letters to Deborah, he claimed it was duty to country, or colony, that kept him in London. Did Deborah believe that? Did Ben? Perhaps. The rational mind, as he observed, is gullible. We can convince ourselves of anything.

Life was good but not perfect. (It never is.) As an American, even a highly respected American, Ben was still an outsider, and one with no proper pedigree or education. He had his nose pressed against the posh windows of London, but he wasn't allowed inside. He was almost a member of the club, but not quite. No wonder he gravitated toward fellow interlopers: Scots like the printer William Strahan ("Straney," Franklin called him) and Quakers like the botanist and electrical whisperer Peter Collinson. Several of his friends were physicians, real doctors, including the royal physician, John Pringle.

London was vibrant and intellectually stimulating, but it wasn't home. It wasn't his soulplace. Ben suffered from bouts of homesickness, assuaged by the growing American presence in London—artists like Benjamin West, fellow colonial agents, and others. Then there was the encroaching American vegetation. Ben would have recognized the sugar maples and hemlock spruces and other native American plants that had sprouted across London, thanks to the work of curious and industrious botanists like Peter Collinson. Ben might have seen American animals—rattlesnakes and crocodiles—stuffed and on display at London's coffeehouses.

If that wasn't enough, Deborah regularly sent packages crammed with his favorite American goodies: cranberries, buckwheat cakes, buckskins, apples (Newton Pippins were his favorite), dried venison, and bacon. Ben sent his wife gifts in exchange: *The Book of Common Prayer* in large type, to spare her eyes; reading glasses set in silver and tortoise shell; shoes; pins; needles; Persian textiles; damask tablecloths; silk blankets; glassware and silverware; a device for coring apples; saucepans from Sheffield. Ben spent freely on himself too, acquiring fine china, leather breeches, a new pair of eyeglasses, Madeira wine, and, of course, books. These spending sprees erupted just as the author of *The Way to Wealth* was gaining a worldwide reputation as the ultimate penny-pincher. Poor Richard's puppeteer may have remained industrious, but he was no longer frugal.

Back home in suburban Washington, DC, I am surprised how much I miss my time at Craven Street. The old house, like the Old Conjurer himself, had wormed its way into my heart. The photos I took remind me of my time there, but there is one image that requires no snapshot for it is engraved in my mind: Naked Ben. I smile whenever I think of him taking his air baths, propriety and neighbors be damned.

Then it dawns on me. It's all well and good to imagine Franklin's air baths, to read about them, but this is mere secondhand knowledge, inferior to direct experience. What if I air-bathed? Why not? I, too, live on a small lane, though the nearest river is not the Thames but a muddy estuary called Sligo Creek. My neighbors are not Aaron Burr or John Quincy Adams but Amy and Barbara.

I wake early one morning, and strip. I step into my home office and open a window. I check my schedule. No Zoom calls. Good. I have company: my dog Parker, who is way ahead of me in the air-bath department and thus unfazed by my little experiment. *It's about time,* I imagine he's thinking.

At first, I feel self-conscious, hyperaware of my nakedness. I begin to breathe funny. I lock my office door even though no one else is home. "Come on," I tell myself. "This can't be so difficult." What could be more natural than a grown man sitting at his desk naked as the day he was born? I take a few deep breaths, elongating the exhalation, as a meditation teacher once advised. Sure enough, the tension in my naked shoulders subsides, and my naked belly expands and contracts more freely. I click on a streaming service and play traditional Scottish folk music, Ben's favorite, fully submerging myself in the air bath.

I fire up my laptop and write. Maybe it's my imagination, but the keyboard feels springier, the blank screen less daunting. The words come more easily. In fact, the ones you are reading right now were written in the nude. Can you tell?

Franklin recognized the power of names. Had he told people he liked to hang around the house completely naked each morning, he would have attracted disapproving looks. The thought of a naked late-middle-aged man is not exactly appealing. But a late-middle-aged man taking an air bath? Okay, it's still unappealing, but less so. An air bath sounds therapeutic, cleansing.

I spend the next hour writing and reading, just like Ben, feeling the cool spring air caressing my . . . arms. Then I return to bed, like Ben, and while I don't experience that sweet sleep he described, I do sink into the mattress with greater ease than usual. My heart rate slows, my breathing deepens. The tasks that lie ahead evaporate like smoke escaping from a Franklin Stove. I believe there is a word for this state I'm experiencing. I believe that word is "relaxation."

Yes, I could get used to this air bathing, I think, closing my eyes. I just might make a habit of it. Better alert the neighbors.

EIGHTEEN

ANGRY BEN

Habits such as air baths helped ground Ben during his London days, and he needed all the grounding he could get. He was on a perilous mission, caught between two worlds: too American for the British and too British for the Americans. I can relate. Returning to the United States after a decade abroad, I felt rootless, a man without a country.

Life in this netherworld is disconcerting but has its advantages too. I never felt more American than in that carpet shop in Kabul. I knew I was representing my country. I had no choice. My Americanness defined me, whether I liked it or not. On visits home, I felt like an outsider too. I was clueless about the latest pop music (a deficiency that has persisted to this day) and paralyzed by the abundance of choice. I once spent forty-five minutes in the bread section of Whole Foods, unable to discern the relative merits of whole wheat versus whole grain versus ancient grain. I gave up and left empty-handed and hungry.

For many years, Franklin thought he could sustain his transatlantic balancing act: thoroughly American yet welcomed (mostly) by London's intelligentsia. It worked. Until it didn't.

. . .

It's difficult to imagine Benjamin Franklin, the cuddliest of the founders, having enemies. But enemies he had, and none more antagonistic than the Penn brothers. It took months for Franklin to get a meeting with them. In the meantime, they launched a whisper campaign aimed at discrediting and belittling "the electrician," as Thomas Penn called Franklin. They spread scurrilous rumors that Franklin was living luxuriously in London and had embezzled public funds. They were hoping Franklin, "a dangerous man," would just go away. He did not, and the Penns finally granted him an audience in early 1758. It did not go well.

Calmly explaining why the Penns should pay their fair share of taxes, Franklin appealed to their sense of fairness and reason. When that didn't work, he evoked their father's memory. When that failed, he pointed to the common interest the men shared with the people of Pennsylvania. Thomas Penn dismissed Franklin's pleas like swatting so many flies, declaring that as proprietors of Pennsylvania, they were free to do as they pleased with the colony. The charter said so. If the colonists felt deceived, "it was their own fault." They should have read the fine print.

Usually Ben would let this sort of haughtiness wash over him like a cool air bath on a spring morning. Not this time. Ben's anger toward the Penns, the arrogant Thomas in particular, was white-hot. He did not express his fury directly but instead resorted to one of his favorite tactics: a cool silence and a searing gaze.

Franklin nursed "a more cordial and thorough contempt [for Thomas Penn] . . . than I ever before felt for any man living." He compared Penn to a "low jockey" who had cheated someone out of a good horse, then chuckled at the deception. When those words got back to the Penns, Franklin doubled down; the men deserved "to rot and stink in the nostrils of posterity." After that, the Penns refused to deal directly with Franklin.

Franklin's anger was uncharacteristic. He prided himself on maintaining his equanimity, even when provoked. He viewed his enemies with the benign indifference of a parent corralling unruly children. Friends admired his Buddha-like "gentle serenity." This set him apart from other founders, like the firebrand Samuel Adams. Ben, ever the utilitarian, managed to render even his enemies useful. The talented learn from their friends. Geniuses learn from their enemies. Or, as Ben put it, "Love your enemies, for they tell you your faults."

But he could not love Thomas Penn. It was not the proprietor's arrogance alone—Ben knew how to handle that type—but how Penn belittled him, meting out what Aristotle called a "down-ranking." Penn considered Franklin, a self-made man, beneath him. The upstart electrician had neither the land nor the heritage to qualify as a "proper gentleman." Franklin was a commoner and, worse, a feral colonist. The Penns' contempt for Franklin was only the most egregious example of treatment he endured time and again at the hands of British officials, a coolness delivered in the form of an unspoken question: *Who do you think you are?* More than anything else, I think, it was this condescending attitude, a preference for pedigree over ability, that fueled the American Revolution.

Ben Franklin had anger issues. Unlike most people with anger issues, he recognized this tendency and worked at it. Hints of Ben's rebellious anger surfaced in his Silence Dogood essays. Silence described herself as "good humour'd (unless I am first provok'd)." Ben would be provoked time and again by people like the Penns and by fellow Americans such as John Adams. Controlling his anger, redirecting that energy toward useful means, was a lifelong struggle. Unlike his plan for moral perfection, he never articulated an anger strategy. There is no "Art of Anger Management" to be found among his voluminous writings. But if I've learned anything thus far, it's that life lessons are sometimes written in invisible ink. They become legible only when exposed to the light.

A bright and good place to start is the Royal Society for the Arts. It's a short walk from Ben's old Craven Street house, a pleasant stroll along cobblestoned streets that Ben made many times. He was an early and enthusiastic member, attending meetings, chairing committees, exchanging ideas. (In his day it was known as the Society for the Encouragement of Arts, Manufactures and Commerce. It didn't get royaled until 1908.)

The society's building looks like a cross between an English bank and a

Greek temple. Like Ben's Craven Street house, it has good bones, though no actual bones, at least as far as I know. I step inside and experience that familiar time-travel jolt of frisson. *Ben Franklin walked here! On this floor!* I say that to myself, but I could probably have said it aloud. I am among history buffs, fellow travelers.

One of them is Eve, a pleasant, gray-haired woman who is my guide to this corner of Franklin land. She leads me down a flight of marble stairs, past portraits of very dead, very White men, former presidents of the society. I make small talk, asking about Franklin's involvement in the society. Was he an active member?

"Oh, yes," she says, "he was very much involved in the society, at least until he went back to America and signed his bit of paper."

Wait. Did she just describe the Declaration of Independence, the founding document of the United States and a beacon of hope for oppressed people everywhere, as a "bit of paper"? I let it slide. The special relationship is more important than the problem.

Eve retrieves a giant folio from a shelf. It must weigh thirty pounds. Inside are original Franklin letters, yellowing but intact. She hands me one. I take it from her carefully as if handling the crown jewels or a Bob Dylan autograph. *I am touching the very paper that Ben Franklin touched.* It's Ben's handwriting all right. I recognize the outsized capital letters, the evenly spaced words. I recognize his signature with its curvaceous *B,* lissome *F,* and whimsical final *N* that curls and loops and pirouettes before sticking the dismount. It's very Ben: methodical and playful at the same time.

Franklin left a long paper trail. He wrote or received more than 15,000 letters in his lifetime. I've read many of them. They range from the silly to the sublime. As a whole, though, they are more elegant and gracious and thoughtful than just about any email today. Franklin took great care with each letter, as the multiple drafts and revisions attest.

The person he wrote to more than any other was his sister Jane, the youngest daughter of the large Franklin family and Ben's "peculiar favourite." Over the course of sixty-three years, he confided in Jane more than anyone else. As other family members began to die, Ben and Jane grew closer. "As our number diminishes, let our affection to each other rather increase," he told her.

Ben was a bona fide citizen of the Republic of Letters, an informal transatlantic network of scientists, philosophers, and other intellectuals of the seventeenth and eighteenth centuries. This virtual republic constituted the Internet of the day. It linked like-minded people separated by accidents of geography. Like the Internet, the Republic of Letters was wondrous—and awful. They had no cat videos, but they did snipe at one another and spread vicious rumors. Franklin often advised friends not to put their ideas into print unless they wanted them to live forever. Like the Internet, the Republic of Letters was not uniformly highbrow. No one—not even a Franklin or a Voltaire—could produce consistently exalted prose.

So it is with the Franklin letters archived here. They address prosaic matters: supplies of potash and sturgeon, an improved compass for surveying land, import duties, receipts for goods shipped, an outstanding balance. The quotidian nature of these letters makes me feel closer, not farther, from Franklin. He wasn't all about scientific breakthroughs and high-stakes diplomacy. He had bills to pay, too.

Ben's correspondence rarely contained even a hint of anger. There were a few exceptions, though. Arthur Lee, a Virginian and fellow diplomat known for his paranoid ramblings and angry outbursts, once wrote to Franklin, complaining that Ben was ignoring him: "I trust too sir that you will not treat this letter as you have done many others with the indignity of not answering it."

Ben wrote a reply the next day: "I hate disputes. I am old, cannot have long to live, have much to do and no time for altercation. . . . If you do not cure your self of this temper it will end in insanity." Ben wrote an even angrier letter to William Strahan, his British friend and member of Parliament who had backed the war against the American rebels. "Look upon your hands! They are stained with the blood of your relations! You and I were long friends: You are now my enemy, and I am, yours."

These two letters have something in common: Franklin never mailed either. They were placebo letters, one of Ben's preferred strategies for diffusing anger. As a rule, he'd wait twenty-four hours or so before mailing a heated letter. More often than not, he wouldn't send it or would dispatch a revised, softer version once the thunderstorm of anger had passed. Ben discharged anger the way his lightning rod discharged electricity, through deflection. Patience was the key. He waited for the storm of fury to pass so he could see more clearly.

Franklin did feel anger, of course. He was human after all. But with few exceptions (see Thomas Penn), his enemies never felt his wrath. Ben's approach surprises me. Like many others, I had long believed we must confront our tormentors if we hope to heal and move on. Over time, though, I've come around to Franklin's way.

Controlling anger doesn't mean remaining silent in the face of injustice. "Where complaining is a crime, hope becomes despair," Ben said. Wrongs must be called out and confronted. The question is how. Franklin responded to injustice not with anger but with justice. Not always, not perfectly, but that was his goal: stopping the cycle of retribution.

In Philadelphia, Ben was upset when a rival publisher, Andrew Bradford, who also happened to be the city's postmaster, refused to carry Ben's newspaper, the *Pennsylvania Gazette*, in the mail. When a few years later Franklin became postmaster himself, he "took care never to imitate" Bradford's pettiness and carried his rival's newspaper. He had arrested the cycle of injustice or, as the Roman emperor and Stoic Marcus Aurelius said, "The best revenge is not to be like your enemy."

Ben approached anger the way he did everything: with an open mind and an eye to the useful. Could anger help him improve himself and the world at large? Ben didn't deny or ignore his anger. He worked hard to master it, lest it master him. That was a luxury he could not afford. Unlike George Washington, Franklin had no troops to command. Unlike Samuel Adams, he had no Sons of Liberty to rouse. His power lay in his ability to persuade, and raw anger never persuaded anyone of anything.

Franklin's mastery of anger was useful. It widened his circle, enlarged his range of motion. Anger-proof, he could engage in heated debate without fear of fire breaking out. He could dine amicably with political rivals and maybe find common ground. Franklin knew what many of us have forgotten: our capacity to tolerate anger—to feel it without acting on it—broadens our world and makes possibilians of us all.

Consider an incident when Ben was a young apprentice printer during his first London sojourn. His fellow printers demanded a five-shilling fee for ale. Ben didn't drink ale so he refused to pay. Soon, strange things began to happen. He found his metal type in the wrong boxes, pages of a manuscript jumbled, and other "mischief done me." When confronted, the other printers feigned ignorance, blaming the mishaps on the printing house ghost.

Ben had a choice: escalate the conflict, perhaps seeking redress from a manager, or soldier on and hope the mischief petered out. There was a third option: pay the fee. He paid, "convinc'd of the folly of being on ill terms with those one is to live with continually." Sometimes that meant yielding on a relatively minor point of principle, as he did in the London printing house. Sometimes it meant forgiving those who had wronged him. The opposite of anger is not despair but forgiveness. Forgiveness dissolves anger. Forgiveness, not living well, is the best revenge.

Ben had a remarkable capacity for forgiveness. He forgave William Keith for sending him, only eighteen years old, on the ill-fated mission to London. He forgave his old boss Samuel Keimer for humiliating him in public. He forgave his brother James for his violent outbursts. He even forgave the British after the war.

Franklin worked hard to reduce friction in his relationships. A consummate negotiator and conciliator, he always sought consensus. He admonished friends and enemies alike to use "*soft words*, civility, and good manners." He always tempered his opinions, eschewing blunt declarations for softer phrases, like "it so appears to me at present." To me, this sort of squishy language sounds antiquated. We don't speak like that. We don't use soft words. We use hard words, the harder the better. Only strident and muscular language can break through the noise, or so we're told. But what if Ben is right? What if softer is better?

·   ·   ·

As I dive deeper into Ben World, I begin to see signs of him and his ideas everywhere. One evening, I'm watching a TV show about a sad sack soccer team up against a formidable rival. Predictably, the sad sack team was down three points at halftime. They were depleted and resigned. Then they watch a video of the opposing team's manager disrespecting them, and their anger is stoked. They walk onto the field furious. The footage slows to highlight the players' scowled faces and tightened muscles. I was sure what was coming next: the sad sack team, fueled by anger, would rage their way to victory.

Only they didn't. Fired up, they committed gratuitous fouls and lost players to red cards. They played aggressively but not skillfully, squandering opportunities, and they lost by an even greater margin. Righteous anger is mindless, and has no off switch.

There is no need to defeat those consumed by anger. They will defeat themselves. When Franklin's son-in-law, Richard Bache, alerted him to a smear campaign being waged against him, Ben was unfazed: "All grieve those unhappy gentlemen; unhappy indeed in their tempers, and in the dark uncomfortable passions of jealousy, anger, suspicion, envy, and malice . . . I take no other revenge of such enemies, than to let them remain in the miserable situation in which their malignant natures have placed them." Anger is the parasite that eventually kills its host.

Whenever Ben felt consumed by rage, he'd go for a swim or lift dumbbells or climb the stairs at Number Seven Craven Street. Or he'd sit in his study, and play the strange instrument he called the glass armonica. If you've ever played a tune on glasses filled with water, you understand the principle behind the glass armonica. The varying amounts of water in the glasses produce different pitches. It's an old idea. The ancient Greeks tapped jars with their fingers or sticks to make distinct sounds. Centuries later, musicians in the Middle East and Asia played glass bowls. In 1638, Galileo observed that different tones could be produced by rubbing moist fingertips across the rims of water glasses.

Franklin's interest in musical glasses began in 1758. He had traveled from London to Cambridge to see Edmund Delaval, a fellow electrician. Delaval, it turned out, also dabbled in musical glasses, which he demonstrated to Ben. Franklin was charmed by the performance but, as usual, was soon thinking of ways to improve glass-based music.

Back in London, he bought a hodgepodge of parts—spindles and glasses and bowls—and got to work. The result was an instrument like no other. It consisted of twenty-three specially blown glasses skewered by an iron spindle. The musician spins the glasses by using a foot pedal while rubbing the edges of the glasses with a moistened finger. Ben's invention was dubbed the "glassy-chord," but he preferred "glass armonica," after the Italian word for harmony.

Ben provided detailed instructions for playing the instrument. First, thoroughly clean both the glasses and the musician's hands with rainwater ("Spring water is generally too hard and produces a harsh tone"). Then close any windows or draw the curtains because sunshine and wind can dry out the glasses. Follow these instructions, he said, and the "tone comes forth finely with the slightest pressure of the fingers imaginable." If only, Ben.

There's a glass armonica at Number Seven Craven Street. It's an odd-looking contraption of a dozen or so glasses or bowls mounted on a long spindle. It looks like a sewing machine with a drinking problem. My attempt at playing it ends in abject failure. I can't coax a single sound from the instrument. I grasped the theory but couldn't make the leap to practice.

Ben had no such trouble. He was delighted with his invention and its "incomparably sweet" tones. I'm not sure about "sweet." To me, the instrument sounds haunting and mournful, like whales grieving. One listener said the music sounds as if it is "coming from nowhere, pervading everywhere," like Franklin himself. There is something wonderfully mysterious and magical about the glass armonica. It's impossible to listen to it without feeling something stir inside you.

I am not surprised Ben Franklin invented a musical instrument. He loved music, particularly simple folk tunes, and played the violin, guitar, harpsichord, and spinet. I am surprised Ben invented *this* instrument. It is wildly impractical. The dozens of glasses required are expensive and fragile. It is not easily transported. It is not a linear instrument like, say, the piano. There is nothing rational about it. It is all raw emotion and passion, an instrument of the heart. People who hear it for the first time are often moved to tears. Was this a fluke, I wonder, or did Ben know something we don't? Was the armonica his relief valve for the roiling anger gathering inside, a way to vent without spewing?

Ben could have invented the armonica and kept it to himself as his private instrument. Instead, he flung it into the world, curious to see how far it would fly. He shared the design with glassblowers, metalworkers, and other skilled tradesmen. They began making armonicas, and soon Ben's invention caught on. Concerts were held throughout Europe and in the American colonies. George Washington attended one in Williamsburg, Virginia. Marie Antoinette, the future queen of France, took armonica lessons while in Vienna. Mozart and Beethoven composed pieces for the instrument. The German physician and debunked hypnotist Franz Mesmer used the armonica in his practice.

When Ben returned briefly to Philadelphia in 1762, he brought an armonica with him. One night, while Deborah was sleeping, he began to play. She woke up, thinking it was the "music of angels." Ben taught his daughter, Sarah (everyone called her Sally), how to play. They performed duets, she on the armonica, he on the harpsichord. He brought an armonica with him to France in 1776 and entertained friends. Of all his inventions, he said, the armonica was his favorite.

Franklin constructed his various inventions with his hands, but the motivation stemmed from his enormous heart. Each one satisfied a need. They were useful. His brother James was suffering from kidney stones, so Ben invented a flexible catheter. The archaic language of the *Book of Common Prayer* confused people, so he drafted a simplified version. His sister Jane was struggling with spelling, so he invented a phonetic alphabet. Sometimes the need was his own. When he was aged and could no longer reach books on high shelves, he invented the "long arm," which did the trick. Necessity may be the mother of invention, but what kind of necessity, and whose? Harsh as it may sound, not all mothers are equally deserving.

Who was the glass armonica's mother? Not pragmatism. The instrument did not alleviate physical pain or speed deliveries or diffuse dangers like lightning. All it did was make music, and a strange kind of music at that. The armonica was invented by and for Sensitive Ben—the Ben who cried when reading poetry or when spotting the American shoreline after a long absence or when hearing an otherworldly sound that surely came from the gods.

The gods are fickle, though, and so is beauty. By the end of the eighteenth century, the armonica had lost its sheen. It was fragile and expensive and ill-suited for the larger concert halls coming into vogue. Rumors circulated that armonica performers went mad or died young, possibly due to excessive stimulation of the nerves in the fingers.

The armonica teetered on the verge of extinction. Then it resurfaced in the early twentieth century and survives to this day. Watch the Harry Potter movies or the Oscar-winning film *Gravity* and you will hear Franklin's glass armonica. A handful of musicians today are proficient in the instrument. I arrange to meet one, a fireplug of a Scot named Alasdair Malloy, Hollywood's go-to armonica player.

I walk a few blocks from my hotel in Waterloo to the Royal Festival Hall on the Thames and spot Alasdair waiting at a table. He has a ruddy complexion and a shock of white hair. He reminds me of Franklin. This has been happening a lot lately. I'm beginning to worry I am losing my grip—the man with a hammer who sees Bens everywhere.

I like Alasdair. I like how he excuses my lack of musical knowledge. I like how he talks about the armonica as if it were a person, one he is intimate with. ("I caress the instrument," he says.) His job, he explains, is not to make music but to "get the bowls speaking." I like how he doesn't so much play the armonica as commune with it.

"I feel all the vibrations coming up through my fingers," he says. "It's an experience completely different from any other instrument I've played, and it's a very personal one." He suspects that was a big part of the instrument's appeal for Franklin. The armonica enabled him to escape his frenzied, high-stakes London life and do something just for himself. Even the most useful person needs me-time.

I tell Alasdair about my failed attempt at playing the armonica. The bowls weren't talking to me. Is there a trick?

"Give the bowls a really good clean," he says. Then I should put a finger (the first joint, not the fingertip) on the far side of a bowl and draw it toward me, first quickly then slowly until I feel a real connection and a sound emerges. A sensitive touch is essential. "It is a very intimate instrument," he tells me, and I picture Ben playing the glass armonica stark naked. He probably did.

I thank Alasdair and head to Number Seven Craven Street. I climb the rickety stairs, then walk across the listing floor like a seasick sailor until I reach the glass armonica. I wipe down the bowls with a sponge, as Alasdair suggested, then turn the instrument on. This one is electric, a modification Ben surely would approve of. I wet a finger then gently touch the far side of a spinning bowl. Slowly I draw my finger toward me. Nothing. I try again, this time alternating the speed I move my finger. Fast, then slow, then fast again. Again nothing. Maybe I am not cut out for this. I am no Mozart. My one attempt at playing an instrument, the trombone, ended quickly and to the great relief of neighbors and their dogs.

I am not optimistic, but I am hopeful. We tend to use the two terms interchangeably, but they are different. The optimist believes that somehow—through their actions or luck or perhaps divine intervention—their future will be bright. The hopeful person makes no claims about the future but does believe it is their actions that make any goodness possible. Optimists believe the odds are in their favor. Hopeful people know the odds are against them but persist anyway. Hope is optimism pumping iron. Ben Franklin was not optimistic. He was hopeful.

I try once more to play the armonica, this time alternating the pressure, light then strong, then light again. And it happens—a sound! It is not a sound you'd want to hear, trust me, but it is a sound, and sound is a half step from music. I have communed with the glass armonica. Did you hear that, Ben? We may not be so different, you and me.

I suspect Ben turned to his glass armonica a lot in 1774, the worst year of his long and useful life. In January, he confronted the greatest test yet of his anger management skills. The brouhaha began when letters were leaked, incendiary letters. In private correspondence, Thomas Hutchinson, the royal governor of Massachusetts, portrayed the colonists as unruly children who needed to be disciplined, lest they veer into "perpetual anarchy and disobedience." What was needed, Hutchinson said, was "an abridgement of what are called English liberties."

Outrage erupted on both sides of the Atlantic, though for different reasons. For Americans, the letters confirmed their worst fears about British intentions. British officials, meanwhile, hunted for the leaker. Eventually Franklin confessed. He was the one who leaked the letters.

On January 29, British officials hauled Franklin before the Privy Council, the king's cabinet. His timing wasn't good. News of the Boston Tea Party had reached London only days earlier. He knew something was amiss as soon as he walked into the small but elegant room called the Cockpit, so named because cockfights were once held there.

On this day, the room was packed with many of London's elite, their patrician eyes trained on the American wearing a simple russet suit of Manchester velvet. The mood was charged, as if those gathered had been "invited as to a bull-baiting." The bull was Franklin. He had walked into an ambush.

What followed was a ritual humiliation of Franklin by Alexander Wedderburn, the king's silk-tongued solicitor-general. He likened Franklin to a common thief who "has forfeited all the respect of societies and of men."

Then Wedderburn, pounding the table, threw Franklin's fame as an electrical scientist back in his face, calling him the "inventor and first planner" of all the troubles between Britain and its colonies. Franklin, he said, sought to "irritate and incense the minds of the King's subjects" in America. Wedderburn then attacked Franklin's most precious possession: his reputation. Doctor Franklin, he said, "moves in a very inferior orbit."

And so it went for nearly an hour. The audience of British lords and other dignitaries ate it up, laughing and applauding, while Franklin remained silent, standing "conspicuously erect, without the smallest movement of any part of his body." If he was angry, no one could tell. His expression gave nothing away. The inquisition complete, Franklin walked across the room and, according to one account, whispered to Wedderburn, "*I will make your master a LITTLE KING for this.*"

Did Franklin really say that? I doubt it, but it makes for a good story, and Ben loved a good story. Even if good stories are inaccurate, they often contain great truths. In this case, it reveals Franklin's approach to anger. On that cold January day in London, he holstered his fury, resolving to convert it into something more powerful and useful.

Ben Franklin became an American the way Ernest Hemingway's character in *The Sun Also Rises* went bankrupt: gradually and then suddenly. Franklin had walked into the Cockpit a loyal, if disillusioned, British subject. He walked out an American rebel.

NINETEEN

REFLECTIVE BEN

Throughout his life, Ben Franklin resided in cities—Boston, Philadelphia, and now London, where he felt at home amid the frenzied shoppers
of Charing Cross and the free-flowing ale and conversation at pubs like the
George and Vulture.

But even the most committed urbanite needs to escape the din and
noise every now and then. Ben had recurring pastoral fantasies. He extolled the beauty of the American countryside and the "continual miracle"
that is farming. The truth is he couldn't milk a cow or hoe a field any more
than I can.

In summer 1771, the pull of the countryside was especially strong. The
London air was smoky and foul, "every street a chimney . . . and you never
get a sweet breath of what is pure, without riding some miles for it into the
country," he wrote to Deborah. It had been "a severe and tedious winter,"
with spring arriving late and half-heartedly.

Ben's mood mirrored the weather. It would be another three years before
his ritual humiliation in the Cockpit, but life was already growing stressful.
Britain seemed determined to milk its colonies dry. In 1765, it enacted the
Stamp Act, which levied duties (requiring an official stamp) on just about

any piece of paper, from legal documents to playing cards. The tax was about as popular with the colonists as the convicted criminals the British sent to America.

Ben, usually attuned to public sentiment, misread the mood on this one. The tax was inevitable, he sighed after it was rammed through Parliament. "We might as well have hinder'd the sun's setting." He even helped a friend, John Hughes, get the job as stamp distributor in Philadelphia, a move both men would regret. Rumors circulated that Franklin was behind the tax (he was not). One day in 1765, an angry mob massed outside his house in Philadelphia. Friends urged Deborah to flee. Instead, she armed herself and, with the help of relatives and a posse of leather-apron men, defended the family home.

Realizing his blunder, Franklin pivoted and argued against the tax. He met with any British official who would listen. He wrote articles and drew political cartoons. In February 1766, he testified at the House of Commons, fielding some two hundred questions. "Franklin of Philadelphia," as he called himself, was brilliant. In firm but measured replies, he delivered a spirited rebuke of the unpopular tax. Shortly after, Parliament repealed the Stamp Act. Ben had salvaged his reputation among Americans.

British officials, though, continued to treat him with contempt. When Franklin presented his credentials to the secretary of state for the colonies, Lord Hillsborough, he refused to accept them. Ben was furious (a controlled fury, of course) but, oddly, remained loyal to the British monarch. The problem, as he saw it, was Parliament, not King George. "Loyalty [to the king] is the most probable means of securing us from the arbitrary power of a corrupt Parliament, that does not like us, and conceives itself to have an interest in keeping us down and fleecing us," he wrote.

By summer 1771, the centrifugal forces pushing and pulling Ben were beginning to take their toll. He displayed rare signs of melancholy, as his friend William Strahan relayed in a letter to Franklin's son. "His temper is grown so very reserved, which adds greatly to his *natural inactivity*, that there is no getting him to take part in *anything*."

This is a side of Ben I had not seen before. I recognize it in myself: the resignation and learned helplessness. When nothing seems to work and new traps await at every turn, the natural reaction is to freeze, to shut down. I have tools at my disposal that Ben did not: therapies and pharmaceuticals galore. I know I should take solace in this, but I do not. The ineffectiveness of these supposed remedies only underscores my powerlessness over the disease.

One remedy that does help: motion. A brisk walk around the block, a slow run—or hopping on a 600 mph Boeing. Change your location, and you can change yourself. Not easily, not permanently, but I'll take what I can get. So did Ben. Not only was London smoky and contentious, but he had a new writing project to begin—not a pseudonymous article or scientific treatise, though; this piece of writing was personal. When his friend Jonathan Shipley invited him to visit Twyford House, his expansive country home near Southampton, Ben didn't hesitate to accept.

Shipley had been appointed Bishop of St. Asaph. Ben may have despised the clergy in general, but he liked individual men of the cloth. Consider his unlikely relationship with George Whitefield, the evangelical preacher who spearheaded the religious revival known as the Great Awakening. He was an entertaining and inspiring speaker who drew large and enthusiastic crowds. "Hearing him preach gave me a heart wound," said Nathan Cole, a Connecticut farmer who traveled miles to hear Whitefield speak.

Whitefield rivaled Franklin in his ability to relieve people of their money for a good cause. After one sermon, Whitefield appealed for donations. Franklin, who was in the audience, hesitated, but the preacher was persuasive and soon, "I began to soften... and he finished so admirably, that I emptied my pocket wholly into the collector's dish, gold and all." Franklin, so expert at nudging people into being more generous versions of themselves, had been out-Franklined.

It was a mutually beneficial relationship. Franklin earned money printing Whitefield's sermons, and Whitefield benefited from the publicity Franklin drummed up in his newspaper. But their relationship was more than mercenary. There was genuine affection between them. When Whitefield was recovering from an illness, Franklin, writing to a relative, said simply, "He is a good man and I love him."

He loved Jonathan Shipley too and counted him among his closest friends. The bishop, his wife, Anna, and their five daughters, ranging in age from eleven to twenty-three, were like family. He was looking forward, he said, to a good chunk of "uninterrupted leisure."

I wanted to see Twyford House myself. Unlike Ben's former London residence, it is not a museum open to the public. It is somebody's home. The house, I discover, is owned by a British family, the Leylands. Were they Franklinistas? I hoped so.

I contact Anna Leyland, explaining my Ben fixation. I am careful to sound sane, eliding such details as my air bath fantasies and fascination with Ben's theory of flatulence. It is a long shot. She and her family have lives to live and probably had no time for a neurotic American writer obsessed with long-dead Ben Franklin. I brace myself for a polite English rejection.

Hi Eric,

We would be very happy to invite you to come to see Twyford House. Could you let me know what days and times might work for you?

Many thanks, Anna.

Once again, I remind myself not to assume the worst of humanity. Ben didn't, and he witnessed far more evil than I have. Anna gives me detailed directions for getting to Twyford House. She asks if I want to take the fast route or the scenic one. A tough choice. I consult Ben. On the one hand, he makes the case for the fast route: *"Lost time is never found again;* and what we call time-enough, *always proves little enough."* Then again, Ben also believed travel lengthens life, so logically the scenic route is the way to go. Yes, that is what I will do.

I slalom through the crowds at Waterloo Station, then board a Southeastern Rail train. We depart on time at 9:53 a.m. and after whooshing past a blur of green countryside arrive eighty-three minutes later. It took Ben a full day's carriage ride to make the same fifty-mile journey. He had recently turned sixty-five and was in relatively good health, so he probably endured the journey well, but as he aged, he suffered from kidney stones, among other ailments, and the jostling of the carriage made such journeys painful.

I disembark at Shawford, a cute-as-a-button English village with a pub and not much else. I follow Anna's directions, so much more personal than anything Google Maps could cook up. I parallel the Itchen River, famous for its trout, and see why Ben savored "the sweet air of Twyford." I take a deep, luxurious breath and confirm that, yes, the air is indeed sweet and the ambiance tranquil. Dogs pass me, soaking wet from the river, their owners trailing close behind and apologizing profusely. I know they don't mean it. Was this dissembling a violation of Ben's virtue of sincerity? I don't think so. Such niceties may be deceitful but they are not hurtful. *Helpful* deceit is the very definition of politeness.

I walk a bit farther before spotting a sign that reads, "Entrance to Twyford House." I step through a gate and onto a gravel driveway. There it is: the house—estate is more like it—is set back from the twenty-first-century road and looks like a scaled-down Downton Abbey. If there are other houses nearby, I don't see or hear them.

I am greeted by Anna Leyland and her husband, Ben (naturally, he's named Ben), and their two children, Alfie and Eira. They all have slim, athletic builds and straight teeth, and they are wearing neatly pressed clothes. *Perfect* is the word that comes to mind, but perfect, I know, is an illusion, a trick that relies on the magic of distance. From afar, people's lives often look perfect, like a gleaming city skyline. Get closer, though, and the smudges and imperfections become visible. Ben Franklin's life was not perfect. God knows mine isn't. And neither, I'm sure, are the Leylands'.

I step inside the house—*the house Ben stayed in*—and immediately like it. The house, large and old, feels like a home, not a museum. I don't know what to say, so I sputter, "What a beautiful old house."

Actually, says Ben Leyland, for Franklin, this house was new, with a cutting-edge design. "It was the equivalent of staying at a glass-and-steel building today," he says. Old. New. These are relative terms, meaningless without context.

The Leylands knew about the Franklin connection when they bought
the house. The real estate agent mentioned it, naturally. What better proof
of history's value? A house with a storied past—Franklin slept here!—in-
creases the price, while a house with a sullied past—people were murdered
here!—decreases it. Real estate and history have a lot in common. Both rest
on the solid ground of location, as well as the shakier ground of perception.

Anna invites me outside. The view stuns me: chalk hills set against a
gray-metal sky and, in the distance, the river I had shadowed. *The same view
Franklin saw.* We sit down for tea and scones. I ask the obvious question:
"You live in the house Ben Franklin visited, a house where the matriarch was
named Anna, and your names are Ben and Anna. Are there some mysterious
forces at work here?"

Ben Leyland insists it is pure coincidence, nothing more. Anna is not so
sure. Nor is she sure about "the man, friendly and nice" whom her son Alfie
used to talk to but nobody else saw. It was probably just the fertile imagination of a young boy, but you never know. Franklin the Possibilian would
keep an open mind. Never close a door until you're certain there's nothing
behind it.

Consciously or not, I slip into the same role Franklin played at Twyford
House: the wise yet slightly cracked uncle. I regale the Leyland kids with my
bottomless reservoir of Franklin trivia. Did you know he invented an instrument called the glass armonica and that it is featured in the Harry Potter
movies? Did you know he could read Italian and Spanish? Did you know
he crossed the Atlantic eight times? Did you know he invented the flexible
catheter? Wait. That last one wasn't exactly age appropriate. I pivot, Ben-like,
and ask Alfie what it's like living in such an old house.

"Well," he says, sounding far wiser than his eight years, "you are really
quite comforted by thinking about what and who was here before." Franklin
couldn't have said it better.

After tea, we walk the grounds. Anna points out an enormous mulberry tree just like the one Ben used to sit under at Franklin Court in Philadelphia. Trees make a mockery of our puny life spans. They reveal their
true nature only over time. The same is true for houses, and people, points

out twenty-first-century Ben. "Character is a pattern," he says. Eighteenth-century Ben would agree. But it is not a randomly acquired pattern. Character doesn't just happen. It is molded and shaped. That's why Franklin strived to acquire good and virtuous habits. He knew that character is never bequeathed, always earned. An eight-year-old—even one as bright and precocious as Alfie—might impress, but we wouldn't say he had character. That demands time.

Twyford House is as rich in character as any, and it's also full of surprises, Ben Leyland tells me. Like that time a ceiling collapsed, or when they discovered it had no central heating. "And the floors are a bit wibbly wobbly," adds Anna. "The higher up you go, the more wibbly and wobbly they get." There have been pleasant surprises too, like the eighteenth-century coat buttons they found scattered on the grounds and the three jigsaw puzzles discovered under a sealed windowsill. The puzzles, now framed and hanging in their living room, are maps of England and France. The date reads 1767. Were they a gift from Franklin to the Shipleys perhaps? A learning project for the Shipley girls? No one knows.

The Leylands make use of the fertile land at Twyford House, growing apples and roses and Annabelle hydrangeas, just as in Franklin's time. Eira plucks a black currant from a tree and hands it to me. I hesitate, making a lame joke about food coming from the supermarket, not trees, before taking a bite. It is sweet and delicious.

We walk down a gravel path before reaching a small cottage with a red brick exterior, white framed windows, and an arched doorway. A vine flowering with pink roses climbs the front wall. This is the place. This is where 250 years ago, Ben Franklin sat down one August morning and, quill in hand, began to write his autobiography, a classic of the American canon.

Ben wrote on large sheets of folio paper, folded in half. Each page measured ten by fifteen inches, roughly the size of a laptop computer. Ben penned a draft on the left side of the page and jotted notes on the right. Each evening, he'd read his day's writing to the Shipleys and their five daughters, the book's first audience.

The words did not come easily, at least at first. Ben made more revisions on the first page than any other. Writing with no clear purpose, he was in uncharted waters. The book begins with these words: "Dear Son." An epistolary hand extended to William. The two were growing apart. William, forty years old, was three thousand miles away in New Jersey, where he was serving as royal governor, a position he owed at least in part to his father's connections. But more than distance separated them. William, London educated and posh, did not share his father's growing antipathy for British rule. He was, and would remain, a devout Loyalist.

Franklin possessed the rare ability to live his life and observe it simultaneously. He could stand apart from himself with bemused detachment, a state of mind Christians call holy indifference. "He speaks of himself as if he were speaking of another person," said his French friend, the Duc de La Rochefoucauld. This skill is one reason the autobiography is such a delight to read. Ben doesn't take himself too seriously. He happily reveals his shortcomings and doubts, often with self-deprecating humor. The same cannot be said of Adams, Jefferson, and other founders whose wooden memoirs elicit nods but no smiles.

Still, Ben's honesty only goes so far. He showed no interest in his interior life. There's no soul-searching akin to St. Augustine's or tell-all confessions like Rousseau's. Ben does not get naked on the page. The autobiography is a useful, do-it-yourself guide to moving up in the world, not only financially but morally too. It is a self-help book, America's first and, I think, still its best. Ben—or, rather, the character Ben created on the page—is funny and smart and ambitious. Most of all, he is resourceful, the first self-made American.

At the time, attitudes about the self were shifting. Once considered mysterious and unknowable, the self was now seen as something that could be unraveled, a code to be cracked. "A mighty maze! But not without a plan," wrote the poet Alexander Pope. Usually that plan doesn't reveal itself until the end of our days, and Franklin wasn't anywhere near his. He was a young sixty-five, with many productive years ahead of him. He exercised regularly. He never smoked and predicted tobacco would go out of style in a century. (Right idea, wrong timing.) And he had good genes. His mother lived until eighty-five, his father until eighty-nine.

At first, Ben's desire to reminisce surprised me. He was a possibilian, and possibility lies in the future, not the past, right? Not exactly. The future needs the past, could not exist without it. You are about to try something and you recall the last time you tried it. Was it a success or failure? Without a sense of the past, you couldn't recognize something, anything, as new. "Enjoy the present hour, be mindful of the past," Franklin said.

A few years earlier, he and William had traveled to the village of Ecton, seventy-five miles north of London and home to generations of Franklins. Ben, the youngest son of ten, marveled at the fact his father was the youngest son too, as was his father, going back five generations. He also discovered he had a doppelgänger. Uncle Thomas, an ingenious problem solver and "chief mover of all public spirited undertakings," died four years to the day before Ben was born. Had he died on the same day, observed William, "one might have suppos'd a transmigration."

Even a futurist like Ben Franklin needed to stand on the firm and reassuring ground of the past. He possessed a deep appreciation of history. When he founded the Philadelphia Academy, the progenitor of the University of Pennsylvania, he included history as one of the core subjects (along with swimming). Yet somehow we've forgotten this side of Franklin and refashioned him as a far-sighted visionary fixated on the future, not the past. Yes, Franklin was forward-looking, but as he sped ahead, he never lost sight of where he had been, never forgot that, as one modern scholar said, "humans are history-bearing animals."

Not long ago, I was talking on the phone with a Franklinista named Nian-Sheng Huang. He grew up in China, and life was hard. During the Cultural Revolution, he spent ten years exiled in Inner Mongolia. He eventually immigrated to the United States and enrolled at Cornell University, where he studied American history, specializing in Franklin. It's no coincidence Huang chose history as his discipline. The Chinese are awash in history, while we Americans wade in shallow waters.

"To many Chinese, America is just a baby," he said. "We Americans don't really care about history; if something is more than ten years old that's ancient. We're constantly looking for something new, something fresh, something different. We really don't have the time to listen to the past. That's why we can move along quite rapidly in many fields. But there are also prices to pay for this attitude."

"What sort of prices?" I ask.

One major cost, he said, is wisdom lost. "The answers are already there. We just don't care to listen anymore." Ben Franklin did listen. The past was another door to knowledge, one he always kept ajar.

Nostalgia isn't what it used to be. For a long time, it was considered a psychiatric disorder, a sign of encroaching dementia among the elderly or neurological damage among the young. Symptoms included uncontrolled weeping, anorexia, and suicidal thoughts. Reminiscing was involuntary. It was not something you did; it was something that happened to you, and that something was awful. Nostalgia, concluded Johannes Hoffer, the seventeenth-century Swiss physician who coined the word, was "a cerebral disease of essentially demonic cause."

This dark view of nostalgia persisted into the twentieth century. British novelist Somerset Maugham captured the prevailing sentiment. "What makes old age hard to bear is not a failing of one's faculties, mental and physical, but the burden of one's memories." But must memories be a burden? Must old age be hard to bear?

No, said psychiatrist Robert Butler, in a groundbreaking 1963 academic paper. He coined a new phrase, "life review," to describe this new interpretation. Far from pathological, reminiscing is "naturally occurring" and therapeutic. Old, unresolved conflicts resurface and "can be surveyed and reintegrated." Life takes on new meaning, and the prospect of death feels less terrifying. Reminiscing, Butler concluded, should be encouraged. He quotes an anonymous seventy-six-year-old man: "My life is in the background of my mind much of the time; I cannot be any other way. Thoughts of the past play upon me; sometimes I play with them, encourage and savor them; at other times I dismiss them."

Many recent studies validate this view of nostalgia. The simple act of reviewing your life—telling your story—has been found to decrease depression and anxiety and increase life satisfaction. It boosts optimism and softens the sting of loneliness. Reminiscing makes us happier. The past may be a foreign country, but it is one we'd be wise to visit regularly.

I like the concept of a life review but not the term. It sounds judgmental, like a performance evaluation conducted by God. I prefer "life story." Reviews don't generally have happy endings. Stories often do.

We can't change our past, but we can change how we perceive it. A life review, or life story, is active, not passive. We may be recalling the past, but that recollection takes place in the present. Memory is subjective, and it is creative, more painting than photography. To tell your life story is to regain a semblance of mastery and control and, if you're lucky, acceptance.

But why does looking back at our lives make us happier? A group of researchers from Guangzhou, China, investigated that question and found the secret ingredient ("mediating factor," in social science speak): gratitude. Looking back at our life, we are often filled with gratitude, not regret. Reading about that study, I couldn't help but think of Ben's invocation: "Be quiet and thankful." That was, I think, what propelled him to Twyford House and the first pages of his autobiography. He was overflowing with gratitude and wanted to share that sentiment with others. More than that, he wanted to supply a road map so that others might reach this happy place too.

At first, I envied the Leylands. I dip in and out of Ben World. They are immersed in it. They sleep in rooms he slept in. They walk the ground he walked. They never know when they might stumble across another Franklin artifact when walking the dog or taking out the trash. That could be me, I think, if I lived here, if—to get to the heart of the matter—I could *afford* to live here. Franklin's namesake, Benjamin Leyland, works in finance. Currency is his currency. Ideas are mine. I wouldn't have it any other way, but I salivate at the thought of writing where Ben wrote.

It is a brief salivation, more of a dribble. After a few minutes, I realize that, no, I wouldn't want to write in the Franklin cottage. It is the last place I would want to write. I recall meeting artists in Florence and philosophers in Athens. They were complete wrecks. Their cities' past greatness weighed them down. A glorious past can inspire. It can also paralyze. I'll take my little home office in suburban Washington, DC, any day.

I check my hybrid watch. I have not yet violated Franklin's famous rule of thumb about visitors. I do not stink like a three-day-old fish, but why push it? Yes, it is time to leave the Leylands to their giant mulberry tree and their Annabelle hydrangeas and their house brimming with character and Ben-ness.

Twenty-first-century Ben offers to drive me to the train station in his electric Mini Cooper. I turn and see Anna and Alfie and Eira smiling and waving as if I were a departing family member. I return their wave, and am caught off guard by the warm feeling welling inside my chest. I don't know these people, not really. We've just met. But I'm going to miss the Leylands, especially Alfie, so bright and curious. He doesn't have character, not yet, but he will.

This is, I imagine, how Franklin felt when he boarded his carriage for the long and bumpy ride back to London. He was leaving paradise, the sweet air of Twyford, and returning to the world of dust and smoke and polite English treachery. I wonder if he experienced the same sinking sensation I do, like a ship taking on water faster than the crew can bail it. I suspect he did not. Ben's emotional buoyancy was portable. He always traveled with it.

On the train back to London, I gaze out the window at the progressively urban scenery and wonder: Why don't I review my life too, à la Ben? I am not that much younger than he was at the time. And I have tools at my disposal he couldn't dream of: a laptop, a camera, ADHD meds.

Yet I find myself resisting this idea. Unlike Ben, I am not a founding father. I am not even a founding uncle or founding third cousin once removed. Then again, neither was Ben when he sat down to write his memoirs in 1771. Yes, he was famous and respected (by most), but he was not yet the larger-than-life Franklin of the Declaration of Independence and the Constitutional Convention.

Still, I resist. Reviewing your life sounds like something old people do, and I am not old. I am not done with life yet, so why would I want to review it?

Somewhere around Clapham Common, the absurdity of my rationalization hits me. Reviewing a life still in progress means you still have time to make course corrections, large and small. Reviewing life is the first step toward improving it. You can't know where you're going unless you know where you've been.

Until now, I have exhibited little interest in my ancestry. What little familial excavation I have done has unearthed a rare and disturbing combination of dullness and drama. I had my DNA tested. It wasn't my idea; I was working on a story for NPR. I spat into the little tube and a few weeks later the results landed in my inbox. I clicked and soon was reading what was surely the dullest ancestry report ever produced. Ninety-five percent Ashkenazi Jewish, mainly from eastern Europe and Russia. My hopes spiked when I saw I am 2 percent South Asian. That is statistically insignificant, though. I suspect the good people at Ancestry.com threw it in to make me feel better.

Yet within this plain-vanilla gene pool, darkness lurks. An uncle committed suicide. Decades later, my father threatened to do so and was briefly hospitalized for depression. I know these demons reside in me too, and honestly, it is a daily struggle to keep them at bay. My demons never sleep. At most, they power-nap. Exhuming my past, I'm afraid, might stir them from their light torpor.

Besides, my impending birthday, the one that features the number six, marks the beginning of an awkward age. The adolescence of senescence. Just as my teenage daughter toggles hourly between fully grown independent woman and helpless child who would really, really like Dad to cook dumplings for her, I toggle between youthful exuberance—I can do anything!—and a sober realization that, while not old by any means, I am no longer young either.

Ben aged without angst. Reviewing his correspondence, I detect no whining or grumbling about the onset of old age. His body was beginning to show signs of wear and tear: kidney stones and gout, to name just two. Yet Ben, unlike me, never let his various ailments disturb his equilibrium. He never became a crabby old man. If anything, he grew more serene with age. Buddha Ben on the ascendance. That same summer of 1771, shortly before decamping to Twyford House, he wrote to his sister Jane. He had witnessed much wickedness, seen how "mankind were devils to one another," he said, but added, "Upon the whole I am much disposed to like the world as I find it."

As my train pulls into Waterloo Station, I wonder: Where did that hopefulness, that stubborn optimism, come from? Was it innate or learned? I sure hope it was the latter.

TWENTY

DECISIVE BEN

How we recall events—as pleasurable or painful—is determined not by how they begin but how they end. Endings carry greater weight than beginnings, studies have found. Ben Franklin's fifteen-year mission to London did not end well. Relations between Britain and the colonies went from bad to worse. Parliament passed a series of laws they called the Coercive Acts and the colonists the Intolerable Acts, lest there be any doubt how they felt about them. The British replaced the civilian governor of Massachusetts with a military commander, the tone-deaf and incompetent General Thomas Gage. He closed the port of Boston and established a new quartering act, military speak for "Our smelly soldiers are going to sleep in your house, okay? Good."

Meanwhile in London, Franklin's anger management skills were tested. In March 1774 a British general boasted within earshot of Ben that with a thousand British troops he would "go from one end of America to the other and geld all the males, partly by force and partly by a little coaxing." Ben remained silent, channeling his anger, as usual, with satire, a biting piece called "A Method of Humbling Rebellious American Vassals."

I try to picture Ben in London that final year. He is sixty-eight years old. He has been humiliated in the Cockpit in full view of Britain's most powerful officials and stripped of his royal position as deputy postmaster for the colonies. He is persona non grata with most of the political elite. His wife, Deborah, is in poor health. Even the sanctuary that was Number Seven Craven Street is upended. William Hewson, the surgeon (and, now, husband to Polly Stevenson), was dissecting a cadaver when his knife slipped. He developed septicemia and died a few days later. In a letter to Deborah, Ben expressed rare anguish: "They were a happy couple! All their schemes of life are now overthrown!" For once, he distrusted providence.

His son William urged him to return to Philadelphia, but he didn't and remained in London for more than a year after his dressing down in the Cockpit. Why? Perhaps he couldn't pry himself from the close friendships he had forged there. Or perhaps those rumored love interests were true. I think there was another, simpler explanation: Ben was stuck. It takes time to process bad news; there's a lag between information and reaction, and the worse the news, the longer the lag. This lag might look like wasted time, but it is not. The lag is what transforms our half-hearted decisions into firm commitments.

Some biographers portray Franklin as a man without principles, a chameleon changing colors to fit the prevailing mood. But he did possess core beliefs, none more steadfast than his faith in unity. The theme permeates every aspect of his life. Unity featured in his science. There were not two distinct types of electrical currents, he discovered, but a single unified one. Unity was nature's preference. It features in his politics too. In 1754, more than two decades before the Battles of Lexington and Concord, the opening salvo in the Revolutionary War, he drafted a plan for colonial unity, called the Albany Plan. "Britain and her colonies should be considered as one whole, and not as different states with separate interests," he wrote. He also sketched the now famous "Join or Die" cartoon depicting a dismembered snake, with each inert piece representing a different colony. The Albany Plan was rejected—by both the British and the colonists. Ben, as usual, was ahead of his time.

The unified entity that animated most of Ben's life was "that fine and noble china vase" otherwise known as the British Empire. Ben couldn't imagine the vase without its largest and most vital piece, the American colonies. When the vase shattered, Ben couldn't accept it. Like a jilted lover who refuses to believe the affair is over, he needed time to adjust to this painful truth.

In London, he continued to meet with friends and visit taverns. He even launched a new group, the Wednesday Club, which met at Craven Street. He corresponded with fellow scientists and began working on a simplified prayer book, a kind of universal liturgy.

He also played the role of colonial interpreter. He'd meet with anyone curious about America, especially potential emigrants. In September 1774, he met a failed corset maker with big ambitions. Franklin saw something in him and suggested he seek his fortune in America. He wrote a letter to his son-in-law, Richard Bache, recommending this "ingenious worthy young man," now en route to Pennsylvania. The man had little education, but would make a good clerk or surveyor. He also could write. The young man's name? Thomas Paine. When Paine later published, anonymously, his incendiary pamphlet *Common Sense*, many people thought it was Franklin's work.

Ben, ever the possibilian, also engaged in some thirteenth-hour diplomacy. He drafted a list of seventeen "hints" for compromise and relayed them to British officials via Quaker friends. Perhaps, he thought, the affair was not over.

One day, a friend, Caroline Howe, invited Ben to a game of chess. When he arrived, he found Caroline's brother, Admiral Richard Howe, waiting and eager to discuss a possible compromise between Britain and the colonies. Alas, the chessboard diplomacy fizzled, as did other last-minute attempts to head off war. The Old Conjurer was out of tricks.

To stay or to go? That is one of life's thorniest questions, the subject of songs and poems and many therapy sessions. Choosing is difficult. We need a method. Ben devised his own. He called it "moral algebra." Too often, he said, people make important decisions based not on the best reasons but the most recent one that pops into mind. He'd draw a vertical line on a piece of paper, listing pros in one column and cons in the other. He also assigned a relative weight to each pro and con. If a pro and a con negated each other, he'd cross them out. Then he'd set the paper aside. If after two or three days, he felt the same way, he knew he had his decision. "This kind of *moral algebra* I have often practiced in important & dubious concerns; and tho' it cannot be mathematically exact, I have found it extremely useful."

Only one example of Ben's moral algebra has survived. Dated 1773, it depicts Ben wrestling with the question of whether to stay in London or return to Philadelphia. At first glance (and second glance too), it looks like gibberish, the scrawling of a madman:

Stay	Go
S. J. P.—Eur.	Recover of F
Finish 5th Edn.	Settle with Do. for Ph.O
—— Piece on New Stove	Get clear of Agys.
—— Dialogue	Repose
Settle with Mrs. S.	Prevent Waste at h
Ohio Business.	Settle with H's Exrs.
Pap. Money	
Boston Agy.	
Beccaria	

Actually, the gibberish is decipherable. "S. J. P.—Eur" refers to an aborted trip to Europe with his friend Sir John Pringle. He still hoped to take that journey, thus a reason to stay in London. "Get clear of Agys" refers to the four colonies he now represented: Pennsylvania, Massachusetts, New Jersey, and Georgia. By going home, he would rid himself of these exasperating assignments. At this time, in 1773, the math favored staying in London. So he did. Two years later, the math changed.

Might Ben's trick, his moral algebra, work for the rest of us? Yes. And no. Listing the pros and cons of any decision is easy; the hard part is weighting them. I can think of many reasons why I should buy a Porsche 718 Boxster: thrills, a sense of mastery, faster commute times. But those reasons do not compensate for the one reason why I should *not* buy the Porsche: I like being married. Moral algebra is an inexact science but useful nonetheless.

How did Ben's wife, Deborah, factor into his calculations? Not very much, it seems. He was fond of her but not fond enough to return home when she fell ill in 1769. She had suffered a stroke. Dr. Thomas Bond, Franklin's friend and cofounder of the Pennsylvania Hospital, wrote to Ben that spring, reporting that Deborah had suffered a temporary loss of memory and other neurological damage. "These are bad symptoms in advanced life and auger danger of further injury on the nervous system," he warned. Franklin consulted with a physician friend in London but did not return home. The task of caring for Deborah fell to their daughter, Sally. Deborah's letters slowed, and by late 1773 stopped. "It is now a very long time indeed since I have the pleasure of a line from you," he wrote the following spring. "I hope however that you are as well as I am, thanks to God."

Deborah was not well. In December, she suffered a second stroke, this time fatal. William attended the funeral of "my poor old mother." (She was actually his stepmother. William was born out of wedlock before Ben and Deborah married; the identity of his biological mother remains a mystery.) Then, on Christmas Eve, William wrote an uncharacteristically harsh letter to his father. "I heartily wish you had happened to have come over in the fall, as I think her disappointment in that respect preyed a good deal on her spirits."

Did William just accuse his father, Benjamin Franklin, of indirectly killing his wife? It might be an exaggeration, but there is some truth to the charge. Ben's letters to his wife had flagged in recent years. His sense of familial obligation tended to flow in only one direction. He wrote emphatically about a son's "natural duties" to his father, but said nothing of a father's reciprocal duties to his son or a husband's obligations to his wife, especially one as loving and faithful as Deborah. Why couldn't Ben get his ass on a boat to Philadelphia and be with his ailing wife?

"You have to accept that there are just some things we will never know," Mitch Kramer, the Franklin interpreter, told me. He was speaking about another mystery in Ben's life—the precise location of his famous kite experiment—but the answer applies equally to many such episodes. Despite the long paper trail he left behind, Ben remains elusive. This was no accident. He cultivated an air of inscrutability, perfected to an art form. Occasionally, though, events proved so momentous, the electrical charge so powerful, that private Ben spilled into public view.

Sometime in March 1775, Ben decided it was time to act. He was comfortable in London, but comfort is never enough. He was going home. Was it guilt over neglecting his ailing wife? Or was it the recognition that he had outlived his usefulness in London; the vase was shattered? Perhaps his motives were more immediate and personal. Rumors circulated that British authorities were preparing a warrant for his arrest.

March 19, 1775, was Franklin's last full day in London. He was with his good friend, Joseph Priestley. They were reading the most recent newspapers, with Ben asking his friend to separate the American ones from the British. Ben read of the horrendous news from back home: the quartering of unwanted British troops in American homes, the trade embargo meant to suffocate the colonies, the fear of further reprisals. Ben had to pause reading frequently, Priestley recalled, because of "the tears literally running down his cheeks." Franklin was an odd fish but not a cold one.

The next day, Franklin boarded the *Pennsylvania Packet* for Philadelphia. He had advanced his departure date by two weeks after receiving a tip that British authorities might take drastic action against him. While at sea, a warrant was issued for his arrest.

I decide to spend my last day in London at Number Seven Craven Street. The timing feels right. It is July Fourth.

I take the Tube to Embankment Station, then stop at a small park to eat the sushi takeaway I had picked up and to collect my thoughts. The English sun is making one of its periodic cameo appearances. I find a seat—a nice beach chair, no less—and soak up the rare ultraviolet rays. I spot a woman sitting on a nearby bench. Her hair is pelican white, her skin ruddy, and her clothes, from the black patent leather shoes to the paisley dress, decades out of fashion. She's reading a tabloid—a *paper* newspaper that, with each turn of a page, emits a distinct crinkling sound. She is the only one reading a newspaper. Everyone else (myself included) is bent over in silent prayer to their smartphones. The woman removes an umbrella from her purse—a simple, black one like the kind street hawkers sell at inflated prices during rainstorms—and uses it to shield herself from the unlikely midday sun. No one notices her. She is invisible.

I find the tableau sad. But why? Is it her age, or my perception of her age? Some philosophers argue there is no difference. Age is perception and nothing more. Chronometric age tells us nothing about a person. It tells us nothing about Ben Franklin who, at nearly seventy, was just getting started.

I walk the short distance to Craven Street, past the Ship and Shovel, "London's Only Pub in Two Halves," and the gym called "The Gym" and the Boris Bikes, neatly lined up, before arriving at Number Seven. The staff has decorated the front door with a red-white-and-blue ribbon. On the first floor, I find Ben, in bust form, wearing a birthday hat held by a string tucked under his chin. The hat would look absurd on other founders, but Ben totally pulls it off. I can hear the small crowd of American tourists in the garden below eating nachos and drinking Yuengling. Once again, though, I have this room, Ben's room, to myself.

After Franklin moved out and his landlady, Margaret Stevenson, died a few years later, the house underwent a variety of incarnations. For a long time, it was a hotel; then in the 1950s and 1960s, it served as the office for a mysterious nonprofit called the British Society for International Understanding. Rumors circulated that it was a front for the CIA. Then, for a while the house was abandoned and used as a flophouse by drug addicts and the homeless. Valuable marble was ripped from the fireplaces.

Finally, a group of Franklinistas, led by American Márcia Balisciano, came to the rescue. There were many twists and turns involving English Heritage and British Rail and even Margaret Thatcher before the house was saved and preserved as a small museum. "I think it has its own will to survive," Márcia, now director of Benjamin Franklin House, told me. She is speaking metaphorically, of course. Or is she? Franklin's homes in Boston,

Philadelphia, and Paris are long gone, but this one still stands. Why? The dedication of people like Márcia Balisciano played a role, but so did luck. *Distrust not providence.* We know less than we think we do, and we control even less.

The *Pennsylvania Packet* enjoyed unusually good weather. It was a pleasant crossing. Franklin, as usual, used the time well, recording his thoughts on his failed mission to London. This time, he dropped any pretense of diplomatic language. British parliamentarians were not qualified to govern "a herd of swine," let alone an entire people. He was speaking of Britain's hereditary legislators, a custom he found absurd. It would make more sense and cause less mischief to have hereditary professors of mathematics. Britain's elected House of Commons were just as corrupt, he said, accepting bribes for their votes.

At some point during the six-week journey, Ben put his quill down and turned to his one dependable diversion: science. He took ocean temperature readings several times a day, part of his ongoing studies of the Gulf Stream. He sketched his ideas about how to design faster, more efficient ships. The weather continued to cooperate and was "constantly so moderate that a London wherry [a light rowboat] might have accompanied us all the way," he said.

On May 5, the *Pennsylvania Packet* docked at the foot of Philadelphia's Market Street. Only then did Franklin learn that while he was at sea, shots had been fired at Lexington and Concord. His worst fears were realized. War had come to America.

TWENTY-ONE

BUSY BEN

Ben was always busy but never busier than in 1775 and 1776. The burst of activity began the moment the *Pennsylvania Packet* docked at Philadelphia harbor. Cheering crowds greeted him as he disembarked. His London mission may have been a failure, but Ben, now a committed rebel at age sixty-nine, was loved by most (not all) of his fellow Americans, future citizens of the not-yet United States.

Ben was home again, but home is a moving target. Philadelphia had changed. Its population had exploded and was now the second largest in the British Empire, after London. Ben's family life had shifted too. Deborah was dead. (Curiously, Ben hardly mentions his loss.) William was still in New Jersey, serving as royal governor and refusing to join the rebel cause. Ben moved into his new house on Market Street, Franklin Court. He had never seen it. It was Deborah who had supervised the construction and furnishing, per Ben's detailed instructions sent from London. "Let papier mâché musical figures be tack'd to the middle of the ceiling; when this is done, I think it will look very well," he wrote in one letter.

You can still visit Franklin's house today, as I did one spring day. Well, *sort of* visit. All that remains is a "ghost house." That's what the National Park

Service, guardians of the historic site, call it. It's just a few steel girders arranged in the same footprint as the actual Franklin house. I ask one of the park rangers, a garrulous man with an unruly beard and Franklinesque girth, why they didn't reconstruct the Franklin house, as they've done with the homes of other historical figures. They almost did, in the 1970s, the ranger explains, but balked. There were no contemporaneous drawings of the original house to work from, and they had been "burned before," he adds enigmatically. Something about the wrong location for one of Washington's homes.

Unlike Mount Vernon or Monticello, Franklin Court didn't last long after its namesake's death. It endured in several incarnations: as a boarding house, female academy, coffeehouse, and hotel before it was carved up into smaller units in 1812 and eventually razed. Franklin Court, home of America's founding grandfather and first scientist, was, like a stolen car or failed dot. com, worth more as parts than whole.

The park service worked with what it had, aiming to re-create the feel of Franklin Court, if not the actual house. They've installed concrete bunkers and portals that enable you to peer at the original foundation. "Fragments of Franklin Court," they call it but, really, it is a bunch of rocks. The entire arrangement—all that steel and concrete—lends Franklin Court an oddly Soviet feel, which might seem peculiar given it was home to the man whose face is synonymous with American capitalism but not so strange when you consider that Franklin held some decidedly socialist views.

Ben liked his new home but had little time to enjoy it. He was busy. The day after his ship docked, the Pennsylvania Assembly elected him unanimously as one of its delegates to the Second Continental Congress. Ben accepted, recalling an old adage about public appointments, "*Never to ask for them,* and *never to refuse them,*" and adding one of his own, "*Never to resign them.*" (This conviction would come to haunt him years later, when he craved repose.)

I've always imagined colonial American life (at least for White male property owners) as pleasantly languid. But there was nothing pleasant or languid about Philadelphia in 1775 or about Ben Franklin's routine. Gone was the late-night socializing of his London days. He went to bed early and rose early, and for good reason. He served on some ten congressional committees, plus a Pennsylvania one, with meetings starting at 6 a.m. and only Sundays off. The demanding schedule exhausted men much younger than Franklin and apparently killed one. Peyton Randolph, president of the Continental Congress, collapsed while dining with fellow Virginian Thomas Jefferson, felled by a stroke. He was fifty-four years old.

Ben was appointed postmaster general. He helped design the new American currency and accelerated the manufacture of saltpeter, needed for gunpowder. In his new roles, Ben deployed his business acumen and charm. He also unsheathed his pen. He wrote essays and songs, mocking British soldiers and urging on the young rebellion. He also wrote a famous war cry, later adopted by Jefferson: "Rebellion to tyrants is obedience to God." Franklin wasn't a religious man, not in the conventional sense, but he never hesitated to invoke the Lord's name if he thought it useful.

By all accounts, Ben was in high spirits despite his busy schedule or, more likely, because of it. We think of busyness as a modern malady. But people were plenty busy in the eighteenth century, and busy people are happier than idle people, many studies have found. This holds true *even if that busyness is forced on them.* As horrible as Sisyphus's fate was, condemned to roll a boulder up a hill, only to have it roll down again and again, it beat being sentenced to an eternity of idleness.

Consider a more modern example. A Houston airport was in a bind. Passengers disembarking in the morning complained about long waits for their luggage. The airport hired more baggage handlers, reducing the wait time to no more than eight minutes. Yet passengers still complained. Officials investigated further and discovered the delay consisted of two parts: a one-minute walk to the carousel and a seven-minute wait for the bags.

What happened next sounds bonkers. Airport officials decided to insert *intentional delays* into the system. They directed arriving airplanes to more distant gates and ensured the luggage carousels were as far away as possible. This increased the walking time (busyness) to six minutes and decreased the waiting time (idleness) to two minutes. Passenger complaints dropped to nearly zero. The same dynamic explains why if I'm stuck in highway traffic I'll take a longer route, even if it means more driving time, just so I can stay engaged and busy. As Robert Louis Stevenson said, "The great affair is to move."

I don't want just any kind of busyness. What I seek is good busyness. Meaningful busyness. When we say we want a happy life, we often mean a *meaningful* life. Happiness is a purely subjective state. Meaningfulness is not. Others have a say. Usefulness directed inward is solipsistic nonsense. We are useful to other sentient beings, and this demands a certain amount of energy, of busyness. Yes, we need time to rest and recharge, but how do we deploy our fully charged batteries? As Ben said, "A life of leisure, and a life of laziness, are two things." Leisure is useful. Laziness is not.

In January 1776, Benjamin Franklin turned seventy years old. That is a not insignificant milestone today. In Franklin's day, when the average life expectancy was thirty-five, it amounted to a miracle. Ben did not, as far as we know, celebrate the occasion. He was too busy.

Not everyone cheered Ben's return to Philadelphia. Some questioned his loyalties. He had spent the bulk of the past seventeen years abroad, on English soil, and had many English friends. Samuel Adams considered Franklin "a suspicious person, designing to betray the cause." Rumors spread that Franklin had returned to America not as a friend but as a spy.

Ben was no spy. The man who spent the past two decades trying to reconcile with Britain, to keep the china vase intact, had flipped, and now displayed the conviction of the converted. Franklin knew the British better than anyone else, and he didn't like what he saw. Writing to a friend, he said, "It is a true old saying, that *make yourselves sheep and the wolves will eat you*: to which I may add another, *God helps them that help themselves*." Ben had gone full rebel.

He won over his doubters. After meeting Ben in Massachusetts, Abigail Adams wrote to her husband, John, saying she found in Franklin "a disposition entirely American," adding that "he does not hesitate at our boldest measures, but rather seems to think us, too irresolute, and backward."

We think of rebels as young and reckless. Ben was neither. He was a methodical septuagenarian, a revolutionary grandfather. It's not as unexpected as it seems. His radicalism had been gestating for a long time. Recall what sixteen-year-old Ben, wearing his Silence Dogood mask, said: "I am naturally very jealous for the rights and *liberties* of my country; and the least appearance of an encroachment on those invaluable privileges, is apt to make my blood boil exceedingly." Ben's rebellious spirit was lying in wait, like a dormant gene ready to be activated.

Besides, the alternative to joining the rebel cause was to withdraw from public life entirely and retreat to a "cool sullen silence." That wasn't Ben's style. He needed to be doing, to be useful. Did he have a lot to lose? In one sense, yes. He had spent years building his reputation and amassing a small fortune. Both could vanish in an instant. Yet, now in his seventies, Ben knew he didn't have that long to live and would "soon quit the scene," as he told George Washington. He found that prospect terrifying—and liberating. As an old man, he was free to listen to his heart, knowing that once the war was over, a new generation would see America flourish "like a field of young Indian corn" battered by wind and rain, but once the storm passed, "shoots up with double vigour, and delights the eye not of its owner only, but of every observing traveler."

I love this about Ben. I love how he could stare into the void that is the future, a Ben-less future, and see not emptiness but meaning. His flame may vanish, but the light still blazes, burning bright in the hearts and minds of a new generation.

I am a decade younger than Rebel Ben yet not nearly as bold. I am not staring down a tyrannical king or outfitting a ragtag army or writing words that animate a revolution, but we don't get to choose our era. This is who I am and when I am. The only question is: What am I going to do with the temporal hand I've been dealt? How am I going to be useful?

I now realize my ego has stunted my usefulness. I help my wife but on my terms, the way I want, not the way she needs. This is not useful, as she helpfully points out. I had forgotten that usefulness is a response to the actual needs of another, not a selfish assertion of one's talents.

Ben rarely fell into this trap. He listened to others, then looked for the intersection of their needs and his abilities. If Philadelphia needed a hospital, he worked toward that, not founding another newspaper, even though journalism lay closer to his wheelhouse than medicine. He holstered his ego and did the needful.

Life was good for Ben Franklin, with one notable exception: his relationship with his son William. The two had been drifting apart for years. Now the drift accelerated, swept along by fast-moving events.

After he was humiliated in the Cockpit, Franklin urged William to resign his royal governorship and take up farming instead. It is, Ben said, a more independent profession and therefore a more honorable one. Franklin warned his son, as fathers are wont to do, that events were unfolding rapidly and not in the younger Franklin's favor. Should William remain a Loyalist, "you will find yourself in no comfortable situation, and perhaps wish you had soon disengaged yourself," Ben wrote. William ignored his father's advice, as sons are wont to do. He stayed on as New Jersey governor, faithful to the British Parliament and to King George.

It is the summer of 1775. Shots have been fired at Lexington and Concord. The British and American forces were careening toward all-out war. We find the elder Franklin firmly on the side of the rebels and the son just as firmly on the side of King George. Something had to give, and it did. Father and son met twice that summer, at a mutual friend's country house in Pennsylvania. No one knows what transpired, but the conversations "ended in shouting matches loud enough to disturb the neighbors." It would be years before father and son spoke again.

History is a series of flukes masquerading as inevitabilities. What today looks like a foregone conclusion was only one of many possible outcomes. For every path taken, there are dozens, hundreds, of alternative routes, enticing what-ifs.

I think about one of these what-ifs every summer. For the past eight years, my wife and I have rented the same cottage in northern Vermont along with two Canadian friends, Martin and Karen. The house is so close to the Quebec border that my friends use a Canadian cell phone service while my wife and I use an American one. For years, we treated the border as a non-entity. We'd cycle across, stopping at a tiny-shack of an immigration post. I'd walk my dog, Parker, along the border, with me on the US side and him in Canada. It was a borderless border, a joke, or so we thought.

Then the pandemic hit, and the joke was on us. The border was shut as tight as the Korean DMZ and remained so for nearly two years. We vacationed without our Canadian friends, which saddened us. I had a lot of time on my hands that summer, so I indulged in a thought experiment. What if there was no border? What if there was no Canada or perhaps no United States, just one giant political entity stretching from Key West to Nunavut? This was Ben Franklin's vision, and he nearly pulled it off. Well, not nearly, not even close, actually, but he tried. That he made the arduous journey from Philadelphia to Montreal through snow and ice, and at age seventy—seventy!—makes him only more insane, and thus more laudable, and likable, in my eyes.

Most Franklin biographers mention the Great Canadian Fiasco only briefly, if at all. That's understandable. The expedition—spoiler alert!—was a failure. It did not alter the course of history, not even a little. Yet I find the Great Canadian Fiasco fascinating. The journey says a lot about Franklin and his bottomless reserves of energy and moxie. It offers a little-known window into what made him tick.

There is, I confess, another reason for my outsized interest in the Great Canadian Fiasco. I have something of a Canada obsession. I can name all the provinces (and territories!), as well as their capitals. I can list most of the Canadian prime ministers. I have mastered Canadianisms like "eh" and "oot and aboot." I know that a loonie is more than a bird. I actively seek, and actually enjoy, Tim Hortons coffee. I am nice but in an annoyingly passive-aggressive way.

Over the years, my Canada obsession has evolved from quirk to deep appreciation. I genuinely like Canadians. To me, they embody all the best of America and none of the worst. I began to fantasize about moving to Canada long before it was fashionable to do so.

Franklin was obsessed with Canada too, but with one important difference. I wanted to settle in Canada. He wanted to acquire it.

Franklin thought about Canada more than most Americans, then or now. "Canada" appears hundreds of times in his correspondence. He saw it as strategically crucial, first to the British Empire and then to the fledgling United States. So when Congress asked him to join an expedition to Montreal, he jumped at the chance. His fellow delegates included Samuel Chase and Charles Carroll, as well as a French printer named Fleury Mesplet. Their mission: to charm the Canadians and persuade them to join the American Revolution. To that end, Franklin and his colleagues were authorized to offer inducements, such as freedom of religion and the press, representation in Congress, and a mutual defense agreement. What they could not offer, unfortunately, was cash.

The mission was a long shot. Most Canadians were Roman Catholic, most Americans Protestant, and the two didn't exactly see eye to eye. The Continental Army, meanwhile, was floundering up north, though to what extent would become clear to Franklin only once he reached Montreal.

It was a long and difficult journey for even a young man, and Franklin was not a young man. At seventy, he suffered from gout, among other ailments, and was seriously overweight. Friends urged Franklin, "in the evening of life," not to embark on such a dangerous expedition. So did William, who, despite their differences, prayed for his father's safe return.

Franklin and his colleagues left Philadelphia in late March, thinking winter was over. They thought wrong. En route, they encountered snow and ice while sailing on small, uncovered boats, riding in horse and carriage over rugged roads, and sleeping in the woods. All the while Ben was suffering from swollen legs and painful boils. Ben feared he wouldn't survive the journey. "I begin to apprehend that I have undertaken a fatigue that at my time of life may prove too much for me," he wrote to Josiah Quincy in Massachusetts. "So I sit down to write to a few friends by way of farewell."

News of his demise was exaggerated. Six weeks after they departed Philadelphia, the delegation crossed a frozen Lake George in New York and at last reached Montreal. They were "very politely received" by General Benedict Arnold. The traitor-to-be was the most senior American officer on Canadian soil.

Ben never got the chance to deploy his considerable powers of persuasion. The Canadians were not in the mood. The Continental Army looked like a losing bet. American troops were outgunned and outmanned. They had not been paid in weeks. American credit was worthless. Food and provisions were running low. Then there was a smallpox outbreak that sidelined hundreds of soldiers. No wonder the British had pushed American forces into full retreat. The withdrawal represented not only a military setback but a public relations disaster. As Franklin and his colleagues wrote, "Our enemies take the advantage of this distress, to make us look contemptible in the eyes of the Canadians."

Perhaps, but the truth is that the Americans had only themselves to blame. Historian Jonathan Dull pinpoints the larger reasons behind the Great Canadian Fiasco: "Believing in the righteousness of their cause the Americans failed to consider that the Canadians had reason to distrust them," a statement as true now as it was then.

Toward the end of his life, Business Ben looked back at the Great Canadian Fiasco and concluded it would have made more sense to buy Canada than conquer it. War-weary, Franklin extended this notion to all conflicts. "It seems to me, that if statesmen had a little more arithmetic, or were more accustomed to calculation, wars would be much less frequent."

There are few traces of Franklin's brief stay in Montreal. There is no monument to the Great Canadian Fiasco. No tome chronicling the expedition. That's a shame. We should commemorate our failures as well as our triumphs, for they are not as far apart as we think. Triumph is failure that made one or two better choices, took a slightly different path.

I dig deeper and unearth a few Franklin fragments in Canada. I tell my Canadian friends Martin and Karen, and they offer to investigate. Being Canadian, they are not only nice but competent too. I knew my research was in good hands.

The border reopened and we rendezvoused at the Vermont cottage once again. There, Martin and Karen shared their notes and impressions of Ben Franklin's foray to their homeland. The site they visited is Château Ramezay.

Built in 1705 as the private residence for Claude de Ramezay, governor of Montreal, it also served as the focal point for the region's commercial and political life. Franklin spent ten or so working days there during the Great Canadian Fiasco. Inside the tan-stoned chateau, docents dressed in colonial-era outfits speak of the "American Invasion" of 1775, which is accurate, I suppose, but I like to think of it as a friendly invasion. The Canadians, I'm sure, didn't see it that way.

The Franklin exhibit is relegated to one corner of the museum, almost as an afterthought. There is a portrait of Ben, wigless with thin strands of gray hair flowing to his shoulders. He is wearing an expression of restrained dismay, as if he were wondering what the hell he was doing in Canada. My Canadian friends wondered too. This "unexpected historical twist," as Karen put it, or "American incursion," as Martin did, is only dimly recalled in Canada. "We've almost written him out of our history," Karen said. I note her use of *almost*. They didn't write Ben *entirely* out of their history. That would not be very nice, or very Canadian.

The small museum, being Canadian, manages to find two bright spots to the Great Canadian Fiasco. On display are papers guaranteeing safe passage to Albany for one Mrs. Walker. She had graciously housed the American delegation in Montreal, making her a target for British reprisals. I'm happy to report she made it across the border to safety.

The other bright spot to an otherwise dark chapter is that French printer Fleury Mesplet stayed behind in Montreal and fired up his printing press. Two years later, after enduring brushes with the British authorities, he founded Canada's first French-language newspaper, later known as the *Montreal Gazette*.

As I put to bed this odd little chapter in Ben's life, an odd little thought occurs to me: I'm glad Franklin failed this time. Had he succeeded, Canada would have become the fourteenth colony, then one of the original states. Most likely, it would have been subsumed by the dominant American culture. Canada would not be Canada. And that, I'm sure, would have been an even greater fiasco.

•   •   •

Franklin returned from Canada exhausted and ill. The gout that plagued him had resurfaced. His legs and feet were swollen and sore. His big toe was red and tender and felt like it was on fire. Walking was difficult and painful. He had to miss several sessions of the Continental Congress.

Gout was especially prevalent during Franklin's time. One medical historian noted wryly that the Age of Reason was also "the Golden Age of Gout." Ben had many risk factors. His diet was meat heavy, and he loved wine, particularly Madeira. He'd regularly down a bottle a day. His skin ailment, most likely psoriasis, also rendered him more vulnerable to gout.

Today we know that gout is caused by a buildup of uric acid in the blood, forming sharp, needlelike urate crystals that accumulate in the joints, causing pain and inflammation. Purines, the source of uric acid, are found in certain foods, especially red meat and alcoholic drinks sweetened with fructose.

Ben tried various treatments, such as they were: a bit of bloodletting and purging. He suggested to a woman he fancied that sexual activity might cure his gout. His rationale: "When I was a young man and enjoyed more of the favors of the sex than I do at present, I had no gout." *So convenient a thing it is to be a reasonable creature.*

When gout struck, Ben did moderate his vices. He drank less wine, ate less meat, and exercised more. He heeded the advice of Poor Richard (i.e., himself): "Be temperate in wine, eating, girls and sloth; or the gout will seize you and plague you both." Perhaps the most potent medicine in his cabinet was humor. After one flare-up of gout, he wrote that hilarious bagatelle, "Dialogue Between the Gout and Mr. Franklin."

> GOUT. I have a good number of twinges for you tonight, and you may be
>   sure of some more tomorrow.
> FRANKLIN. What, with such a fever! I shall go distracted. Oh! eh! Can
>   no one bear it for me?
> GOUT. Ask that of your horses; they have served you faithfully.
> FRANKLIN. How can you so cruelly sport with my torments?

GOUT. Sport! I am very serious. I have here a list of offenses against your
own health distinctly written, and can justify every stroke inflicted
on you.

The Gout proceeds to scold Franklin for his gluttony and sedentary lifestyle until, finally, he agrees to eat less and exercise more. The Gout isn't
buying it: "I know you too well. You promise fair; but, after a few months of
good health, you will return to your old habits." The dialogue's takeaway: to
defang your maladies, poke fun at them. Humor saps them of their power
over our minds, if not our bodies.

At age seventy-one, Ben inventoried his health, writing in the third
person as if he were a real doctor assessing a patient. He notes the gout, of
course, as well as the scurf, the boils, and "some small spots on his hands and
face." He ends his clinical report on an upbeat note. "[The patient's] health
is otherwise good. He feels on comparison no diminution of his strength,
but is as capable of bearing labour as he was at 50. His legs particularly seem
stronger since the swelling left them, and he can walk much without weari-
ness. His digestion is good."

Old Ben's healthiest habit was his attitude. He never whined or complained; he had no interest in comparing notes with other older people, engaging in what a friend of mine calls "organ recitals." Ben's uric acid may have
hardened but not his heart. He treated his body with kindness and gratitude.
As he wrote in 1790, some three weeks before his death, "I do not repine at
my malady, though a severe one, when I consider . . . how many more horrible evils the human body is subject to; and what a long life of health I have
been blessed with, free from them all."

Ben was accepting but not resigned. He consulted with physician friends
and invented medical devices such as bifocals. He was stoic in his outlook,
changing what he could, accepting what he could not. "There are in life real
evils enough, and it is a folly to afflict ourselves with imaginary ones," he told
his sister Jane.

I have far fewer real ailments than Ben but far more imaginary ones. The
IBS, a touch of sleep apnea, the occasional AFIB, and something to do with

my bladder that I'd rather not discuss. Overall, my health is good. Yet I complain prodigiously and with alarming gusto. I worry too. Every chest pain is
a heart attack, every headache an aneurysm. This chronic hypochondria is
not sustainable. When I do pass that milestone, the one that prominently
features the number six, I know that my body, no longer under warranty, will
begin to act up. Parts will need to be repaired, possibly replaced. My body
will emit strange, indeterminate sounds, even more than it does now, and I
will worry even more.

There is hope for me, though. Poor health need not demoralize. Some
people maintain high levels of happiness even when facing chronic health
challenges, a recent study found. The keys are friends and perspective, recognizing that all things considered, you are doing well. This was Franklin's
way. He had many close friends and was genuinely grateful for his reasonably
good health. Gratitude, like sincerity, cannot be faked.

Many people grow happier as they age, even in the face of adversity,
another study found, provided they possess one trait: a flexible sense of
self. The happy elderly consider flexibility central to who they are. When I
stumbled on that study, I thought of Ben and his bagful of masks. The man,
even at age seventy, was remarkably flexible. He was that rare and wonderful
human who grew more, not less, nimble with each passing year.

History is to Americans as water is to fish—an all-pervasive, life-sustaining
substance that somehow evades notice. The fish doesn't appreciate water
until it's deprived of it. The American doesn't appreciate history until it bites
him in the ass.

I am just as fishy as my fellow Americans; at least I was for a long time.
Should history be thrust upon me, I would not reject it, but I rarely sought it
out. A case in point. I've been living in the Washington, DC, area for the past
fifteen years yet not once have I visited the National Archives Museum. How
can this be? Laziness only partly explains my oversight. The disturbing truth
is I haven't gone because I haven't cared. There, I said it. But now I do care,
thanks to Ben, the futurist with a rearview mirror.

I take the Metro, Washington's sad subway, to the Gallery Place station, then walk a few blocks through Chinatown before arriving at the museum. I climb the prodigious stairs and step inside slowly, reverentially, as if entering a cathedral or mosque. That's understandable. The documents housed inside are precious. America's secular scripture. I am interested in only one.

The Declaration of Independence is located in the Rotunda for the Charters of Freedom, a serious room with serious pillars, a high-domed ceiling and marble everywhere. America's founding document is encased in glass and mounted in a gold frame. It is larger than I expected, about the size of a small coffee table. The parchment is intact but so faded that only a few phrases are legible: "When in the course of human events . . . we, therefore, the Representatives of the United States of America . . ." It is credited to a lone man, but the declaration was a group effort.

No writer likes to be edited, and Thomas Jefferson was no exception. To make matters worse, he was edited by a committee: the fifty-six delegates to the Second Continental Congress. Each man had an opinion about what the document proclaiming American independence should and should not say and how it should or should not say it. Some delegates objected to "two or three unlucky expressions," Jefferson whined. (Incredibly, one of those "unlucky expressions" was a call to abolish the slave trade.) After Jefferson excised these objectionable passages, the nitpickers found other alleged faults. Jefferson bristled at these "mutilations" of his pristine words, sounding less like a founding father and more like a touchy writer.

Fortunately, he had made a new friend: Ben Franklin. The two sat next to each other during the congressional sessions. They were an odd pairing. Ben was world famous; Jefferson was a nobody, at least outside the American colonies. Ben, the son of a soap and candle maker, had two years of formal education. Jefferson, the son of a landowner and "gentleman," studied law at William and Mary College. Ben was seventy years old, Jefferson thirty-three. But they both shared a love of the written word and a distrust of the spoken one. And both men saw themselves as outsiders. They got along swimmingly.

Franklin sensed Jefferson's irritation (it was impossible to miss) at seeing his words maimed and tried to comfort the young lawyer from Virginia by deploying his favorite tactic: humor. Committees make terrible editors, Ben said. Then he relayed a story from his Boston days.

There was a local hatter named John Thompson who was about to open his own shop. He needed a signboard, so he composed these words: "John Thompson, Hatter makes and sells hats for [cash]." There. Thompson liked it, but thought he'd consult with a few friends.

"'Hatter' and 'makes hats' are redundant," said one friend. Thompson deleted the latter.

"You really don't need the part about 'for cash,'" said another friend, since that form of payment was customary. Thompson cut those words too.

"You don't really need 'sells hats,'" chimed a third friend. "Nobody will expect you to give them away."

And so it went until the sign was reduced to simply, "John Thompson" accompanied by a drawing of a hat.

I can picture Jefferson chuckling, the tension draining from his neck and shoulders. He was not the first or the last writer to bristle at editorial suggestions. Fortunately for him, Franklin, recovered from gout, was assigned to the five-person team tasked with drafting the declaration. Jefferson wrote the document. Franklin and the others edited it. Ben was a rigorous but kind editor, a rare combination.

Click. Click. I zoom closer and closer, straining to read the digitized 248-year-old document more clearly. On my laptop, I am looking at an early draft of the Declaration of Independence. It contains dozens of edits: deletions and insertions, scratches and scrawls. It looks less like American scripture and more like American graffiti. Scholars have tried to distinguish the marks and identify who made which. Was it John Adams or perhaps one of the other delegates? Or was it the work of Ben's meaty printer's hands?

Franklin's handwriting, thankfully, is distinctive, so we have a good idea which revisions are his. They are not mutilations but, I think, improvements. The original Jefferson draft read that Americans "should declare the causes which impel them to threaten separation." Franklin scratched out "threaten," thus simplifying the text and at the same time making the split irrevocable.

The most important Franklin edit appears early. Jefferson's original draft reads, "We hold these truths to be sacred & undeniable; that all men are created equal." An assertive pen stroke—most likely Franklin's—struck through "sacred & undeniable," replacing it with "self-evident." *We hold these truths to be self-evident.* The best-known seven words of the Declaration of Independence. It might seem like a minor revision, a more concise wording of the same idea, but it is more than that—much more. It is, I believe, the greatest edit of all time. Jefferson's original wording appeals to religious authority. These truths are sacred. They are undeniable, presumably *because* they are sacred. This was a fine seventeenth-century argument but not an enlightened eighteenth-century one, a time when appeals to sacred sources were on the decline.

By revising the passage to read "self-evident," Franklin invoked a different and, he believed, higher authority: human reason. The idea was in the air, thanks to the English philosopher John Locke. His fingerprints are all over America's founding documents, especially the Declaration of Independence. Locke rejected the long-standing belief that ideas are innate. We are not born with any knowledge, he believed, but are like a blank sheet of paper waiting to be written on. Experience, acquired through our senses, is the source of all knowledge. A self-evident truth is one deduced from direct experience. You don't need to be a philosopher or even educated at all to grasp a self-evident truth. Anyone, even a child, can see it.

Locke lists several examples of self-evident truths. That "it is impossible for the same thing to be and not to be," that "white is not black," that "a square is not a circle," that "bitterness is not sweetness," and so on. Locke calls this "intuitive knowledge," though it is more a kind of seeing than knowing. Just as the eye detects light, the mind detects a self-evident truth. No proof is needed. What is self-evident "strikes the mind as immediately and perpetually true" and "leaves no room for hesitation, doubt or examination," Locke said. Self-evident truths are beyond—or, rather, above—debate.

This is where it gets tricky. It is crucial we get these truths right, for once declared self-evident, they are no longer in play. On the one hand, this can be wonderfully liberating. For instance, it is self-evident that I love my daughter. I know it so thoroughly and so deeply I need not waste time questioning or "proving" it. It just is. Another of my self-evident truths is that I am overweight. I don't need a scale to tell me. I know it every time I try to squeeze into a pair of jeans.

The drafting committee for the Declaration of Independence faced a similar bugaboo. Jefferson named a number of supposedly self-evident truths: "that all men are created equal, that they are endowed by their Creator with certain unalienable Rights, that among these are Life, Liberty and the pursuit of Happiness," and that people have the right to abolish an unjust government. To eighteenth-century readers, though, these were not self-evident at all, certainly not in the reductionist hot-is-not-cold way John Locke had in mind.

Jefferson and his editors attempted something audacious. They hoped that by proclaiming these truths as self-evident, they would become so. "We *hold* these truths to be self-evident" was less an observation than an assertion, a wish. They wanted to extend self-evident truths from the world of perception—up is not down, hot is not cold—to the world of morality: might is not right, equality is better than inequality. This evolution remains a work in progress, as the state of race relations in America shows, but with Jefferson's draft and Ben's sagacious pen strokes, the two steered us in the right direction.

The same month Franklin began editing the Declaration of Independence, news of a much more personal nature reached him. New Jersey rebels had arrested Franklin's son William, the last of the royal governors, on charges he had "discovered himself to be an enemy of the liberties of this country." On the day his father signed the Declaration of Independence, July 4, William was moved to Connecticut where he would spend the next two years in jail, including eight months in solitary confinement. Conditions were harsh. He was imprisoned in a dark and bare cell with only straw to sleep on. In September, William wrote to Connecticut's revolutionary governor, Jonathan Trumbull: "I suffer so much in being thus buried alive, having no one to speak to day or night, and for the want of air and exercise, that I should deem it a favor to be immediately taken out and shot."

William's wife, Elizabeth, was distraught. She worried about her husband and was in poor health herself. She wrote to Ben, pleading with him to use his clout and intercede. "Consider my dear and honored sir, that I am now pleading the cause of your son, and my beloved husband," she wrote, adding a plaintive note: "If I have said, or done anything wrong I beg to be forgiven." Ben did not reply.

Their dispute came down to a knotty question. What is the higher duty—a father's unconditional love for his son or a son's undying loyalty to his father? On this question, Benjamin and William Franklin could not agree.

I'm not sure if it's my nascent Franklinian hopefulness or perhaps my covert Canadianness, but I desperately want to salvage a lesson from this sad affair. I dig into the historical record, scouring Ben's correspondence and William's too. Nothing. If there is a truth to be gleaned, it is far from self-evident.

I've seen this before. Mahatma Gandhi, Winston Churchill, Martin Luther King Jr., and others: great men who shaped history but were terrible parents and spouses. Why these lapses in humanity, and with those closest to them? It is not, I'm sure, a matter of excessive busyness, but something else, some character flaw that manifests not on the world stage but at the family dinner table, those quiet moments when the klieg lights fade and, for a moment, it is simply a husband and wife, a father and son, alone with each other. For Ben, I suspect, the intimacy proved uncomfortable, and he yearned to escape. Once again, he heeded the call of the open seas.

I am standing in front of an unremarkable colonial-era building, red-bricked with white, arched windowpanes, and a small cupola sitting atop its A-frame roof. There is nothing the least bit grand or monumental about Carpenters' Hall, so-named because it was (and still is) home to Philadelphia's carpentry trade guild, yet a lot of history happened here. This was where the First Continental Congress convened in 1774. For a while, it was also home to two Franklin creations: the Library Company of Philadelphia and the American Philosophical Society. It is also where, in late December 1775, a series of clandestine meetings took place that altered the course of Benjamin Franklin's life and that of the not-yet United States.

One of those in attendance was Julien Alexandre Achard de Bonvouloir, a shabbily dressed, disabled twenty-six-year-old who had recently arrived in Philadelphia. He claimed to be a French military officer on sick leave and enthralled by the American cause. He was actually a French secret agent, dispatched by Louis XVI to assess the viability of the American rebels.

His timing was good. Congress had recently formed the Committee of Secret Correspondence. I love the name. It sounds like something a gaggle of twelve-year-old boys dreamed up while huddled in a tree house. The committee was, in fact, quite serious, the forerunner of the US State Department. Its mission was to identify foreign governments willing to back the American rebellion with either money or arms or, ideally, both.

France was an obvious prospect. The country was still smarting from the thumping it received by the British in the Seven Years' War, a brutal, sprawling conflict that also ensnared the other great powers of Europe and felt longer than its name implies. France was eager to avenge its loss but wasn't yet ready to commit. The war had dented its economy and decimated its military. There was also the sticky issue of a monarchy like France backing a rebellion whose stated aim was the ouster of another monarch. Who knows? The French people might get ideas.

Bonvouloir was instructed to seek out one man in Philadelphia: Ben Franklin. Ben had visited France and, like many other first-time visitors, was instantly smitten. France made him feel twenty years younger, he said.

Once in Philadelphia, Bonvouloir made some discreet inquiries and before long was sitting down with Franklin and three other members of the Committee of Secret Correspondence. They met at night and, recalled Bonvouloir, "each one of us took a separate path" to Carpenters' Hall.

The two sides, French and American, sniffed each other like two dogs meeting for the first time. Bonvouloir wanted to know if the Americans were being truthful about the upstart Continental Army's ability to wage war. Franklin and his fellow Americans wanted to know if Bonvouloir might be a double agent, possibly working for the British secret service. Over the course of the three meetings, they grew to trust one another and the sniffing subsided. At least one "deliverable," as diplomats say, emerged from these meetings: Bonvouloir promised to provide George Washington with two French army engineers, which he desperately needed, and the Americans agreed to continue the conversation. It was the beginning of a mercurial but beautiful friendship.

After the meetings, Bonvouloir fired off a report to his handlers in Versailles. He described the American forces in rosy, breathless terms. "Everyone here is a soldier, the troops are well clothed, well paid and well armed.... They are more powerful than we could have thought, beyond imagination powerful; you will be astonished by it. Nothing shocks or frightens them, you can count on that."

Bonvouloir's assessment was exaggerated, but it served a useful purpose. Versailles and Philadelphia inched closer. By spring 1776, the French began to secretly supply the Americans with much-needed gunpowder. Congress dispatched a representative to France. Silas Deane, a Connecticut merchant and congressional delegate, sailed with diplomatic instructions from Franklin, a handful of letters for Ben's French friends—and vials of invisible ink, presumably so the Committee of Secret Correspondence could live up to its name. (John Jay, Deane's handler, was given solvent that could render the ink visible.)

Congress soon realized they needed a more prominent representative in France. They asked Franklin. This made sense. He was America's most experienced diplomat and its only international celebrity. His electrical experiments were received enthusiastically everywhere but nowhere more so than in France. The French adored Franklin.

It was a dangerous mission, though, beginning with the ocean crossing. Should the British capture Franklin, he surely would be arrested and possibly hanged. Assuming he made it to France, a viper's pit of politics and British spies awaited him.

Ben accepted the assignment without hesitation. His philosophy of public appointments—*Never to ask for them* and *never to refuse them*—helps explain his decision, but I suspect there was something else going on. Two

2

decades earlier, in a letter to his friend the preacher George Whitefield, Ben explained his approach to ageing in theatrical terms: "Life, like a dramatic piece, should not only be conducted with regularity, but methinks it should finish handsomely," he said. "Being now in the last act, I begin to cast about for something fit to end with." Of course, that was not Ben's last act, not even close. The man had more last acts than the musical *Cats*. He was not about to play the role of the distinguished but irrelevant elder statesman. He wanted to go out with a bang, and the mission to France was just the sort of fireworks he craved.

I'd also like to go out with a bang, or at least a gong. Too many otherwise rich and meaningful lives end with a bland mélange of golf, early bird specials, and nagging ennui. Ageism is nothing new. It's been around for as long as there have been old people and young people to mock them. Yet the idea that old age is *necessarily* a time to disengage from active life is relatively new. It began in the 1940s, with a theory called structural functionalism. If the elderly were unhappy, this theory posited, it was because they suffered from "adjustment problems." They couldn't cope with the "natural" process of ageing and the accompanying loss of relevance. Books with titles like *Growing Old: The Process of Disengagement* suggested the elderly simply do less and aim for what the Roman philosopher Cicero called *otium cum dignitate*, "leisure with dignity." Only relatively recently have attitudes shifted and the elderly encouraged to stay active.

Not all busyness is equal. There is a difference between bingo busy and revolutionary busy. One is meaningful, the other is not. Franklin enjoyed games, especially chess, but I can't see him withdrawing to a chess-themed retirement home. Nor do I see myself doing so, and not only because I can't play chess. Pleasure alone is rarely a good enough reason to do anything. Purpose is a far more powerful engine.

In late October 1776, Ben visited friends to say farewell. He did so discreetly. His mission to France was a secret, though not a very good one. Philadelphia was gossipy and lousy with British spies. On October 27, Franklin boarded an American naval vessel, aptly named *Reprisal*. Ben was accompanied not by two enslaved people, as he was en route to London two decades earlier, but by his two grandchildren, seven-year-old Benny, his daughter's son, and sixteen-year-old Temple, the son of still-imprisoned William. Ben had more or less raised Temple. The two lived together in London and, now, in Philadelphia. For Ben, Temple was a reliable presence in an unreliable world.

At the helm of the *Reprisal* was a young but capable captain named Lambert Wickes. The Committee of Secret Correspondence handed him sealed orders to be read only once at sea. They urged him not to tarry, to obey Dr. Franklin, and to "keep totally secret where you are bound . . . or what is your business." To avoid detection, Franklin and his grandchildren boarded not in Philadelphia but at Marcus Hook, several miles downstream.

Normally Franklin loved long sea voyages, but not this time. The *Reprisal* was "a miserable vessel," the autumn seas were rough, the quarters cramped, and most of the food too hard for his aged teeth. Ben was also plagued by boils and the scurf, "extending over all the small of my back, on my sides, my legs, and my arms, besides what continued under my hair." Then there was the constant fear of capture. Two weeks into the voyage, the crew spotted a pair of British men-of-war. Captain Wickes took evasive action, barely eluding the enemy ships. Ben no doubt recalled his sister Jane's plaintive plea that he never cross the Atlantic again. "Don't go, pray don't go."

By the time the *Reprisal*'s crew spotted the French coast on November 28, Ben was weak and malnourished. The journey, he said, "almost demolish'd me." Unfavorable winds prevented the ship from reaching its intended destination, the port town of Nantes. For four days, they loitered off the coast until Franklin, exhausted and frustrated, convinced Captain Wickes to hire a small fishing boat to bring him ashore.

On December 4, 1776, Benjamin Franklin, seventy years old, landed at the fishing village of Auray. This time, there were no cheering crowds. Nobody was expecting him.

TWENTY-TWO

FULL BEN

It took Ben more than a month to reach the fishing village of Auray. It took me less than twelve hours. If progress is measured by speed, then, yes, this is progress. My journey was more comfortable than Ben's and with significantly less drama. I did not suffer from the scurf or boils. British warships did not shadow me. The food, while not gourmet, was edible. The journey fatigued but did not demolish me.

Yet Ben and I shared one harrowing experience: a brush with ageism. For him, it came in the form of whispered misgivings about whether, at age seventy, he was fit for such a challenging assignment. For me, it came while transiting at Frankfurt International Airport. I was on a bus shuttling from terminal to airplane, and the bus was crowded. Standing room only. A young guy, wearing jeans and an attitude, offered me his seat—no, *insisted* I take his seat. He did so loudly and melodramatically, lest there be any doubt about the size of his vast and potent generosity.

"No thanks," I said curtly. "I'm good."

A few seconds later, he offered again, even more dramatically, and I repeated, "I'm good," though in a tone that conveyed another sentiment: *fuck you.* So this is how it's going to be? People offering me their seats.

Carrying my bags. Taking pity on me. I won't have it. Why should I? Ben didn't.

I came across this story about Ben when he was well into his eighties. A visitor to his Philadelphia home, Manasseh Cutler, asked to see a particular book in Ben's library. The volume was heavy, and Ben struggled to lift it. Cutler offered to help, the library equivalent of offering your seat. Ben demurred and, recalled Cutler, "with that senile ambition common to old people . . . insisted on doing it himself, and would permit no person to assist him, merely to show us how much strength he had remaining." Good for you, Ben. Senile ambition? There's another word for that: *moxie*.

I like Auray. I like how the town hugs the harbor like a warm blanket and how it wears its age nonchalantly, like a septuagenarian with nothing to prove. I like the dark and imposing Church of Saint-Sauveur, perched atop a hill, overlooking the old houses and cafés, listing this way or that, and the waterfront that has changed little since Benjamin Franklin and his two grandchildren washed ashore here nearly 250 years ago.

Ben did not share my fondness for Auray—a wretched place, he supposedly called it—and couldn't leave fast enough. This hasn't deterred the town from exploiting its moment of Ben. He's everywhere, as I discover after two minutes. I walk past Franklin Quai and the small plaque marking the spot where a nearly demolished Franklin came ashore. I continue past the giant, colorful mural of Franklin splashed across a wall, past the ice cream parlor featuring a Franklin flavor (lemon with cassis and peach) before arriving at Bar Franklin. I can't blame the good people of Auray for going full Franklin. Places don't get to choose their historical cred. They work with what they have.

Dark wood pillars and pale stone blocks support Bar Franklin, barely. It is old and slanting and reminds me of something from *Willy Wonka & the Chocolate Factory*. On this summer day, Bar Franklin is doing a brisk business. The waiter is busy. Ben busy. I get his attention and order a beer and savory crepe. From my vantage on the terrace, I can survey all of Auray: the wooden sailboats bobbing in the small harbor, the black-roofed buildings contrasting nicely with the day's cottony clouds, the sidewalk booksellers who arrange their offerings in neat, loving rows. The Brittany town doesn't seem wretched at all. It has a pleasant, vaguely mystical feel, perhaps owing to its Celtic influence.

Maybe Ben's grim assessment of Auray stemmed from his exhaustion (he could barely stand), or maybe it was here where the immensity of his mission hit him. George Washington's Continental Army was in desperate need of ammunition, supplies, engineers, warships, and even uniforms. All of this cost money, and the young United States had virtually none. It had no credit either. French support wasn't optional. The Americans couldn't win the war without it.

Convincing the French to join the American cause would not be easy. France had fought four colonial wars with Britain in the past century and Louis XVI was reluctant to get entangled in a fifth, especially one whose stated goal was the ouster of a fellow monarch. French officials did not want to provoke their old rival, not yet, so they were unwilling to be seen in public with Franklin. Ben's was not an impossible mission, but it was close.

With each passing year, Ben grew more, not less, bold. He took chances, tilted at a few windmills. Too many people play it safe as they grow older. They no longer tackle the impossible or indulge in the frivolous. Why? If anything, you'd think old age is the perfect time to experiment, take up scuba diving and windmill tilting. What do you have to lose? As I walk along Auray's pleasant waterfront, gazing at the wooden boats and licking a scoop of Franklin, I vow to age boldly and recklessly. I will take chances, even dangerous ones. And I will stand, not sit, on buses—no matter what some smug punk thinks.

Ben was eager to get to Paris and dive into his mission. There was a hitch, though. His luggage was still aboard the *Reprisal*, floundering offshore. I'm surprised how often the problem of lost luggage appears in Franklin's writing. I always thought of it as a problem born of the twentieth century, the enfant terrible of the jet age, but apparently not. Ben spent a lot of time searching for wayward luggage, either his own or that of fellow Americans abroad.

Another problem that's not as new as I thought: disinformation. Even

before Ben arrived in France, the British embassy was busy spreading rumors about him and the American war effort. Most were unfounded. One
of the first letters he wrote from French soil was to an old friend, Jacques
Barbeu-Dubourg, warning him not to believe everything he heard. "I see you
have had some bad news about our business in America; but they are not
true."

Actually, in this case, they were. The war was going poorly for the Americans. The redcoats had pushed George Washington's ragtag army out of
Long Island and into New Jersey, in full retreat. It wasn't looking good. Ben
knew he had to spin the war news if he had any hope of gaining French support.

Ben and his grandsons soon departed Auray for nearby Nantes. It was
another uncomfortable and dangerous journey. The carriage was "miserable," the horses tired, and the road rife with bandits. The entourage kept a
low profile, and for reasons beyond safety. Ben's mission demanded secrecy
so as not to embarrass the French government or, should they reject American overtures, "subject ourselves to the hazard of a disgraceful refusal."

Ben tried not to call attention to himself but soon realized that was about
as likely as a lightning rod not calling attention to lightning. In Nantes, word
leaked that the famous American was in town, and Ben was flooded with
invitations to balls and other social events. "I am made extremely welcome
here," he wrote to the Committee of Secret Correspondence in a massive understatement. "America has many friends." So did Ben. When he arrived in
Paris just before Christmas Eve 1776, a few hundred of those friends greeted
him. Cheering crowds lined Rue de l'Université.

How to explain Benjamin Franklin's enormous, borderline messianic
fame in France? Was it genetic perhaps? "Some think we are of a French extract, which was formerly called Franks," Ben's father once speculated. Or
was it his electrical experiments, which resonated in France, the epicenter of
the Enlightenment, more than anywhere else? Was it his cheeky Poor Richard persona, dubbed *Bon Homme Richard* in France?

Partly by design, partly by happenstance, Franklin fulfilled a French
wish for a certain archetype: the wise backwoodsman philosopher. Ben

embodied Rousseau's theory of the innate goodness of primitive man, the "noble savage," but spiced with Voltaire's urbane wit. An irresistible combination.

Chameleon Ben dressed the part. Gone were the gentleman's suits of London. Instead, he donned a plain brown jacket, white stockings and shirt, and a marten fur cap he had acquired during the Great Canadian Fiasco. And most shocking of all, no wig. Writing to his friend Emma Thompson, he describes his new look: "Figure me in your mind as jolly as formerly, and as strong and hearty, only a few years older, very plainly dress'd, wearing my thin grey straight hair, that peeps out under my only coiffure, a fine fur cap, which comes down my forehead almost to my spectacles. Think how this must appear among the powder'd heads of Paris." People mistook him for a simple Quaker. (He was not.) Franklin didn't lie about his identity. He simply didn't correct people's misimpressions.

Ben stayed at hotels for a few months before finding accommodations befitting his stature and mission, an elegant and tranquil residence that would serve not only as his home for the next eight years but also as the de facto US embassy. Another first.

I am having breakfast at the Aero Café, a name I'm sure Ben would like. He was an early aviation enthusiast. Having witnessed a balloon ascension in Paris, he predicted not only air travel but aerial warfare as well.

I am in Passy. A separate village in Ben's time, today it's a posh enclave in Paris's 16th arrondissement. Passy is the kind of neighborhood where no one walks. They stroll, so I do too.

I stroll past the impromptu book stalls where each volume is displayed with great care and—let's call it what it is—love. Printer Ben no doubt appreciated the French passion for books. I stroll past pricey boutiques and nail salons. I stroll past a scrum of utility workers, leather-apron men, wrestling with a tangle of cables. These are Ben's people, not mine. My idea of manual labor is plugging in my laptop. I stroll past well-coiffed Parisians and their equally well-coiffed dogs. I stroll to the Marché de Passy, a covered market featuring an array of gout-inducing food: sides of beef, cuts of veal, wheels of cheese the size of my head. No wonder Ben had trouble resisting.

I notice a profusion of opticians in Passy. Very Ben, I think, given his invention of bifocals. A sign! Or is it my rational mind tricking me into seeing what I want to see? I note that possibility and continue my stroll. Soon I come upon Maison Balzac, the erstwhile home of the writer Honoré de Balzac that is now a small museum. The two great men didn't know each other. Balzac was born nearly a decade after Franklin died, but he was a thoroughgoing Franklinista. He once remarked that Franklin had invented the lightning rod, the hoax, and the republic.

I stroll down Rue Franklin and then a sloping street, Rue Raynouard. I look to my left, and there's the Eiffel Tower, materializing out of nothingness, or so it seems. Ben never saw the Parisian landmark, which wasn't built for more than a century after his stay in France. He did see the Seine River, of course, a constant and reassuring presence. The world may be going to hell, but there was the trusty Seine, flowing serenely through the heart of Paris and neighboring Passy.

In another block or two, at last I spot it: a small plaque marking the spot where the Hôtel de Valentinois once stood. The sign references the building's sybaritic heritage. The previous owner, the Countess of Valentinois, hosted gallant parties for her "libertine friends because 'in Passy one enjoys one's self.'" Lest there be any doubt, sex parties were once held at the Hôtel de Valentinois, but this was long before Ben chose it as his new residence and the makeshift US embassy.

The mansion was ideally situated—close to Paris but far enough away to give Ben some breathing space, and on the road to Versailles, the seat of government. It overlooked vineyards sloping toward the Seine. It had a wine cellar. (Ben's collection would grow to more than 1,200 bottles.) Even more than his beloved Number Seven Craven Street, Ben adored the Hôtel de Valentinois, a sentiment he relayed to his sister Jane in early 1777.

I live in a fine airy house upon a hill, which has a large garden with fine walks in it, about ½ an hours drive from the city of Paris. I walk a little every day in the garden, have a good appetite and sleep well. I have got into a good neighbourhood, of very agreeable people who appear very fond of me; at least they are pleasingly civil: so that upon the whole I live as comfortably as a man can well do so far from his home and his family.

The Hôtel de Valentinois, like the Craven Street house, was more than a residence. It was a refuge, an oasis, his safe space (though it was not safe from British spies, as I soon learned). Ben installed a lightning rod on the roof and a printing press in the basement.

The new owner of the mansion, Ben's landlord, was a wealthy arms dealer named Jacques Donatien Le Ray de Chaumont. He was sympathetic to the American cause and refused to accept rent from Franklin. As Ben moved in, Chaumont was already supplying American forces with much-needed gunpowder.

Ben loved his little village. He delighted in the fresh spring water, filtered through sand, and far healthier than anything in London. Passy checked off many of Ben's Thirteen Virtues, and a few of his vices too. He marveled at the clean (virtue number ten) streets fit for walking, and the tranquil gardens (virtue number eleven) and the way they struck a balance, an order, between business and pleasure (virtue number three). If the French fell short when it came to temperance (virtue number one) and chastity (virtue number twelve), Ben cut them some slack, just like he did for himself.

Franklin maintained a low profile, but he was no recluse. He was a regular at the salons, especially those hosted by one Madame Helvetius, widow of a renowned philosopher and an intellectual force in her own right. Her cat-filled house in Auteuil, a short carriage ride from Passy, was called the Nine Sisters, after the Nine Muses, and the intellectuals and *philosophes* who gathered there were known as l'Academie d'Auteuil. Ben often played chess there late into the night, as long as the candles held out. He occasionally cheated, some said, and would throw his opponent off balance by drumming his fingers on the table.

Another favorite companion of Franklin was Madame Brillon. She was a talented harpsichordist and composer who played and sang for Ben, accompanied by her two daughters. "My opera," Ben called it. It was Madame Brillon who dubbed Ben *mon cher papa*, a term of endearment adopted by most of his close friends in Paris, including the men. By this point, everyone knew he was the US representative, which only enlarged his fame.

It's time to address the elephant in the salon: Ben Franklin and the ladies of France. Was he, as fellow American Arthur Lee alleged, "a wicked old man" who had converted the American mission into "a corrupt hotbed of vice"? No. First, Ben was not unfaithful to his wife, Deborah. She had died two years before he landed in Auray. Also, Franklin was in his seventies and bedeviled by kidney stones, gout, and other ailments. Some days, he could barely get out of his own bed, let alone hop into others. "There is no shred of evidence" Ben actually had affairs with French women, conclude two historians who wrote the definitive account of Franklin's private life.

For fleshly and fluid Ben, "that hard-to-be-govern'd passion of youth" had subsided. Good riddance, he said, before indulging his latest diversion: flirtation for its own sake. In France, he elevated it to an art form. He flirted in the salons and he flirted in the music chambers. He flirted on the rivers and he flirted in the gardens. He flirted in the daytime and he flirted at night. Kissing cheeks or lips was not fashionable at the time. Not to worry, Ben wrote to a friend. "The French ladies have however 1000 other ways of rendering themselves agreeable; by their various attentions and civilities, & their sensible conversation." The brain remained Ben's favorite organ.

At least one Franklin scholar, Lorraine Pangle, believes Ben's flirtations were an extension of the skill set that enabled him to charm the French government and help win the Revolutionary War. "He had an instinctive knowledge of how to reach people, disarm them, draw them out, and win them over, and it is perhaps inevitable that a man with such talents would be incorrigibly flirtatious."

Ben was popular with everyone, not just women. He was constantly buttonholed by "projectors, speculators, and adventurers of all descriptions," including writers, philosophers, runaway teens, would-be immigrants to America, country priests, and, one day, an ex-convict with a quixotic "plan for perpetual peace." Pierre-André Gargaz arrived at Franklin's doorstep dirty and disheveled, having walked from a village in the south of France. Most diplomats, most people, would have sent Gargaz packing, but not Ben. He welcomed him and read his possibly visionary, possibly crackpot plan for world peace. He found it contained "some very sensible remarks"—Gargaz is the first person to use the term "United Nations"—and printed several copies at his own expense. Ben at his most possibilian.

Negotiating with the French was his most important task, but it was not his only one. He helped Americans track down lost luggage, disposed of booty snagged by privateers, and hosted weekly dinners for fellow Americans in Paris.

Let's pause for a moment and survey Ben's situation. He is nearly seventy-one years old and, once again, beginning life anew. Not only did he face a nearly impossible mission; he had to adapt to a new culture, language, and political scene. And he did. Whether it was a matter of disposition or world-view or some ineffable chemistry, Ben and his new home proved remarkably compatible. The French loved Ben, and he loved the French. France, he said, is "a most amiable nation" and without a "national vice." That wasn't exactly true. France did have a national vice—several—but they meshed perfectly with Ben's: his love of laughter and music and wine and, yes, women. Perhaps never before have a person and a place so wholly complemented each other as Ben Franklin and the nation of France.

At first, the French government was reluctant to bet big on the Americans. They doled out just enough to stay in the game: one million livres ($200,000) funneled through a dummy company set up by the playwright Pierre Beaumarchais, author of *The Barber of Seville* and *The Marriage of Figaro*. And so it went for more than a year. The French dispensed a trickle of aid, enough to placate the Americans but not so much as to infuriate the British.

All that changed on the morning of December 4, 1777. Word reached France of a major American victory in Saratoga. Some eight thousand British troops led by General John Burgoyne surrendered to George Washington's Continental Army. The Americans now looked like a much better bet. Franklin entered talks with the French foreign minister, Comte de Vergennes, about

a possible alliance. Firmly pro-American, Vergennes was a careful and professional diplomat and, thankfully for Ben, a good judge of character.

Franklin succeeded in France, spectacularly so. In a few short years, he
negotiated two treaties, managed to extract more than 48 million livres
($1.4 billion today) in loans and gifts, not to mention direct military aid in
the form of French warships and soldiers. America would not have won the war
without the Old Conjurer's diplomatic magic. How did a seventy-something
overweight man who hated begging for money and detested conflict of any
kind immerse himself in a doozy of one—a conflict within a conflict, a Matry-
oshka doll of enmity—and emerge not only victorious but with his trademark
sanity intact? If anything, Franklin grew more sane during his time in France.
Serene is the word many French friends used to describe him.

I could use some of that Franklinian serenity. Early one morning in Passy,
I wake to find my right leg red and swollen. Worried, I consult Dr. Google,
who is even less of a real doctor than Ben or me. The not-so-good Dr. Google
informs me it might be deep vein thrombosis, which might lead to a blood
clot, which might be fatal. Or it could be a touch of skin irritation.

I'm not taking any chances. I call my real doctor back home, the time difference be damned. He sounds annoyed for some reason but calms me and
suggests I drop by a local pharmacy for an antibacterial cream.

It turns out it was not deep vein thrombosis. It was not even a skin in-
fection. It was—what is the proper medical terminology?—nothing. Ben
didn't suffer from such chronic hypochondria and he had a lot more to be
hypochondriacal about. What did he know that I don't?

Being a non-French speaker in France is a lot like being old. The world is familiar yet not, as if viewed through a funhouse mirror. You pick up dribs and
drabs, linguistic scraps, but little more. You understand just enough to confuse you. You occupy a netherworld, simultaneously present and absent. Even
the most innocuous encounters make you sweat. Most people ignore you. A
few are nice, but you suspect they're motivated by pity, not kindness. You live
in constant fear that something will be asked of you that you cannot do, like
convey the correct time or give directions. When you speak, people strain

to understand. A few look physically pained by the sounds you emit. Others offer to help, to speak your language, but you refuse such entreaties, clinging to your last scraps of pride the way Ben clung to that heavy book in his library.

Ben learned French the way he did everything else: socially, with a playful attitude and a willingness to make mistakes. His spoken French wasn't fluent, but it was more than adequate. This gift irked John Adams (also in France at the time) who dutifully spent hours—days!—hunched over grammar textbooks and grim tomes such as Bossuet's *Funeral Orations*, all the while grumbling about Franklin's ungrammatical French and the undeserved praise it received.

In large gatherings, Ben had trouble following the conversation, so he remained silent (virtue number two). People mistook his reticence for wisdom. Women, in particular, talked to him for hours on end "without noticing that he understood little because of his limited command of our language," observed his friend Abbé Lefebvre de la Roche.

I reach the sad conclusion that at my age (older but *not* old), I will never learn to speak French, not even poorly. I will never climb Mount Everest or star in a Broadway play or even an off-off-Broadway one. I will never spelunk. A stanza from a poem by Donald Justice comes to mind: *Men at forty/ Learn to close softly/The doors to rooms they will not be/Coming back to.* I am well past forty, and the doors are slamming shut so rapidly I am beginning to feel trapped.

Doors closed for Ben too. The swimming door (though it never shut completely), the sex door, and eventually even the walking door. Yet he never succumbed to despair and continued to derive joy from the doors that remained open, or at least ajar. Even closed doors have their advantages. They enable you to focus on the ones that remain open, the ones that truly matter, like the "doors of wisdom," which, Ben noted, never close.

Ben remained active but did not cling to youth. He did not mimic the young or envy them. He fully accepted his age, celebrated it even. He owed his vigor, I think, to the fact that his life wasn't only busy; it was meaningful. In the American Revolution, Ben found the purpose—the home—he had been looking for. And at age seventy! Maybe, just maybe, I still have time.

I reach into my rucksack and retrieve a book. It contains a collection of portraits of Ben. My favorite was rendered by a French artist named Anne-Rosalie Bocquet Filleul, a neighbor of Franklin in Passy and a friend. Her painting is different from the stiff and lifeless portraits popular at the time. Franklin is dressed casually in a white open-neck shirt and a green, fur-lined gown. He is wigless, his thinning light brown hair spilling nearly to his shoulders. His left arm rests on his lap while his right hovers above a map and a pair of spectacles (bifocals perhaps) sitting on a table. His palm is open and gesturing generously, as if conceding a point mid-conversation. His lips are turned slightly upward in just a hint of a smile. It is his eyes that I find most arresting. They are at once self-assured and vulnerable. He looks like a man you want to know.

Ben was seventy-two when he sat for the portrait, yet he does not look old. He doesn't look young either. He exudes a quiet vitality, a rawness and—I'll just say it—lustfulness I've never associated with a septuagenarian. The painting fills me with admiration, and hope.

I return to the Great French Enigma. How did Ben pull off the ultimate diplomatic feat? I scour historical records: treaties, financial documents, portraits, contemporary accounts and letters, lots of letters. I trace Ben's footsteps, from the streets of Passy to the tables of Café Procope (Paris's oldest café and one of Ben's favorites) and the banks of the Seine, and eventually unearth the answer—or *answers*.

Franklin's mission to France was his masterpiece, his White Album. Success demanded not one tool but the entire kit. It was all Bens on deck. Angry Ben was there, as were Social Ben and Busy Ben and Funny Ben, and the others. A few new Bens showed up too.

Franklin needed a method for everything. It was how he converted his sizable but scattered energy into productive, useful ends. He had his Thirteen Virtues for leading a good life, and what he called Articles of Belief for leading a spiritual one. He also had a method for diplomacy, for winning people over. He never named it explicitly, but I do. I don't think Ben would object. He was always open to new ideas, new formulations.

HOW TO CHARM THE FRENCH AND WIN THE
REVOLUTIONARY WAR IN SEVEN NOT-SO-EASY STEPS

1. Work with What You Have

Ben had little with which to work. There was no US embassy or staff awaiting his arrival. He had to invent the American Foreign Service from scratch, and in secrecy. Never before or since has a US diplomat been so alone, and so needed. Today, the State Department keeps its ambassadors, especially those serving in sensitive posts, on a short leash. Not in Franklin's day. It took three months to pose a question to Congress and receive a reply. Franklin was very much on his own. This proved to be more blessing than curse. It gave him the time and space to do what he did best: improvise.

Since he had no staff, he appointed his grandson Temple, William's son, as his private secretary. People dubbed him "Franklinet" because of the physical resemblance and the fact that the two were inseparable. Temple, Ben said, "is my right hand."

Ben improvised in other ways. The United States had no national emblem yet, so Ben and his fellow commissioners sent official documents with Franklin's personal seal, his adopted coat of arms. The embassy had no printing press, so Ben set up one, churning out US passports, legal documents, and invitations to embassy receptions. He also printed his bagatelles and gave them to friends. Ben compensated for his lack of social standing by tapping into several French social networks, like the scientific community and the Freemasons.

He had something else working in his favor, something intangible but potent: fame. To say the French loved Ben Franklin is like saying Americans love big portions. A massive understatement. France was a nation of panting Franklinistas. When Ben attended sessions of the French parliament, applause greeted him. Every French painter and sculptor wanted Ben to sit for them, and he usually obliged. Soon his image was everywhere. As he told his sister Jane, "My face is now almost as well known as that of the moon."

This fame delighted Franklin but irked his fellow American diplomats. John Adams moaned about "a scene of continual dissipation" that permeated Franklin's daily routine, the parade of acolytes who "come to have the honour to see the great Franklin, and to have the pleasure of telling stories about his simplicity, his bald head and scattering strait hairs." Abigail Adams, on a visit to France, was also shocked. She attended a dinner with Franklin and his good friend Madame Helvetius, whom she describes as "once a handsome woman" (ouch!) with "a careless jaunty air."

Then, reports Abigail Adams, something truly scandalous transpired. "When we went into the room to dine she was placed between the Doctor and Mr. Adams. Madame Helvetius carried on the chief of the conversation at dinner, frequently locking her hand into the doctor's and sometimes spreading her arms on the backs of both the gentlemen's chairs, then throwing her arm carelessly on the doctor's neck." The topper: "After dinner, she threw herself upon a settee where she showed more than her feet." *Quelle horreur*!

The Adamses failed to grasp that Ben's social and professional lives were of a piece. He was meeting the French on their own terms. What his prudish colleagues saw as indulgence and depravity, Ben saw as gentle persuasion.

John Adams worried aloud that all this fame had gone to Franklin's bald head and he was too much under the French influence. Thomas Jefferson replied, coolly, that the good doctor had earned the confidence of the French and "it may truly be said, that they were more under his influence, than he under theirs."

Fame is a powerful force. It can be used for good or ill. Franklin used it for good.

2. Be Empathetic

Arthur Lee and the other American commissioners saw the French government as a giant cash dispenser. Franklin did not. He saw the world through their eyes, understood their desires and fears. He didn't ask for money when it suited the Americans. He timed his requests to the workings of the French budgetary system. Franklin, observed one historian, "had the common sense not to annoy the French."

Ben's empathy made him a perceptive diplomat and an extremely useful one. Vergennes, the French foreign minister, preferred dealing with Franklin in confidence and one-on-one. He liked Franklin and considered him wise and collaborative, even if a bit old and odd. He found John Jay vain and ill-humored. As for John Adams, he refused to have anything to do with him. (In 1779, Congress appointed Franklin sole plenipotentiary, de facto ambassador.)

Where did Ben's empathy come from? His upbringing explains a lot. Unlike many of the founders, Ben was not born into privilege. He was a skilled laborer, a leather-apron man. His profession, printing, deepened his empathy. Printers had to handle writings that expressed a variety of viewpoints. And recall that typeface was arranged upside down and backward. Printers like Ben were accustomed to seeing the world from different perspectives.

3. Ignore Your Enemies—Or, Better Yet, Ridicule Them

Franklin didn't seek enemies, but they found him. George III called him an "insidious man." Confronted with such barbs, Ben's usual strategy was to ignore them. He wasn't going to fan the flames of enmity by responding to hatred with hatred. Instead, he responded with humor.

Lord Stormont, the British ambassador to France, was a chronic pain in Ben's ample backside. He schemed to undermine Franklin's reputation and cast doubts on the prowess of the American army. At one point, rumors circulated that six battalions of the Continental Army had surrendered. Asked if these reports were true, Ben replied, "No, it is only a Stormont." The gibe stuck, and soon a new word reverberated across French high society: *stormonter*, "to tell a falsehood."

Ben made it a point not to alienate those with whom he disagreed. He always kept doors open and bridges unburned. This approach served him well, but sometimes he was too trusting. Consider the case of Edward Bancroft, an amiable friend, fellow member of the Royal Society, and unofficial secretary at the unofficial American embassy. He was also a British spy. For more than eight years, Bancroft slipped into Paris's Tuileries gardens every Tuesday at 9:30 p.m. and placed a sealed bottle inside a hollow tree, to be retrieved later by a British agent. Classic dead drop. Bancroft betrayed his fellow Americans for the usual reason: money—four hundred pounds a year, to be precise. No one, not even the leery John Adams, suspected him. Historians would not uncover Bancroft's double dealings until the latter part of the nineteenth century.

4. Appeal to People's Bigness

Franklin appealed to the French in a number of ways. One was their self-interest. He reminded French officials and business owners of the vast market that awaited them in an independent United States, and he dangled the prospect of a trade treaty that would open American ports to French ships. (He didn't need to remind the French that an American victory would weaken their longtime rival, Britain; it was understood.)

But he knew self-interest alone was rarely enough to sway people. He made other, more high-minded appeals, best articulated in a letter to his friend Samuel Cooper. "'Tis a common observation here, that our cause is *the cause of all mankind*; and that we are fighting for their liberty in defending our own." Aiding the Americans was more than a mercenary move. It was a noble one. It was a case of "moral beauty," that elevated, ineffable feeling we experience when witnessing an act of pure selflessness. It is, as Ben knew, a powerful motivation. It's what he had in mind when, years earlier, he extolled "the beauty and usefulness of virtue." It's a rare combination today, beauty and utility, but one that defined Franklin's philosophy, and his life.

There was another dynamic at work, a quirk of human nature today known as the Ben Franklin effect. He stumbled across it in 1736 when serving as clerk to the Pennsylvania Assembly. A powerful new member of the assembly, "a gentleman of fortune, and education," didn't care for Franklin and threatened to make life miserable for him. What to do? Ben could have kowtowed to this member and attempted to win him over with flattery. He took a different approach.

Having heard that the man owned a rare and valuable book, Ben asked if he could borrow it for a few days. The man agreed, and Ben returned it dutifully with a nice note. "When we next met in the House he spoke to me, (which he had never done before) and with great civility," Ben recalled. The two became fast friends. Ben's takeaway: "He that has once done you a kindness will be more ready to do you another, than he whom you yourself have obliged."

It sounds counterintuitive, even a little loopy, I know. Wouldn't we favor those who do us favors? Not necessarily. As Franklin discovered and recent studies confirm, the opposite is true. We don't like people who are nice to us. We like people to whom we are nice. Why? One explanation is cognitive dissonance. It's difficult to hold two contradictory thoughts at the same time. It makes us uncomfortable. We resolve this tension by changing our mind. *I don't like Joe, but I am doing a favor for Joe, so maybe I do like him after all.* There is a simpler explanation: We like being useful and, by extension, we like those who give us the opportunity to do so.

5. Deploy Energy Strategically

Despite what his detractors said, Ben was no slacker. He clocked twelve-hour days and hardly took a vacation. He worked hard, but he also worked smart. In his seventies, Ben knew he had to conserve energy. A good swimmer is efficient, never squandering momentum. Franklin sensed when to propel and when to glide, when to apply (subtle) pressure and when to ease up.

I can't help but think of Franklin's main electrical discovery: the theory of conservation of charge. Electrical currents, like a flowing river, seek balance, neither a surplus of positive or negative charges. Likewise, Ben saw Britain and France as two counterweights, positive and negative charges seeking equilibrium, whether they knew it or not. Ben was not beyond exploiting this balancing act and playing one side off the other. Before sailing

for France, he drafted a dummy peace proposal between the American colonies and Britain. He knew this would worry the French and could be used to
pressure them into supporting the Americans. He kept it in his pocket, just
in case, but never used it.

6. Be Grateful

Franklin's fellow American commissioners saw no need to thank the French
for their support. They viewed gratitude as a sign of weakness. If anything,
the French should thank the Americans for giving them a chance to invest
early in this promising start-up called the United States of America. Franklin
didn't see it that way. He thanked the French every chance he had. "Such an
expression of gratitude is not only our duty but our interest," he said. Virtue
and utility fused once again.

Franklin's philosophy of gratitude paid off, both for the young United
States, which continued to receive support from France even after the war,
and for Ben. To this day, Franklin is revered in France. As for the others, well,
let's just say there is no Rue Adams or Rue Lee.

7. Maintain Perspective

While in France, Ben wrote a bagatelle titled "The Ephemera." It's told
from the perspective of a mayfly, or *ephémère*, which has a life span of only a
single day. "I have seen generations born, flourish, and expire," the fly says.
"My present friends are the children and grandchildren of the friends of my
youth, who are now, alas, no more! And I must soon follow them; for by
the course of nature, tho' still in health, I cannot expect to live above 7 or 8
minutes longer."

The fly is bereft. What is the point of doing fly things, like collecting
honeydew, if there is no time to enjoy it? The fly's friends try to console him,
reminding him that he will leave a name behind. "But what will fame be to an
ephemere who no longer exists?" the fly says, channeling Ben.

It was, I think, this keen awareness of the transience of life that enabled

Franklin to weather storms that would have broken anyone else. He knew the stakes were both extremely high and not high at all.

Franklin's advanced age was not incidental. I don't think a younger Franklin would have succeeded in France. He was too green, and too arrogant. He cultivated his methods, his habits, over a lifetime, so when it was time to go Full Ben, he knew what to do.

On a cloudy summer day, I wake early. Ben rarely did. He was still industrious (virtue number six) and resolute (virtue number four) but strictly on French time. He knew dinner, not breakfast, was when plans were discussed, ideas aired, deals struck. There was no point in waking early. If anything, it made you suspect in French eyes.

I cross the Seine at Pont de Grenelle, the sky brightening while a light breeze stirs the river below. A not-unpleasant briny odor fills my nostrils while a boat called *Yacht de Paris* glides by. Ben swam in the Seine—not as often or as fast as he once did, but he swam, and that was something. He would swim alone or sometimes with his grandson Benny, whom he taught how to swim. Passing the torch.

I try to picture Franklin here, wrinkled and flabby, plunging into the river, naked. Did Naked Ben attract curious looks or sneers of disapproval? I doubt it. What the British found shocking, the French found perfectly normal and hardly worthy of comment. They glossed over Franklin the (alleged) fornicator and focused on Franklin the scientist, Franklin the philosopher, and Franklin the man—in all his naked glory.

After a few wrong turns, I find the station and board the train for Versailles. It takes thirty-five minutes. Ben made the same journey, by carriage, many times. It took several hours, and the rough, bumpy ride aggravated his kidney stones.

The train arrives at the Versailles station and deposits me into a cornucopia of Americana: KFC, McDonalds, and Starbucks. What would Ben make of this unholy trinity? He'd smile, I'm sure, pleased that his prediction proved correct. American culture was indeed ascendant. "The arts delight to travel westward," he said. Fast food, apparently, travels in the opposite direction.

I walk along a gravel, tree-lined path. Some 250 years ago, a trio of Americans, led by Ben, came to Versailles, hat in hand, looking for money and guns. Today Americans come by the thousands looking for trinkets and Instagram pics and, perhaps most of all, a whiff of the royal scent that, inexplicably, we children of rebels can't seem to get enough of.

I skirt the crowds, heading to one room. Markedly smaller than the others and furnished more simply, the Council Room is among the palace's least popular draws. I see why. The ceiling is bare, the few mirrors small and dirty. The floors are simple parquet, like something you'd see in a basement rec room, not a French palace. On one side of the room is a fireplace and, above it, two vases depicting Mars, the Roman god of war, and Minerva, the goddess of wisdom. In the center of the room is a small and simple wooden desk. King Louis XVI conducted business here.

I can't picture Ben in Versailles's over-the-top spaces, but I can picture him here, in this simple and serious room where sleeves were rolled up and important decisions made. It was here where, on March 20, 1778, the first day of spring, Benjamin Franklin had an audience with King Louis XVI. They were commemorating the two treaties France and the infant United States had signed six weeks earlier. No more half measures or clandestine operations or dummy companies. France was now all in with *les insurgens*, as they called the Americans. After more than a year of furtive courtship, France and the United States had taken their relationship public.

Ben was lucky he got this far. The king was not a fan. He didn't trust Ben and bristled at the simple American's outsized popularity. Franklin's visage was ubiquitous in France, so the king added it to one more location: the bottom of chamber pots, which he gave to friends. Thankfully, cooler voices were whispering in the king's ear—namely, his foreign minister, Vergennes, who persuaded Louis to back the Americans.

Marie Antoinette was a bit less Ben-skeptical than her husband. The queen "was amazed to find so much genius behind such genuine simplicity amid the opulent ministers of the great European powers," recalled Franklin's friend Abbé Lefebvre de la Roche. One day, the queen asked a courtier what Franklin's profession was before becoming ambassador.

"Foreman of a print shop," he said.

"Is that so?" replied the queen. "In France he would have become no more than a bookseller."

She was charmed, though, and deigned to allow Ben watch her at the gaming table. We don't know if cake was served, but I bet it was, and eaten too. And so went the French aristocracy's relationship with Ben. They were at once repulsed by and attracted to his simple dress and folksy wisdom.

Legend has it that when Franklin met the king, he wore a russet velvet coat, the same one he had worn during his ritual humiliation in the London Cockpit. Payback. Most startling, though, was what he was not wearing. No wig. No ceremonial sword. This was a breach of court etiquette, but one the courtiers of Versailles delighted in.

I spot an American couple nearby—their Skechers give them away—and decide to play unsolicited tour guide. This is the room where Franklin met the king, I inform them before reaching higher. "This," I say, pausing for dramatic effect, "is where the American Revolution succeeded." An exaggeration? Perhaps, but not by much. Had Franklin not sealed the alliance with France, the Continental Army would not have had the resources it needed to defeat the British. It is that simple.

I'm exiting the palace when it occurs to me that the last time I was here was almost forty years ago. I was on a break from college, touring Europe with a wildly incompatible girlfriend. Am I the same person I was then? In a physical sense, no. My younger self had a lot more hair and many fewer pounds. On a cellular level, too, I am not the same person. Most (not all) cells in the human body regenerate on average every seven to ten years so, technically, I am at least six times removed from my younger self. In other ways, too, I am different. My younger self had his whole life ahead of him, open doors as far as the eye can see. All I had to do was choose which ones to enter. Surely, though, some vestige of my twenty-year-old self remains, a psychological through line that links younger and older me.

Older Franklin was, of course, also different from young Ben. His muscular swimmer's body had morphed into rolls of fat encased in flaky, reddish skin. His hairline had traveled north, and not to Canada. He moved more slowly, careful not to trigger an attack of "the stone" or any of his other ailments. He was a softer person in other ways too. Less saucy and provoking, more conciliatory and agreeable. So, yes, he was a different Ben, but he was also the same. He never lost his belief in equality (even if he didn't always live up to it) or in the power of compromise or the primacy of personal experience or the quiet dignity of leading a useful life.

On my last full day in France, I return to Rue Franklin. At one end of the street is a bronze statue of Ben. He is seated, upright and alert, as if he might spring into action at any moment. His left hand is clutching an armrest, his right a sheath of papers. His expression is bright and attentive, his lips revealing a trace of a smile, as if he is reprising one of the bawdy jokes he liked to tell. At the base of the statue, a tablet reads: "The man whose genius raised America's standards, whose wisdom spilled over to Europe, the man two worlds claim as their own."

I want to touch Ben but can't. The statue is set back some twenty yards from the sidewalk, behind a chain-link fence. This seems wrong. Ben, a man of the people, should be more accessible. I won't stand for this, I declare silently, with unaccustomed conviction. I try to open the fence, but it is padlocked shut. I try shaking it open. Nothing.

I consider jumping the fence. That is what Samuel Adams would do. He'd grab hold of the metal fence with both hands and hoist himself over, the rules be damned, then demolish the fence for good measure. John Adams would curse the fence and the system that installed it—a rigged system that was *at this very moment* scheming to undermine him. Thomas Jefferson would write eloquently about the unalienable right of all men (except enslaved ones) to live fence-free and happily, but leave the fighting to others.

What would Ben do? I look at him for an inordinately long time, as if a statue could supply the answer. Then it dawns on me. Franklin would find the local fence authority and, in charmingly broken French, make the case that it was not only in Ben's interest to open the fence but in the man's interest too. Ben would do this patiently but persistently, for as long as it took, until the fence man happily opened it for him, as if it were the American who was doing him a favor and not the other way around. Then Ben would join a few friends for Madeira and chess and amuse all by recounting tales of his fence diplomacy.

I take the Metro to St. Germain, then I walk—no, I am *walked*, swept along by the crowds on the sunny summer day. I catch snippets of English. "The sun feels good," says an older (but not old) woman. "I mean, there's no air-conditioning in Paris," says another, with a New York accent. Two older (not old) men with Texan accents are, I swear, talking about oil prices. I turn onto Rue Bonaparte and walk a few more minutes before realizing I've overshot my destination and make a disruptive U-turn. *Pardon, pardon.*

I see why I missed 59 Rue Bonaparte. It is an ordinary Parisian building, four stories high with Juliet balconies and fronted with peeling white paint. Immediately adjacent is a window display, though "display" is generous. It's just a pile of random books: *The American Heritage Dictionary, Ecole et Inté-gration des Immigrés*, and, for some reason, a smattering of titles in Russian and Chinese. One sign informs me that this is currently a printing house. Of course, I think. Print followed Ben everywhere. Another sign reveals the building's historic significance. "In this building, formerly the Hotel of York, the 3rd of September 1783, David Hartley, in the name of the King of England, Benjamin Franklin, John Jay, John Adams, in the name of the United States of America, signed the definitive peace treaty recognizing the independence of the United States."

The war was over. Franklin, along with Jay and Adams, spearheaded the peace negotiations. They culminated in the summer of 1783, an unusual time when Europe hardly saw the sun. A blue haze and dry "blood-colored" fog blanketed the continent for several months. People had trouble breath-ing. Ships, unable to navigate, remained at port. Ben speculated the strange weather was caused by either a meteorite or a volcano. His second suppo-sition was correct. In June of that year, an Icelandic volcano had erupted, spewing billions of tons of sulfur dioxide into the atmosphere.

The negotiations were long and contentious, stretching to nearly two years. But Ben stayed cool under pressure. He was in no hurry. He would wait until the British came around and signed a peace treaty on America's terms. He was such a cool customer that in the midst of the negotiations, he somehow found time to send a friend a twenty-page letter on the effects of lightning.

Ben's patience paid off. In late July 1783, the new British prime minister, Lord Shelburne, eager to strike a deal and realizing the Americans would accept nothing short of full independence, relented on this sticking point. Franklin and the other negotiators secured a treaty that was incredibly favorable to the Americans, including a western border that stretched all the way to the Mississippi River. Ben suggested the British also cede Canada to the Americans. They did not, but I admire Ben for trying.

Franklin did make one blunder. The Continental Congress had explicitly instructed him to consult with France about the negotiations. He did not. Once the peace treaty was signed, Franklin made the bumpy journey to Versailles to meet Vergennes and grovel. Ben was an excellent groveler. He was sorry, very sorry, he told the foreign minister, and hoped an otherwise perfect treaty would "not be ruined by a single indiscretion of ours." It was not. Vergennes forgave Franklin and even agreed to a new loan for the now fully independent United States.

Ben was ready to go home. He had been ready for some time and, despite his rule to never quit public positions, had submitted his resignation. Congress refused to accept it and insisted he stay in France. This is the downside of being extraordinarily useful. You get little rest. "It seems my fate, constantly to wish for repose, and never to obtain it," Ben sighed.

His health was deteriorating. "I feel the infirmities of age coming on so fast, and the building to need so many repairs, that in a little time the owner will find it cheaper to pull it down and build a new one."

In 1785, Congress finally relieved Franklin of his duties, dispatching Thomas Jefferson to succeed him. "Having finish'd my day's task, I am going home *to go to bed*," he told David Hartley, his British counterpart at the peace negotiations. But there was no guarantee he would survive the long journey to Philadelphia. Not only was there the perilous ocean crossing, but first he had to get from Passy to the port town of Le Havre, 146 miles away. His kidney stone had migrated south to his bladder and was now more painful than ever. Walking even short distances resulted in excruciating pain. Riding a carriage over rough cobblestone was out of the question.

Stay, his French friends pleaded. Spend the rest of your days here, attended by skilled physicians and in the company of those who love you. It was tempting, and Ben considered the idea. He had a fierce case of place attachment. I am the same way. Wherever I go, I ask myself, "Could I live here? Could I be happy here?" More often than not, the answers are yes. Yet I do not move there, wherever "there" is. I go home. And in the end, that is exactly what Benjamin Franklin decided to do.

Thomas Jefferson was relieved. He was worried Franklin might die during surgery in Paris, and he'd have a lot of explaining to do. Ben's French friends were saddened, as was he. He implored them not to add to his sorrow. "Help me sustain the spirit I need to leave. My task is unfinished."

Ben explained his difficult decision in a letter to his friend, the sea captain Nathaniel Falconer. "The French are an amiable people to live with: They love me, and I love them. Yet I do not feel my self at home, and I wish to die in my own country." This is the true definition of home—not where you want to live but where you want to die.

His decision was made—he was going home—but a sizable problem remained: how to get to Le Havre. Typically, taking a barge up the Seine was a viable option, but the summer of 1785 was not typical. It was hot and dry. The water levels were low and the river unnavigable. Ben considered floating in a balloon from Passy to Le Havre. It's not as far-fetched as it sounds. Just six months earlier, two intrepid aviators (including fellow American John Jeffries) had completed the first crossing of the English Channel by balloon. This option was possible but risky.

Queen Marie Antoinette came to the rescue. She lent Ben her royal litter and two of her best, most sure-footed mules. The litter, suspended on long poles and attached to the mules, was curtained, with a couch where Ben could sit or recline.

It was time to say goodbye. Ben, like me, dreaded them. My wife claims I once said farewell in India by hurling her backpack at her, then walking away. I don't recall this episode, but it sounds plausible. I come from a long line of crummy goodbye-ers. My father was the worst. Dropping him off at his Florida home, he would regularly exit the car *before* it came to a complete stop. I wish I were making that up, but I am not. Ben wasn't much better at goodbyes. The outpouring of raw emotion overwhelmed him.

In early June 1785, workers began packing Ben's belongings: a total of seventy-seven crates that included books, a dismantled printing press, scientific instruments, and jugs of mineral water from the Passy springs. Finally, on July 12, it was time to leave. A large crowd of friends and well-wishers gathered to see him off, a moment chronicled by Franklin's grandson, Benny. "My grandfather mounted his litter among a great number of people at Passy. A solemn silence reigned around him, interrupted only by sobs." Thomas Jefferson, also on hand, said it looked as if Passy had lost its patriarch.

Franklin tolerated the overland journey well. Marie Antoinette's royal litter proved not only elegant but useful too, swaying gently with each step the mules took. Within a week, the Franklin caravan had reached Le Havre. One last letter from Madame Helvetius awaited him: "I picture you in the litter farther from us at every step, already lost to me and to those who loved you so much and [miss] you so. I fear you are in pain. . . . If you are, come back, *mon cher ami*, come back to us!"

But Ben was not coming back. His voyage across the English Channel and then to Philadelphia was about to begin. Benjamin Franklin, a man with a deeply Gaelic soul, would never step foot on French soil again.

I depart France not by royal litter but by SNCF, the French railway, then by ferry across the English Channel. Two German women staying at my hotel suggest we share a taxi to the train station, and I agree. One speaks excellent English and, starved for conversation in my mother tongue, I find myself blabbing about my Franklin fixation and how I see him as a role model—for people everywhere but especially for my fractured homeland. I tell her how I have retraced his steps from Auray to Passy and, now, was heading to Southampton, England, where he would briefly see his estranged son William one last time.

"But how is he a role model if he broke with his son?" she asks. "What if every American family did that when they disagreed politically?"

I'm not sure how to respond. I mumble something about Ben not being perfect. She nods politely, but I can tell she finds my answer inadequate. So do I.

We say goodbye, bon voyage, but her question stays with me. It follows me aboard the train and then the ferry. I turn it over in my mind again and again. How can Ben be a role model for an entire people when he wasn't even one for his own family?

By the time the ferry docks at Portsmouth harbor, the summer light fading, I am exhausted, but still have no answer. I vow to revisit the question. Soon, after a good night's sleep.

TWENTY-THREE

FLOATING BEN

I can't sleep. I'm not sure why. Maybe it's the lingering spell of seasickness from the Channel crossing. Maybe it is the hotel. I am staying where Ben stayed. The Star Hotel (Star Inn during Ben's time) in Southampton is either charmingly old or decrepitly old, depending on your perspective. Opinions are divided, as a quick scan of Tripadvisor reveals. "Loved the location and the historical style of the hotel," cooed one reviewer. "They say that Benjamin Franklin stayed here in 1785," noted another, dryly. "I hope he got a better night's sleep than we did!"

We like the idea of old places but not the reality. We need our twenty-first-century comforts and doodads. A few inns claim to provide both, boasting of their "storied history and modern conveniences" or some such nonsense, but the truth is old places demand a trade-off, a sacrifice. Heritage comes at a cost, a history tax exacted in the form of sleepless nights and comforts denied.

At the Star Hotel, the history tax is steep. In the lobby, peeling paint and faded paisley wallpaper clash with highlighter-yellow pandemic-era tape warning, "Keep a Safe Distance!" It looks less like a hotel lobby and more like a crime scene. My room is a vast hodgepodge of eras. Ornate chandeliers and oversized antique mirrors compete with harsh fluorescent lights and particleboard dressers.

I toss and turn on the too-soft mattress, clutching the too-hard pillow. I can't pin all the blame for my restlessness on the Star Hotel. Sleep and I have always had a volatile relationship. It's never there when I need it but always there when I don't. I regularly slip into a midday torpor but am wide awake at midnight.

I turn to Ben for help. Late in life, he penned a little ditty called "The Art of Procuring Pleasant Dreams." Dreams are important, Ben tells me. "If while we sleep, we can have pleasing dreams, it is, as the French say, *tant gagné*, so much added to the pleasures of life." I agree, Ben. I could really use some *tant gagné*. But how?

Start with the body, fleshly Ben advises, "for when the body is uneasy, the mind will be disturbed by it; and disagreeable ideas of various kinds, will in sleep be the natural consequences." His detailed advice that follows sounds remarkably modern: get lots of exercise but only before eating, never after. Don't eat heavy meals before bedtime. Ensure there is plenty of air flow in your bedroom. Wear thin and porous pajamas. I have done all this but still can't sleep. What to do, Ben?

"Beat up and turn your pillow, shake the bedclothes well with at least 20 shakes, then throw the bed open and leave it to cool."

Check. Still wide awake. What now?

"Continuing undress'd, walk about your chamber till your skin has had time to discharge its load. . . . When you begin to feel the cool air unpleasant, then return to your bed; you will soon fall asleep, and your sleep will be sweet and pleasant."

I do as you say, Ben, but experience no sleep, sweet or otherwise. What is wrong with me?

I turn to the last sentence of Ben's prescription. All becomes clear. "What is necessary above all things, a good conscience." That must be it. My conscience is defective. To be clear, I have not murdered anyone or stolen classified documents or placed nonrecyclables in the recycle bin. My crimes are imagined. I am a not-good-enough son, an impatient father, and a feck-less friend. Not true, mostly, but that doesn't matter. Imagined crimes generate real guilt. Ben slept well and, by all accounts, procured many pleasant dreams. Can we assume he had a good conscience?

Not necessarily. During his brief stopover in Southampton en route to Philadelphia, Ben met many people—old friends mainly, but also his estranged son William. They had not seen each other for nearly a decade and had corresponded only once, in 1784. William initiated the conversation, and I admire him for it. It took courage. "Dear and Honoured Father," he begins. "Ever since the termination of the unhappy contest between Great Britain and America, I have been anxious to write to you, and to endeavor to revive that affectionate intercourse and connection which till the commencement of the late troubles had been the pride and happiness of my life."

William then explains why he had remained faithful to King George. "I can with confidence appeal not only to you but to my God, that I have uniformly acted from a strong sense of what I conceived my duty to my King, and regard to my country, required," he said, adding plaintively, "If I have been mistaken, I cannot help it."

What William does not mention is the active form his loyalty to the Crown took. Once released from a Connecticut prison in 1778, William traveled to New York where he ran a spy network on behalf of the British and was, by some accounts, the city's leading Loyalist figure. In 1782, with the war all but over, he sailed for London, never to step foot on American soil again.

William explains but doesn't apologize. Given similar circumstances, he would act the same again. But he clearly hoped to reconcile with his father. He heard he'd be stopping in England on his way home to Philadelphia. Could they meet?

It took Ben Franklin several weeks to reply. When he did, he composed what is, I think, the most heartbreaking of the thousands of letters he wrote. It begins optimistically enough. "Dear Son, [I] am glad to find that you desire to revive the affectionate intercourse that formerly existed between us," he writes. "It will be very agreeable to me." Then he turns bitter. "Nothing has ever hurt me so much and affected me with such keen sensations, as to find myself deserted in my old age by my only son; and not only deserted, but to find him taking up arms against me, in a cause wherein my good fame, fortune and life were all at stake."

Ouch. Ben may have been gentle and amiable, a conciliator, but he could also play the guilt card as effectively and ruthlessly as any Jewish mother. Okay, Ben concedes, William felt he had a duty to his king. "We are men, all subject to errors. Our opinions are not in our power; they are form'd and govern'd much by circumstances that are often as inexplicable as they are irresistible." But, he continues, twisting the knife, *"there are natural duties which precede political ones, and cannot be extinguish'd by them."* In other words, William's duty to his father trumped his duty to his king. Having made his point, Ben withdraws the knife and retreats from the emotional combat. "This is a disagreeable subject," he says. "I drop it." Ben did agree to meet William in Southampton. The lines of communication were frayed but still open.

Ben's few days in Southampton were busy. There was the prelaunch frenzy that precedes any journey, then and now, and the matter of Ben's luggage, which had gone missing somewhere in France. He met several old friends, such as the Shipleys of Twyford House, reminiscing about happier times, before the war.

Amid all this activity, Ben managed to find time to visit Martin's Salt Hot Water Baths. Spas like this were gaining in popularity, as the rest of the world caught up with Ben's almost evangelical belief in the therapeutic benefits of water. Floating on his back, the noon sun high in the sky, Ben fell fast asleep for nearly an hour, motionless and at peace. It was, he records in his journal, "a thing I never did before, and should hardly have thought possible. Water is the easiest bed that can be."

Floating intrigues me. It strikes me as swimming but without the effort, or the fear. Yes, I must float, like Ben. I try tracking down Martin's Salt Hot Water Baths, but it has sunk without a trace. I feel silly. What was I expecting? It has been more than two centuries. I regroup and double my efforts. My research—okay, Googling—turns up an establishment called Limitless Float. I like the name and the infinite ease it suggests. I click to learn more.

"Do you know how to unplug from the world and just BE?"

Obviously not. Why else would I be reading this?

"Our body can heal itself but without the proper environment to do so we continue to reach breaking point."

I hear you. I am familiar with said breaking point and, as a place person, have spent a lifetime searching for that "proper environment." Can we get to the floating bit please?

"Floating provides an opportunity for our mind to rest, re-connect, and recover."

Apparently floating also enhances alliteration. Stop, Eric. That is cynical. Not very possibilian. Not very Ben. *Trust your experience*, he would advise. I make an appointment at Limitless Float.

It's a pleasant summer evening, so I decide to walk. Limitless Float is not easy to find. I turn this way and that, blindly following Google Maps into cul-de-sacs and dead ends. Finally, I find it, hiding in an industrial park, sandwiched between an auto parts store and a dance school.

I step inside and am greeted by Daniel. He is young and clear-complexioned and disturbingly serene—in other words, just the sort of person you'd expect to work at a place called Limitless Float. Normally, I hate people with perfect pores and serene countenances, but I like Daniel. He has the skin but not the subtly smug attitude that so often accompanies it.

Daniel guides me into a room, illuminated with blue lighting and with a *Star Trek* feel, as if Captain Kirk were dipping into a spa on Omicron Delta. On one side of the room is a shower stall and on the other a white, egg-shaped pod topped with a large, hinged lid that looks as if it dislodged from the USS *Enterprise*.

Daniel tells me what to expect. Perhaps it's protocol, or perhaps he senses my trepidation, but he spends a lot of time reassuring me about the risk of claustrophobia. The lid on the pod does not lock, will not lock, *cannot lock*, he tells me with the same tone one might use with a terrified toddler. I am relieved, but still wary.

Daniel leaves. He'll be right outside, he reassures me. I shower, then insert the earplugs he recommended, and enter the water the way I always do, tentatively, unsure whether it is friend or foe. The water is warm, set to a constant 97.7 degrees Fahrenheit, Daniel had informed me. So that's why the pod feels so familiar. It reminds me of a place where I spent nine blissful months, at the same temperature, floating effortlessly, oblivious to the harsh world that awaited me.

I hear Ben in my head: "You will be no swimmer till you can place some confidence in the power of the water to support you." That is the problem. I've never acquired that confidence.

Until now. The highly salinized water in the pod is so buoyant I don't need to stroke or flail or do anything at all to stay afloat. Nature does all the work. Floating effortlessly, eyes closed, earplugs inserted, I realize how different this is from my usual state. I fret and strain constantly, as if my worrying somehow propelled the clouds across the sky, made the rain fall, the Earth spin. Now I realize how silly this is. Nature doesn't need my puny exertions. It can support itself just fine—and me too.

What I experience in my pod is a taste of the Enlightenment. Like today's scientists, those of the eighteenth century studied nature in the hope it might reveal its secrets. Those insights enabled us to tame nature and thus improve our lives. Unlike most scientists today, those of the Enlightenment retained a religious, or at least spiritual, motivation. By studying nature, they hoped God would reveal his secrets too—not only about the physical world but the moral universe as well. Witness the phrase that appears early in the Declaration of Independence about the "laws of Nature and of Nature's God." This is the deism that Franklin subscribed to off and on. God reveals his majesty through his works—that is, nature—and has endowed humans with the power of reason so they can uncover these natural laws. Nature, and by extension God, can be known, and what can be known can be trusted.

I decide to take this exercise in trust a step further. I practice dying. That sounds a bit unhinged, I know, but stay with me. Floating in my pod, eyes closed, I inhale deeply and with each exhalation try to expand that trust. I rehearse letting go of . . . everything. I let go of expectations and of striving. I let go of all distinctions, between success and failure, wealth and poverty, health and illness—even the distinction between life and death. Dying, I realize, is nothing more or less than the ultimate test of trust. Do you trust in—call it what you like, God, the universe, nature, science—or do you not? It is that simple, though not at all easy.

I had, until now, kept the lid of my pod ajar, just in case Daniel was less than truthful about it not locking shut. Now, high on trust, I decide to close the lid and see if I can tolerate the darkness. I immediately experience a jolt of fear, a primal panic, and push the lid open just a bit. I must have pushed too hard, though, because it pops open, and I have to stand to close it. That's when I realize I have been floating not in an unfathomable body of water but in a space-age bathtub perhaps two feet deep. I feel foolish. Maybe all fear is like that. To use a different analogy, we spend a lifetime afraid of falling from a great height, only to discover late in life the drop was only a foot or two. We spend decades cowering in fear of an illusion, a nothing.

I am pondering all this, when New Age music begins to play, indicating my float is, alas, not limitless. My sixty minutes are up. I towel dry and emerge to find Daniel, offering me green tea. Of course.

"How was it?" he asks.

"Religious," I say, without hesitation.

Why did I choose that word? I'm not sure. I meant it not in the traditional sense but the Franklinian one. What was the term he used for God? Powerful Goodness. I like that. Powerful Goodness is what heals a wound, lights a dark sky. Powerful Goodness is what keeps you afloat, and without even trying.

Benjamin and William Franklin met several times at the Star Hotel. These must have been tense, heart-wrenching encounters, but the sad truth is we don't know what transpired. In his journal, Ben records only the most perfunctory of observations. "Met my son, who had arrived from London the evening before." William is equally reticent.

We do know the two Franklins conducted business. With his father looking over his shoulder, William transferred the deeds of his property in New Jersey and New York to his own son (Ben's grandson), Temple. William was told never to contact his son again.

Clearly, there was no reconciliation between Ben and William. Why not? They were once as close as any father and son. The war was over. William was willing to put the acrimony behind him and move on. His father was not.

This is not Likable Ben. This is not Admirable Ben. This is Despicable Ben. Why couldn't you forgive your son, Ben? Clearly, he still loved you, and you still loved him. Yes, he chose the wrong side during the war, but you are far from blameless. Recall how you hurt your own father by absconding at age seventeen. What about *your* "natural duties"? Why demand William be a better son than you were? Besides, Ben, you clearly have a great capacity for forgiveness. You forgave William Keith, the governor who sent you on a fool's errand to London. You forgave many of your British friends who sided with the Crown during the war. Why not forgive your own flesh and blood? I can't imagine my daughter doing anything, *anything*, that would cause me to disown her.

The German woman's question resurfaces in my mind: "How is he a role model if he broke with his son?" I still don't have a tidy answer. I can't dismiss Ben's refusal to forgive William as a minor personality flaw, as if an otherwise perfect Ben cracked his knuckles or whistled annoyingly. He disowned his one surviving son. I notice Ben doesn't list his estrangement with William among his errata, those correctable mistakes of life. Some mistakes cannot be corrected, no matter how many future editions are published. I get that. What disappoints me is that when it came to his son, Ben didn't even try.

On July 27, 1785, Ben received word that his ship, the *London Packet*, would soon sail for Philadelphia. Passengers included Ben and his two grandchildren, Benny and Temple; a French sculptor named Jean-Antoine Houdon, en route to Mount Vernon to render a likeness of George Washington; and two angora cats, presents from Madame Helvetius. Not on board was Ben's luggage. It had been located in France but was detained at a customs house in Le Havre. (Franklin wouldn't be reunited with his luggage for several months.)

That evening, Ben and friends enjoyed one last meal together at the Star Inn, then continued the festivities aboard the *London Packet*, anchored just offshore. Franklin's journal entry for the following day consists of a single sentence: "When I waked in the morning found the company gone, and the ship under sail." That's it. No mention of his state of mind or what he left behind: a country he once called home and a son who, despite everything, still loved him.

Benjamin Franklin, his long and useful life nearing its final act, would never see either again.

TWENTY-FOUR

DOUBTING BEN

Friends urged Ben to use the long voyage home to finish his autobiogra-
phy. He instead passed the time measuring the temperature of the North
Atlantic waters and writing treatises on maritime navigation and the problem of smoky chimneys. It was Franklin's favored form of procrastination.
We all have one. I shop for bags online. Ben wrote scientific papers. Different methods, same results: an unfinished manuscript and boatloads of self-
recrimination.

Franklin tolerated the Atlantic crossing remarkably well. He felt better
after the journey than before. On September 13, 1785, the *London Packet*, flying the new American flag, sailed into the Delaware Bay, the "water smooth,
air cool, day fair and fine," Ben noted in his journal. He had returned, at long
last, to his "dear Philadelphia."

While Ben was at sea, rumors had spread that he had been captured and
enslaved by Barbary pirates, so it was with both elation and surprise that
crowds gathered at the Market Street wharf greeted Franklin. Cannons re-
sounded. Bells rang. Tears flowed. Benny Bache, more demonstrative than
his grandfather, chronicled the homecoming: "The joy I received at the ac-
claim of the people, in seeing father, mother, brothers and sisters can be felt,

not described." At Franklin's home, his daughter, Sally, was waiting for him on the doorstep, along with four grandchildren he had never seen. He had been abroad so long he was now "almost a stranger in my own country."

Ben imagined himself free of politics and able to "welcome again my dear philosophical amusements." He was wrong. There would be no philosophical amusements. No retirement or repose. Busy Ben was back, and by popular demand. People needed him. He was soon elected chief executive (governor, in effect) of Pennsylvania, serving three terms. He was also president of the American Philosophical Society and a trustee of the University of Pennsylvania, two institutions he founded. Then, in 1787, he was named a delegate to the Constitutional Convention.

He didn't need to accept any of these assignments. Now nearly eighty years old, he had by any measure lived a long and useful life. He had advanced a new science, helped win a war, and made an international name for himself. Surely he had earned some rest.

Ben had his reasons. He wanted to remain faithful to his own tenet that when it came to public positions, one should *never ask, never refuse, never resign*. Then there were those smoldering embers of ambition he thought were long extinguished. Ben wanted to remain relevant, useful. He needed to be needed. But what about his advanced age and the fact that he likely had only a few years left? His rejoinder, in so many words, was *pffft*. "It has always been my maxim to live on as if I was to live always," he told a French friend. "It is with such feeling only that we can be stimulated to the exertions necessary to effect any useful purpose."

I'm not sure what to make of this. The Old Conjurer had concocted another illusion—in this case, immortality. He didn't really believe he would live forever but pretended anyway. It was, I realize, another helpful deceit.

Growing old is never easy, not now and not during Franklin's time. Some respond to creeping senescence by "acting their age," whatever that means. Others stubbornly refuse to conform to society's notion of how an old person is "supposed" to behave. Benjamin Franklin fell squarely in the latter category.

Andrew Ellicott, one of the surveyors of the Mason-Dixon Line, recalls visiting "this Venerable Nestor of America" at his Philadelphia home. Ben began to heat some water so he could shave. Ellicott offered to help, but the Nestor demurred. He was going to do it himself or not at all. "He was determined not to increase his infirmities by giving way to them," Ellicott recalled. To his astonishment, Franklin worked the razor with the ease and skill of a much younger man. Shaving was one of those small pleasures that made life worth living, Franklin said. "I think happiness does not consist so much in particular pieces of good fortune that perhaps accidentally fall to [a person's] lot, as to be able in his old age to do those little things which, was he unable to perform himself, would be done by others with a sparing hand."

Ben was determined not to outsource his happiness. He would do what he could for as long as he could.

By mid-May 1787, delegates from twelve of the thirteen states (Rhode Island abstained) began to arrive in Philadelphia. Ben was not a typical delegate. He had traveled far more widely than the others. He had less formal education but more honorary degrees. Among the fifty-five delegates who traveled to Philadelphia, thirty-four were lawyers, ten were "planters," and a handful were physicians. Franklin was one of the few tradesmen and the only journalist.

What really set him apart, though, was his age. At eighty-one, Franklin was old enough to be the father of all the others and the grandfather of most. The youngest delegate, New Jersey's Jonathan Dayton, was twenty-six. Ben had a grandson older than that. When Franklin had first argued for colonial unity in 1754 (his so-called Albany Plan), James Madison was three years old.

The founding grandfather's mind was as sharp as ever. One visitor, Manasseh Cutler, was struck by "the brightness of his memory, and the clearness and vivacity of all his mental faculties, notwithstanding his age." Fellow delegate William Pierce said Franklin possessed "an activity of mind equal to a youth of 25 years." One possible explanation is that as a young man, Ben invented magic squares, a kind of early sudoku, to occupy his mind during tiresome Pennsylvania Assembly sessions, a pastime he continued for the rest of his life. Perhaps this helped keep his mind sharp, the way crossword puzzles do today.

Ben's age made him the object of both veneration and ridicule. The younger delegates admired Franklin's past accomplishments but not necessarily his present contribution. "They listened to his suggestions, then with little or no debate quietly voted the other way," one historian said.

The delegates, like many before, underestimated Benjamin Franklin. True, he did not play a major role in shaping the Constitution. That task fell to younger delegates, like James Madison and Alexander Hamilton. Ben was no political theorist, but we should not confuse a lack of theories for a lack of principles. Ben had many. He just didn't broadcast them, embodying, as he did, the seventeenth-century jurist John Selden's dictum: "They that govern most make [the] least noise."

Franklin was the Hippocrates of American politics. First, do no harm. He liked to tell the story of the farmers and the blackbirds. New England farmers were convinced blackbirds were harming their crops, corn in particular. They mercilessly wiped out the blackbird population, only to discover that a species of worm, free of its natural predator, began to devour the farmers' precious grass. "Then finding their loss in grass much greater than their saving in corn they wished again for their blackbirds," Ben said. This was the type of earthy wisdom Franklin brought to the convention.

He brought something else too: a dispassionate curiosity. Comfortable in his own wrinkled skin, he had nothing to prove. During the proceedings, he maintained a quiet detachment. Buddha Ben was back. This didn't mean he was uninterested in the proceedings—quite the contrary—but it did mean he could hover above the dust and noise of the convention hall and see what others could not. A man of a certain age, he said, "looks out upon the noisy passersby without becoming involved in their quarrels." This mindset proved tremendously useful. With less ego invested in the outcome of the convention, Franklin was able to play a mediating role, nudging and cajoling competing factions toward compromise.

•   •   •

The summer of 1787 was unusually hot. Ben considered traveling to the convention site each morning by balloon. He was joking. Sort of. With Ben, you could never be certain. Most days, he walked the block or two to the Pennsylvania State House (now Independence Hall). Occasionally, when his gout resurfaced or "the stone" acted up, he was carried in a sedan chair. It had enclosed, glass-paneled doors and was conveyed on long poles by four muscular bearers. More common in Europe than America, the chair was, like the man riding in it, an object of public curiosity.

The convention schedule was grueling. The delegates met in the sweltering summer heat for more than five hours a day, sometimes longer, and with little time for lunch or even a coffee break. The deliberations were often as heated as the weather. Nearly everyone was screaming to be heard.

Not Ben. Never a good public speaker, he said little during the convention, adhering to his virtue of silence. But when he did speak, it was "with great pertinacity and effect," said James Madison, who sat near him. Ben also injected some levity into the tense deliberations. He told jokes—with a serious point, naturally—about two-headed snakes and Scottish lawyers and French sisters. At one point, he opened a cache of porter ale.

Ben proposed several intriguing ideas. He suggested, for instance, that members of the executive branch, including the president, receive "no salary, stipend, fee, or reward whatsoever for their services." There are, Franklin explained, two passions that rule men: ambition and avarice, "the love of power, and the love of money." Separately, each is a powerful force. Together they have "the most violent effect." In London, he had witnessed firsthand the corrupting influence of money in politics. Surely America could do better.

Indeed, it already had, in the person of George Washington who, during eight years as commander of the Continental Army, never accepted a single dollar in compensation. To those who say Washington was a rare and exceptional man, Franklin parried, "I have a better opinion of our country." The United States will never want for "a sufficient number of wise and good men" willing to serve their country without salary. "The less the profit, the greater the honor."

The delegates listened politely to Franklin's suggestion—more out of respect for the man than the idea. In the end, the motion failed. Franklin had overlooked its obvious flaw. By denying a salary to government officials, only the wealthiest of citizens could afford to serve. That ran counter to his own beliefs. Despite his age and stature, he was the most populist and egalitarian of the delegates. From his earliest writings, he expressed a love of equality, a fondness that deepened with age. Did he always live up to his own egalitarian ideals? Absolutely not, as his long-suffering wife, Deborah, or the people he enslaved would attest. Yet it would be a mistake to dismiss Franklin's ideals out of hand simply because he failed to live up to them. He and the other founders laid down the markers for us to meet—or if not us, then our children, or their children. This is the way it has always been. One generation identifies the target (the higher the better) and the next takes aim.

Ben did score a few bull's-eyes at the convention. He helped pass a motion that allowed for impeachment of the president and defeat one that would have restricted the right to vote and hold public office to property owners. Franklin knew a government's legitimacy never rested on raw power alone. "There must be maintain'd a general opinion of its *wisdom* and *justice*, to make it firm and durable." On that age-old question of whether it is better for a leader to be feared or loved, Franklin fell squarely on the side of love.

By late June, the proceedings had grown even more acrimonious. The delegates were deadlocked. Not to worry, Franklin said. This is merely "melancholy proof of the imperfection of the human understanding." Admit your fallibility, your humanness, he urged. "We indeed seem to feel our own want of political wisdom, since we have been running all about in search of it."

Then Franklin proposed something wholly unexpected. Each session, he said, should open with a prayer, "imploring the assistance of heaven" and "humbly applying to the Father of Lights to illuminate our understandings."

This did not seem Ben-like. Among all the delegates, he was probably the least religious, at least in the conventional sense. Look more closely, though, and you see it was not at all out of character. Franklin may not have been a churchgoer, but he always believed in the social utility of religion. If sermons and scripture motivated people to do good, then he was all for them. And in suggesting the delegates look outside themselves for political wisdom, he revealed another side of himself: Irrational Ben. He was, of course, a great proponent of reason as a means to navigate life, but he also knew it was an imperfect compass. Reason can lead us astray just as surely as emotions can. He "almost wish[ed] that mankind had never been endow'd with a reasoning faculty, since they know so little how to make use of it, and so often mislead themselves by it." Besides, he said, there is an alternative: "a good sensible instinct." Ben possessed that instinct and knew when to deploy it. Reason alone rarely swayed anyone. You must appeal to their passions too.

The delegates again listened respectfully, but few backed Franklin's proposal. There was no money for a chaplain, one delegate said rather lamely. The larger concern, no doubt, was the optics. The people of Philadelphia already suspected the convention was floundering. Seeing a chaplain enter the hall would confirm that suspicion. Franklin's prayer motion flopped (it was not even put up for a vote), but it did pause the rancor for a beat or two, just long enough for the delegates to cool off a bit. Ben's speech had also reminded the men gathered inside that hot and airless convention hall of the importance of their task and the necessity for humility. In other words, it was useful.

Two days later, Franklin tried a different tack. In urging compromise, he deployed the metaphor of a carpenter fashioning a table. "When a broad table is to be made, and the edges of planks do not fit the artisan takes a little from both, and makes a good joint," he said. "In like manner here both sides must part with some of their demands, in order that they may join in some accommodating proposition."

When gauging the value of institutions, Ben deployed the eye of a craftsman. He poked and prodded, held up various parts to the light to see if they fit properly, and made alterations where necessary. His was a "manipulative, hands-on approach to the world."

This is very different from my hands-off approach to, well, more or less everything. Given a choice, I would much rather think about something than do it. I now realize this approach is not very useful, and not very American. The United States was a child of the Enlightenment, and a willful child at that. The young nation didn't only borrow ideas. It advanced them, manifested them. America's founders built what European thinkers such as John Locke had only theorized about. If Europe was the Enlightenment's library, America was its workshop.

Later, Ben proposed a more formal cooling-off period—a three-day recess. Delegates should spend the time, he suggested, mixing with colleagues they disagree with and lending a patient ear. His advice has a contemporary ring. On the one hand, this is reassuring. The states have never been fully united. We've always lived in silos. On the other hand, it raises a troubling question: Why have we evolved so little since Franklin's day? You'd think our patient ears would have grown to elephant size by now, but if anything, they have shrunk. We don't listen to one another. This would deeply worry Ben. Listening, he knew, is the most important part of any conversation.

Franklin also knew you can't win over everyone, no matter how closely you listen. Friction is inevitable, but as a scientist and electrician, he appreciated friction's helpful role: if harnessed wisely, it is a powerful force. "By the collision of different sentiments, sparks of truth are struck out, and political light is obtained."

By early July, some six weeks into the convention, a dispute over representation threatened to torpedo the entire experiment. Larger states wanted population alone to determine representation in the new Congress. Smaller states insisted it be allocated by state, regardless of population.

In July, Franklin was appointed to the Grand Committee of Compromise. (What a marvelous name for a committee! I suggest we resurrect it.) After several days of closed-door deliberations, the committee lived up to its name, emerging with the Great Compromise. One body, the House of Representatives, would be determined by population, while another, the Senate, by state. The plan, whose conception Madison credited to Franklin, saved the day, and the infant nation.

On September 17, the convention was drawing to a close. The summer heat had finally abated. Morning light flooded the south windows of the convention hall. Franklin had prepared a speech but too weak, or perhaps too shy, to deliver it himself, he asked fellow delegate James Wilson to do so.

It is, I think, one of the greatest speeches of all time. It is a political speech, yes, but it is more than that. It is an impassioned plea for something rarely celebrated: doubt. Franklin doubted whether the Constitution drafted over the past few months was the best version possible. He doubted whether it was worth signing. Addressing George Washington, president of the convention, he explained why he was going to sign it anyway.

> I confess that I do not entirely approve this constitution at present, but Sir, I am not sure I shall never approve it: For having lived long, I have experienced many instances of being oblig'd, by better information or fuller consideration, to change opinions even on important subjects, which I once thought right, but found to be otherwise. It is therefore that the older I grow the more apt I am to doubt my own judgment, and to pay more respect to the judgment of others.

Franklin's speech naturally contained a story, a brief one about a French woman embroiled in a dispute with her sister. "I don't know how it happens, sister," she said, "but I meet with no body but myself that's always in the right." Did the other delegates laugh when they heard this? I bet they did. A knowing laugh.

Franklin's message is as vital today as it was in 1787. *More* vital. Doubting the views of others is easy. The real test of character is doubting your own positions. Doubt everything, including your own doubt. Don't grow too attached to your intellectual castles, Franklin warned. They might be built of sand. What he once said of scientific theories holds true for political ones as well. "How many pretty systems do we build, which we soon find ourselves oblig'd to destroy!" The mark of a mature democracy is not only the institutions and policies it constructs but its readiness to modify those institutions and policies to fit new circumstances.

There's much to recommend an open and fluid society like America, but there's one significant downside: a "necessary uneasiness." Franklin could live with that uneasiness for longer than most. He had a capacity that the English poet John Keats later called "negative capability": the capacity to sit with uncertainty and doubt "without any irritable reaching after fact & reason." That was pure Ben. If only it were us as well.

A life guided by doubt need not be a timid, circumspect one. It is possible, as Franklin's life attests, to possess extreme self-confidence *and* continuous self-doubt. That unlikely admixture is what all great people and civilizations possess.

Whenever people assemble, Franklin's speech continued, they assemble their prejudices, passions, failings, and selfishness too. The Constitutional Convention was no exception. "From such an assembly can a perfect production be expected? It therefore astonishes me, Sir, to find this system approaching so near to perfection as it does." It will astonish America's enemies too, Franklin added, salivating as they were at the prospect of the young states "cutting one another's throats."

Franklin then urged each of the delegates, self-assured men not prone to misgivings, to "doubt a little of his own infallibility" and "put his name to this *instrument*." Not a document. An instrument. The word choice was no accident (it never was with Ben). A document is a product. An instrument is a tool—not an end, but a means. Franklin saw the Constitution as an instrument, like a scalpel or fountain pen, an inert object in need of a skilled practitioner.

Ben's European friends were eager to hear about this new nation and its new constitution. Would it stick, or would America backslide into monarchy? That was always a possibility, Franklin knew. "There is a natural inclination in mankind to kingly government," he said. Later, in a 1789 letter to Jean-Baptiste Le Roy, his former neighbor in France, Ben deployed what is perhaps his most memorable observation, though the context is often overlooked. "Our new Constitution is now established and has an appearance that promises permanency," he said, "but in this world nothing can be said to be certain except death and taxes."

As the delegates filed out of the convention hall in late September, a local woman, Elizabeth Powel, is said to have buttonholed Franklin and asked, "Well, Doctor, what have we got, a republic or a monarchy?"

"A republic," Franklin replied, "if you can keep it."

The United States Constitution, messily and courageously crafted during that broiling Philadelphia summer, was not a gift or an entitlement. It was not even a finished product. It was a work in progress, a challenge to future generations and, most of all, an instrument—precisely as good and useful as those who wield it.

TWENTY-FIVE

BELATED BEN

Spend enough time with someone, even someone you love, and they inevitably disappoint you. And so it was with Ben and me. Over the past few years, I've grown to like and admire Ben, maybe even love him, yet he disappoints me. He disappointed me when he failed to rush to his dying wife's side and he disappointed when he couldn't bring himself to reconcile with his son William. Nowhere does he disappoint more, though, than when it comes to slavery.

I wanted Ben to be different from, better than, other founders like Washington and Jefferson, who enslaved hundreds of people and, in the case of Jefferson, never freed the vast majority of them even upon his death. In the end, Franklin was better, but he took a good long while getting there. For much of his life Benjamin Franklin was an enslaver and a middleman who profited off the slave trade. Franklin enslaved at least seven Black people over the course of about four decades, records show. (By comparison, Jefferson enslaved more than six hundred people.)

In later years, Franklin no longer enslaved people; he became a cautious abolitionist and, shortly before his death, a vocal critic of slavery. It is this

change of heart on which I hang my hopes for Ben—a glimmer of light, perhaps, in an otherwise dark aspect of his life.

Try as we might, we never fully rise above the blind spots of our era;
we are all prisoners of a particular time and place. Benjamin Franklin was
no exception. He inherited all the prejudices and fallacies of his time. This
is not to excuse his words and actions. Ben wouldn't excuse himself. "The
man who is so *good* at making an excuse," he once said, "is seldom good at
anything *else*." So, Ben, I will not attempt to justify your actions. I will try to
understand them.

Ben owned and edited the *Pennsylvania Gazette* for nearly twenty years.
During that time, the newspaper ran many advertisements for enslaved persons and for runaways, including absconding apprentices, as young Ben
once was. These ads make for disturbing reading. What is most unsettling
is their matter-of-fact tone, appearing alongside, and sometimes embedded
in, ads for rocking chairs, fishing boats, and goose feathers. Here is one ad
from 1734: "Two likely young Negroes, one a lad about 19: the other a girl of
15, to be sold. Inquire of the printer." The printer, of course, was Benjamin
Franklin. This heartbreaking ad Franklin ran in 1733: "There is to be sold a
very likely Negro woman aged about thirty years who has lived in this city,
from her childhood, and can wash and iron very well . . . and also another
very likely boy aged about six years, who is son of the abovesaid woman. He
will be sold with his mother, or by himself, as the buyer pleases. Enquire of
the printer."

Franklin had no qualms about running these ads, "being no more reluctant to advertise a runaway slave than a runaway horse," says historian Gary
Nash. Ads like these accounted for a sizable chunk of the *Gazette*'s revenue
and helped make Franklin a wealthy man able to retire (at least for a while)
at age forty-two.

The editorial side of Franklin's newspaper was hardly more enlightened.
In one news story, about a smallpox outbreak in 1731, Franklin reports that of
the 288 people who died, 64 were enslaved Blacks. Then he engages in some
appalling math: "If these may be valued one with another at £30 per head,

the loss to the city... is near £2000." That is all he had to say about those who died. To him, they were property, not people.

It's true, as I said, that these reprehensible attitudes were common at the time. Most printers ran stories and ads like Franklin's. Not all did, though. Christopher Sauer, publisher of a German-language newspaper in Pennsylvania, refused to accept any advertisements for enslaved persons. Why couldn't you be the exception, not the rule, Ben?

Franklin also printed early abolitionist tracts, such as Benjamin Lay's fiery 1738 pamphlet *All Slave-Keepers That Keep the Innocent in Bondage, Apostates*. Lay was an odd bird. A Quaker and a dwarf, standing just over four feet tall, he lived in a cave and was shunned by much of Philadelphia. He was arguably the first modern American abolitionist. He considered slavery the "mother of all sins," believing it corrupted the entire community, not only enslavers. Lay was determined to rouse people from their moral stupor—and by any means necessary. At one Quaker meeting in Burlington, New Jersey, he drove a sword into a Bible, splattering worshippers with fake blood (red pokeberry juice) and shouting, "Thus shall God shed the blood of those persons who enslave their fellow creatures!"

Franklin admired Lay's abolitionist essay, but it was Deborah who was the true devotee. She hung an oil painting of Lay in the Franklin home. Did Deborah shape her husband's evolving views on slavery? We don't know for sure, but it is certainly possible.

I was hoping Ben's decision to publish abolitionist tracts in the 1730s and 1740s represented a sea change. It did not. I detect no other signs that Ben was at all sympathetic to the plight of enslaved persons, or Africans in general. In the 1747 pamphlet *Plain Truth*, a rallying cry to defend the Pennsylvania frontier, he warned Whites that "your persons, fortunes, wives and daughters, shall be subject to the wanton and unbridled rage, rapine and lust, of *Negroes, Molattoes*, and others, the vilest and most abandoned of mankind."

I want to know more about these people Franklin and his family enslaved but find little. We know their first names—Joseph, Jemima, Peter, Bob, George, Othello, and King—but not much else. History is written by the enslavers, not the enslaved. The Franklin Museum in Philadelphia includes many portraits of Ben and his male friends and family, but far fewer of the women in his life and virtually none of the people he enslaved. They are invisible, making only fleeting appearances in Ben's voluminous writings. Yet they were a constant, often comforting, presence in his life. When Ben and William traveled to the Franklin ancestral home in Ecton, England, it was enslaved Peter who scrubbed the moss-covered tombstone of their ancestor.

In the 1750s, Ben began to slowly, cautiously question the institution of slavery. His initial concerns, though, were based on economic, not moral grounds. It was the welfare of Whites, not Blacks, that worried him. Whites who depend on slave labor grow lazy and "enfeebled" and their children "proud, disgusted with labour, and being educated in idleness, are rendered unfit to get a living by industry." In a 1751 essay, Franklin fretted about the growing number of enslaved Africans in the colonies—not because it was morally repugnant but because it would "darken" the complexion of America. "Why increase the Sons of Africa, by planting them in America, where we have so fair an opportunity, by excluding all Blacks and Tawneys, of increasing the lovely White and Red?" Franklin's blatant racism is tempered slightly by the next sentence: "But perhaps I am partial to the complexion of my country, for such kind of partiality is natural to mankind."

A glimmer of light. This marked, I think, the beginning of Ben's transformation. By acknowledging his prejudices, he had planted the seeds of doubt, and as we saw at the Constitutional Convention, from those seeds mighty trees grow.

There were more specks of light. In 1757, just before sailing for England, Ben revised his will, directing the manumission of enslaved Peter and his wife, Jemima, in the event of Ben's death. The next year, King, a man enslaved by William Franklin, ran away to the English countryside and was taken in by a kindly woman who taught him to read and write. Ben and William could have demanded his return but did not. Did that reflect a softening of Franklin's heart? Or was it simply convenient to let King go since, as Ben told Deborah, "He was of little use, and often in mischief." It's difficult to say. Even the glimmers of light are dim and murky.

Stepping back and surveying a wider swath of Ben's life, I see clearer signs of his shifting position on slavery. In his 1751 essay "Observations Concerning the Increase of Mankind," Ben wrote how "almost every slave being by nature a thief..." Eighteen years later, he revised it to read, "almost every slave being from the nature of slavery a thief..." It may seem like a small change, but it is, I think, significant. The "thief" is a product of nurture, not nature.

The real sea change came in the early 1760s. Franklin was approached by an Anglican group, Bray Associates, who wanted to open a school in Philadelphia for Black children and requested Franklin's advice. Ben obliged, eventually becoming chairman of the group's board. A visit to the Philadelphia school in 1762 dramatically changed his view of Blacks. He now "conceiv'd a higher opinion of the natural capacities of the black race, than I had ever before entertained. Their apprehension seems as quick, their memory as strong, and their docility in every respect equal to that of white children."

Franklin's revelation seems so obvious, so self-evident, today as to be patronizing, even racist. Yet the idea that Blacks were intellectual equals to Whites was, sadly, not at all self-evident at the time. It certainly wasn't to Thomas Jefferson. Two decades *after* Franklin's visit to the Philadelphia school, Jefferson defended slavery in his *Notes on the State of Virginia*. He couches his racism in pseudoscientific jargon, which only makes it worse. Blacks need less sleep than Whites, he says, tolerate heat better and have "a very strong and disagreeable odour." Their memory is equal to that of Whites but "in reason much inferior, as I think one could scarcely be found capable of tracing and comprehending the investigations of Euclid; and that in imagination they are dull, tasteless, and anomalous." Jefferson concludes that Blacks "are inferior to the whites in the endowments of both body and mind."

Benjamin Franklin may have shared Jefferson's bigoted views at one point but when confronted with contrary evidence, Franklin, unlike Jefferson, changed his mind. It was his "empirical temper" at work. He was always open to experience and was willing to modify his views based on that experience.

By the early 1770s, Franklin was speaking out publicly against slavery. In 1772, he wrote an article for the *London Chronicle* in which he asked whether the "petty pleasure" of drinking sweetened tea could "compensate for so much misery produced among our fellow creatures, and such a constant butchery of the human species by this pestilential detestable traffic in the bodies and souls of men?"

Franklin's change of heart was reflected not only in word but deed. Revising his will, he essentially purchased the freedom of a man enslaved by his son-in-law, Richard Bache. He had sailed for London in 1757 with two enslaved people; nearly twenty years later, he sailed for France with his two grandchildren and no enslaved people. In France, his abolitionist views gelled further, thanks in part to the French intellectuals whispering in his ear.

By the time he returned to Philadelphia for the final time in 1785, Ben, now nearly eighty years old, was an all-in abolitionist. No, he did not splatter anyone with ersatz blood or deploy other confrontational tactics. That wasn't his style. He worked hard, though, to change minds in his own way. He was appointed president of the Pennsylvania Society for Promoting the Abolition of Slavery and, in 1787, just before the Constitutional Convention, signed an antislavery petition declaring that God had made "of one flesh, all the children" of the world. Writing in 1789, a year before his death, he struck his toughest abolitionist stance to date. He called slavery "an atrocious debasement of human nature" and, perhaps for the first time, put himself in the shoes of an enslaved person.

> The unhappy man who has long been treated as a brute animal, too frequently sinks beneath the common standard of the human species. The galling chains that bind his body, do also fetter his intellectual faculties, and impair the social affections of his heart. Accustomed to move like a mere machine, by the will of a master, reflection is suspended; he has not the power of choice; and reason and conscience, have but little influence over his conduct: because he is chiefly governed by the passion of fear. He is poor and friendless—perhaps worn out by extreme labor, age and disease.

Benjamin Franklin's final public writing, penned less than a month before his death, was a biting satire of the institution of slavery. He wrote it in
response to the angry tirade of a Georgia congressman who had objected
to an abolitionist motion brought before the first federal Congress. In his
satire, Ben dons one last mask: that of Sidi Mehemet Ibrahim, an Algerian
prince who defends the practice of enslaving Christians captured by Barbary pirates. If we end our practice of enslaving Christians, Ibrahim/Frank-
lin asks, "who, in this hot climate, are to cultivate our lands?" Surely not
us, says Ibrahim, for then we would "be our own slaves." Besides, he says,
we are actually *improving* the lives of these enslaved people by introducing
them to the infinite mercy of Allah and providing "an opportunity of making themselves acquainted with the true doctrine, and thereby saving their
immortal souls."

Ben had taken every American justification for the institution of slavery
and turned it on its head. He accomplished the satirist's goal, and with dev-
astating effect. Rather than shine a light directly on injustices like slavery, he
held a mirror to them. The reflection was not pretty.

I return one last time to the Franklin Museum. By now, I am a regular, though
not the only one. Washington and Jefferson have scholars. Franklin has fans.
I head directly to the last exhibit. "Did Franklin oppose slavery?" it asks. The
museum doesn't answer the question but instead kicks it back to the visitor:
"You be the historian; weigh the evidence and decide."

I am then presented with ten moments from Franklin's life—such as his
early role as a go-between for enslavers and his later writings against slavery—and asked which way each tipped the scales. My final score: seven in
favor of Franklin the Abolitionist, three against. There, it is settled.

Or is it? Walking back to my hotel, I wonder whether historical verdicts
are ever so clear-cut. Might someone else, an African American for instance,
review the same set of facts and reach a different conclusion? Also, I know I
am invested in my conceit of Ben as a guide for our troubled times. Have I
fallen into the trap of confirmation bias, seeing only Good Ben while down-
playing Bad Ben? My eighteen-year-old daughter said as much when I told

her about Franklin's involvement with slavery. "He enslaved people, Dad. How can we learn anything from him?"

At the time, I had no answer for her, but now, walking down Chestnut Street in Philadelphia on a warm spring day, I think I do. There is no excuse for Ben's past as an enslaver. Slavery is wrong now, and it was wrong then. But to conclude we have nothing to learn from him is, I think, a mistake. Great people—and I do believe Franklin was a great person—teach us by both positive example and negative. Object lessons are still lessons. Sometimes they are the most valuable of all.

Rather than demythologizing a founder like Benjamin Franklin, we should, I think, *remythologize* him. We need myths. Not myths as in falsehoods but myths as Joseph Campbell defined them: animating stories that inspire. All cultures need these kinds of myths. They wouldn't be a culture without them. So, let's look at Benjamin Franklin unflinchingly, flaws and all, and rather than ask whether he was perfect or not, pose a different question. Is the story of his long life, the good *and* the bad, useful? If not, move on. If yes, I think we owe it—not to Ben but to ourselves—to sit up and pay attention.

TWENTY-SIX

ETERNAL BEN

Ben lived for thirty-one months to the day after the conclusion of the
Constitutional Convention. His mind remained sharp, but his body was,
like an old house, beginning to creak and buckle. The plumbing was acting
up too. "People who live long, who will drink of the cup of life to the very
bottom, must expect to meet with some of the usual dregs," he said. That
is a bracingly positive take on a process I have always associated only with
decline and loss. At the same time, Ben is realistic. He doesn't deny the bitterness of the dregs, but rather than viewing them as an injustice sees them
for what they are: the natural outcome of a long and useful life.

Considering all the maladies that can afflict the human body, Ben said,
he was lucky to suffer from only three incurable ones: the gout, the stone,
and old age. He did not dwell on his sundry aches and pains. He recognized
his illness for what it was: an exit ramp "kindly intended to wean him from a
world, in which he was no longer fit to act the part assigned to him," said his
physician, John Jones.

Franklin knew we don't own our bodies. We merely borrow them
for a while. They may give us pleasure and help us do some good in this
world, but "when they become unfit for these purposes and afford us pain

instead of pleasure," nature supplies a way out. "That way," said Franklin, "is death."

We know this intuitively. We willingly choose a "partial death," as Franklin called it, when amputating a mangled limb or parting with a diseased tooth. Death is merely the logical extension of this mortal calculus. In the end, concludes Franklin, we are not our bodies: "We are spirits."

In the time he had left, Ben focused on what he could enjoy: "reading or writing, or in conversation with friends, joking, laughing, and telling merry stories." He added a three-story wing to Franklin Court, including a dining room that could seat twenty-four and his pride of place: a library "lin'd with books to the ceiling." It was a rare rash act from the typically cautious Franklin but, as he told his sister Jane, "we are apt to forget that we are grown old, and building is an amusement."

Repose, at long last. Surrounded by his inventions and the numerous honors bestowed upon him, Ben took stock of his life. It was long, no doubt, but was it truly useful? He wondered aloud "whether I have been doing good or mischief." He didn't dwell on that question for long, though, for he knew it was not for him to decide. Only others, peering backward, are qualified to take the measure of a life. "I only know," said Franklin, "that I intended well, and I hope all will end well."

Intended well? What an odd statement coming from a man who placed so little value on intentions and so much on results. Was this a change of heart, I wonder, a deathbed conversion to the virtues of good intentions? And might it signal a larger conversion? Was Benjamin Franklin, so critical of scripture and the clergy, now banking on an afterlife?

When his friend Ezra Stiles, a minister and president of Yale, solicited Franklin's thoughts on religion and, in particular, the afterlife, Franklin's reply was characteristically sly. "It is a question I do not dogmatize upon," he said, "having never studied it, and think it needless to busy myself with it now, when I expect soon an opportunity of knowing the truth with less trouble." Classic Ben. Witty, in the best sense, it also points to one of his core principles: Experience trumps theory. Every time.

To other correspondents, Ben embraced the prospect of life after death. Drawing on his electrical experiments and especially his greatest discovery, the law of conservation of charge, he notes that nature doesn't destroy or waste anything, "not even a drop of water," so why would she annihilate souls or waste millions of minds? It makes no sense. That is why, concludes Franklin, "I believe I shall in some shape or other always exist."

Back at Franklin Court, I traverse a brick-lined entrance and a sign informs me Franklin used to walk the same route to his house. I notice an illustration depicting Market Street and its explosive growth from Franklin's arrival in 1722 to his death in 1790. When he arrived in Philadelphia, people still recalled when settlers lived in caves along the Delaware River. By the end of his life, Philadelphia was a thriving scientific and cultural capital, the Athens of America.

I notice an oval plaque on the ground and stoop to read it. "Benjamin Franklin Privy Pit. 1787." The sign could have just as easily read: "Ben Franklin shat here." Too bad. Ben would like that.

Spotting a bench, I sit under a mulberry tree, just like the one Franklin liked to sit under during the warm Philadelphia summers. I close my eyes and try to picture Benjamin Franklin's final days. It was April, the season of rebirth. In the eighteenth century, a time of rapid, unsettling change, people looked to the seasons as a comforting metaphor. Seasons change, but they don't change randomly. There is an order, a reassuring predictability, to the cycle. Franklin was attuned to the seasons, the flux of all things. One of his favorite poems was "The Seasons" by James Thomson. It "brought more tears of pleasure into my eyes than all I ever read before," he said.

Franklin believed anything worth doing was worth doing with others, and this predilection extended to death. He did not die alone. At his side were his daughter, Sally ("the comfort of my declining years"), a brood of grandchildren, and his old friend and protégé, Polly Stevenson.

One day, Polly found Franklin "in great agony." When the pain subsided, she asked if she should read to him. Yes, he said, so she picked up a book of poetry and turned to Isaac Watts, one of Franklin's favorites. She thought it would lull him to sleep, but instead, "it roused him to a display of the powers of his memory and his reason." He recited several of Watts's poems verbatim, and reflected on their sublimity. I see why Franklin liked the English poet. A Congregational minister who wrote a book on logic, Watts, like Franklin, toggled effortlessly between head and heart.

In his final days, the Old Conjurer kept everyone guessing. He would slip into a torpor and then regain his strength, buoying hopes. One day, Ben sat bolt upright and asked that his bed be made up so that he might "die in a decent manner." Sally told him she hoped he would recover and live many years longer.

"I hope not," he replied calmly.

Shortly afterward, Benjamin Franklin breathed his last breath, marking the end of the longest and most useful of lives.

I arrive at the Christ Church Burial Ground at Fifth and Arch Streets on a pleasantly cool spring day. I pay my five dollars and enter a small, leafy cemetery. Ben's grave is located in a corner, near a busy intersection. Of course. A city boy to the end.

The marble tombstone reads simply, "Deborah and Benjamin Franklin, 1790." Scattered on top are a handful of pennies, along with a few quarters and crumpled dollar bills. It's a tradition no doubt born of the famous though oft misquoted line about "a penny saved is a penny earned." (Ben actually said, "a penny sav'd is a penny *got.*")

Across the street is a massive gray bunker of a building. What is that soulless monstrosity, I wonder? I look more closely and see the sign: "United States Mint." Poor Ben. Even in death, he can't escape his monetary reputation. I don't think he'd fret about it. He knew who he was. As he said, dirt sticks to mud walls but not to polished marble.

I'm about to leave the cemetery when I notice an engraved rendering of the epitaph Ben wrote for himself at a young age while suffering from a serious case of pleurisy.

The Body of
B. Franklin,
Printer;
Like the Cover of an old Book,
Its Contents torn out,
And stripped of its Lettering & Gilding,
Lies here, Food for Worms.
But the Work shall not be wholly lost:
For it will, as he believ'd
appear once more,
In a new & more perfect Edition,
Corrected and amended
By the Author

Amended and perhaps expanded too. Even the longest and most useful of lives is incomplete. We exit the stage too soon, leaving behind a basketful of disappointments, regrets, and stillborn dreams—journeys not taken, books not finished, words not said.

Ben was not immune from the sad incompleteness of life. He never did write that book he had long talked about, *The Art of Virtue,* and God knows we could use it. Ditto the Society of the Free and Easy and the Party of Virtue. Most glaring of all, Ben never finished his autobiography. It trails off when he had just turned fifty-one and life was really getting interesting. Why couldn't he finish it? Sure, he was busy, but too busy to fully chronicle a singular life, the template for the American dream? Come on, Ben. What happened?

The answer, I think, lies in the first two words of history's most famous incomplete work: "Dear Son." He began the book as a letter to William. But there was no more William, not as far as Ben was concerned. After the war, he rarely mentioned his son and when he did it was with acid bitterness. In his will, he left William nothing of value, only a few books and papers William already possessed and some worthless land deeds. By explanation, Ben said coldly, "The part he acted against me in the late war ...

will account for my leaving him no more of an estate he endeavoured to deprive me of."

For Franklin, the conflict with Britain was, at its heart, a family quarrel, and nothing hurt him more. Ben couldn't finish his autobiography without thinking of William, and that was too painful. A wound even the great Dr. Franklin couldn't heal.

Is Ben still with us? Not only on the bills we use to buy Afghan carpets or the signs advertising Philly cheesesteak subs or in his pithy sayings, but in a deeper sense? I'm tempted to speak of his "legacy," but I don't care for that word. It is lifeless and inadequate and contains more than a whiff of staleness, like your grandfather's old suit still hanging in the closet, unworn and unloved. "Legacy" doesn't do justice to the lasting influence of a great and flawed man like Benjamin Franklin.

Our footprints fade but never disappear. Some, like Franklin's, grow more pronounced with time. Franklin is the least dead of the founders. Perhaps it's his love of technology. Unlike Washington or Jefferson, we can picture Franklin sitting in front of a laptop or listening to a podcast with noise-canceling headphones. Heck, I can see Franklin *inventing* noise-canceling headphones. Perhaps it is something more profound. Perhaps it is how Franklin lived, the values he embraced and actions he took that explain his surprisingly robust afterlife.

It is only a few blocks from the cemetery to my hotel, but those few blocks contain much Ben-ness. The touchstones where Ben lived, studied, joked, dreamed, drank, wrote, convened, cajoled, mourned, experimented— and experienced. More vital than these, though, are the living manifestations of his useful life. The Library Company of Philadelphia is thriving, as is the American Philosophical Society, the Pennsylvania Hospital, and the University of Pennsylvania (now located across the Schuylkill River). A fire engine races by, sirens blaring and lights flashing, and that is Ben's doing. A feisty newspaper? Ben. Streetlights? Ben. A public vaccine drive? Ben.

As I walk, the sun dipping low on the horizon, a thought bubbles up. Maybe the past doesn't vanish entirely. Maybe it lingers, like radioactive particles after a nuclear explosion. Only what if—and this is where we get downright possibilian—the past is not harmful, like radiation, but the opposite: an unseen but salutary force, like the good bacteria in your gut or the ozone layer blocking harmful ultraviolet rays.

We speak of the "weight of the past," but what if it isn't heavy at all? What if the past is unimaginably light—no, more than light, buoyant, lifting us, supporting us, keeping us afloat?

Surely that changes everything.

BEYOND BEN

Dear Ben,

I know how much you love a good correspondence, communing with a faraway mind, so I figured you wouldn't mind one more letter.

I wish you could see me. I am naked. Okay, not exactly naked but close. I am wearing something called a "bathing suit." Imagine an undergarment you wear in public—a partial air bath. You'd question the need for this invention, I'm sure. That which conceals also constricts.

Anyway, I digress, and I know how you hate that. Brevity, always. Picture, if you will, a man of a certain age plunging into Lake Michigan one summer morning in search of a hard-boiled egg. Are you with me, Ben?

Of course you are. It was your idea. Surely you recall the advice you gave a friend, Oliver Neave, who wanted to know if, as a middle-aged man, he could learn to swim.

Absolutely, you replied, without hesitation, and supplied detailed instructions. Find an egg, you counseled, and drop it deep in the water. Then swallow your fear and dive for it. You will not drown, you assured Oliver. Instead, "you will find that the water buoys you up against your inclination," you said, before adding a sentence that has stuck with me. "It is not so easy a thing to sink as you imagined." I want to believe you, Ben, honest I do, but I struggle, even after these past few years I've spent with you, the most sanguine of possibilians.

I procure a hard-boiled egg at a Greek diner, then toss it into the lake, as you suggested, and follow close behind. Submerged in the unseasonably cool water, I pump my arms and legs in a controlled flail I call swimming when a familiar fear flashes across my brain like an electric shock. It's nothing I can name, this trepidation, but I have associated it with water for as long as I can remember. I nearly abandon my attempt to reach the egg when I recall your words: "Feel the power of the water to support you, and learn to confide in that power."

It was easy enough to confide in that power, that Powerful Goodness, when I was floating in two feet of highly salinized water at a spa in southern England. It is a different story here, in the twelve-foot depths of brisk and saltless Lake Michigan. This is the paradox of water. We need it. We *are* it. Yet it can kill us.

I persist. Legs frog-kicking, arms arcing, I dive deeper and deeper. It dawns on me that the lake doesn't want me to sink. It wants me to swim—or at least not drown, and as far as I'm concerned, that is good enough.

I am not alone. Others have gathered lakeside for an early morning swim. Most are older than me, including my friend Barbara, a Chicago transplant and retired newspaper columnist. You'd like her, Ben, and not only because of the printer's ink coursing through her older (but not old) veins. She is an avid swimmer and loves the water as much as you do.

As I dive for the egg, I am vaguely aware of Barbara and the others. Humans gliding next to me, over me, *through* me, or so it seems. Up there, on the surface, they were specific persons with specific identities. Down here, they are nameless mammals, indistinguishable from one another and from me. Up there, they had wrinkled, walrus skin, varicose veins, arthritic knees, scar tissue, keratoses, artificial hips, pacemakers, dentures, and other stigmata of bodies in decline. Down here, their oldness, their otherness, disappears, dissolved in the welcoming waters.

Old. Young. Adolescent. Middle-aged. Late-middle-aged. These are

labels, roles we assume for a short while. Like all labels, they are not meaningless, but they mean less than we think. Time, formless and fluid, refuses
to play our category game.

It is not so easy a thing to sink as you imagined. In the months since we
parted ways, Ben, life has tested your proposition. I have buried my mother,
sent my only child to college, undergone surgery, and turned sixty. There, I
said it!

I'd like to report I navigated these turbulent waters with your easy equanimity, Ben, but that would be a lie, and not a helpful one. The truth is I
fought the riptides. I distrusted providence. Yet I did not sink. I did not swim
either. I floated. Despite it all. Because of it all.

I don't know what lies ahead for me, Ben. An overflowing cup or the
dregs? Obscurity or fame (perhaps a celebrity that extends beyond the ter-
ritorial waters of Bulgaria)? I do know choppy seas await me, such is the way
of the world. But you will be there, in some form or another, nudging me,
buoying me, sharing a laugh with me.

I see why you suggested an egg. Bright white, it gives me something clear
to aim for. A beacon. I kick once more, then stretch my right arm and in a
surprisingly fluent motion, pluck the egg off the lake bed. Then I pivot, like
you did so many times, and kick again. Up, up, up, I glide, the lake lifting me,
pulling me, willing me toward the surface, and the light.

I rub my eyes and shake the water from my ears like a dog after a bath.
The air is soft and plump with the sounds of a city stirring. I spot Barbara.
She is standing on shore, clearly relieved to see me intact, a smile on my face
and a hard-boiled egg in my hand. I raise it triumphantly above my head, as if
it were the Nobel Peace Prize or an honorary degree from Bulgaria's second-
most-prestigious university.

You were right, Ben. All in all, it is a pretty good sort of a world.

Acknowledgments

Benjamin Franklin, impressive as he was, was not self-made. He had help. So did I. Like Ben, I benefited from the generosity of friends and strangers near and far and, like Ben, I am deeply grateful.

On the road, I was blessed with friends who graciously supplied not only a room of my own but boatloads of bonhomie as well: Mark Landler and Angela Tung in London; Barbara Brotman and Chuck Berman in Chicago.

In the spirit of Ben, several Franklinistas generously shared their wisdom. Roy Goodman is as passionate about Franklin as he is knowledgeable. Marty Mangold, a Franklinista of the finest kind, spent many days hunkered in his extensive library, unearthing elusive facts and attributions. In Paris, Ellen Leventer helped me track down, and interpret, Franklin landmarks. In Montreal, friends Martin Regg Cohn and Karen Mazurkewich were my eyes, ears—and heart. Canada's finest.

I am particularly indebted to the guardians of the Ben Franklin House in London. Márcia Balisciano and Michael Hall made me feel at home and let me roam where Ben roamed. Writer in residence George Goodwin shared his extensive knowledge—first by Zoom, then over salmon salad and ale. Playwright in residence Mike London also shared his many insights.

In Philadelphia, Franklin interpreter (never call him an impersonator) Mitch Kramer not only looks like Ben but also embodies the same generous spirit. Michael Barsanti, director of the Library Company of Philadelphia, was equally charitable with his time.

In Seattle, Caroline Sayre, Catherine Hunt, Lisa Blume, and the rest of the city's Ben Franklin Circle graciously welcomed me as one of their own. Back home, during the long, dark exile known as writing, I was buoyed by the warm companionship of fellow scribes Jacki Lyden, Eliza McGraw, David Grinspoon, Florence Williams, Leeya Mehta, Kris O'Shee, Matt Davis, Juliet Eilperin, and Josh Horwitz.

John Lister, Gwydion Suilebhan, and Mark Rennella read early drafts of this book and offered valuable suggestions. My agent, Sloan Harris, believed in the project from the get-go, skillfully steering me away from the aliens and toward Franklin. I am grateful to Carolyn Kelly and the rest of the terrific staff at Avid Reader Press for shepherding Ben & Me from rough manuscript to finished book. I am especially indebted to my editor, Ben Loehnen, who cajoled, cheered, and condensed with all the skill and grace of his namesake. He is my favorite living Ben.

At home, my daughter, Sonya, rooted for me and graciously tolerated the fountain of random Franklin facts I spewed. My brother, Paul, supported me throughout; the Franklin bust he gifted me was a constant companion. My wife, Sharon, deserves, if not sainthood, then a billboard on I-95. She served as cheerleader and comforter, idea-backboard, draft-reader, and frontline editor. I could not have written this book without her.

My biggest booster was my mom. During our regular Monday calls, she'd always ask how the book was coming along. "Swimmingly," I lied. When I finally entered the home stretch, my mom fell gravely ill. I finished this book near her bedside, writing the final sentence mere minutes before she passed away. She knew it was okay to let go. This book is also dedicated to her.

Notes

Most of the quotes by Benjamin Franklin come from three sources: Yale University's *The Papers of Benjamin Franklin* (forty-three volumes), Norton's edition of Franklin's *Autobiography*, and the Library of America's two-volume collection of his writing. In the interest of brevity, I have not included endnotes for Franklin quotes that come from these sources but have done so for those that come from elsewhere. I have also attributed quotes from Franklin's many interlocutors. Much of this correspondence appears in the *Papers*.

INTRODUCTION: ALIEN BEN

xv   *one UFO encounter in particular*: Adam Reilly, "Western Mass. Debates a UFO Monument—and How to Commemorate the Inexplicable," WGBH, June 14, 2018.

xv   *"Our Founders, Alien Obsessed"*: Matthew Stewart, "Our Founders, Alien-Obsessed: Adams and Franklin Had a Thing—Really!—for Extraterrestrials," *Salon*, July 4, 2015. See also "Aliens in New England? A Timeline of UFO Sightings and Unusual Encounters," New England.com, April 15, 2022.

xvi   *"Fleshly, worldly, fluid"*: Betsy Erkkila, "Franklin and the Revolutionary Body," *ELH* 67, no. 3 (2000), 717–741.

xvi   *He signed all four documents*: the Declaration of Independence (1776), the Treaty of Alliance with France (1778), the Treaty of Paris Establishing Peace with Great Britain (1783), and the US Constitution (1787).

xvi   *He invented the lightning rod, bifocals*: Most historians credit Benjamin Franklin with inventing bifocals, but a few believe others may have preceded him in the invention. For an overview, see Charles Letocha, "The Invention and Early Manufacture of Bifocals," *Survey of Ophthalmology* 35, no. 3 (1990), 226–235.

xvii   *"the perfect model of sanity"*: Ormond Seavey, *Becoming Benjamin Franklin: The Autobiography and the Life* (University Park: Penn State University Press, 1990), 99.

xviii   *"To forget our mistakes is bad"*: Neil Postman, *Building a Bridge to the 18th Century: How the Past Can Improve Our Future* (New York: Vintage, 1999), 6.

ONE: RESTING BEN

1   *recorded by Polly Stevenson*: Her married name was Mary Hewson, but Franklin, like other close friends, called her "Polly" and still thought of her as a "Stevenson."

1   *"No repining, no peevish"*: Polly Stevenson (married name: Mary Hewson), cited in John Bigelow, ed., *The Works of Benjamin Franklin* (New York: Knickerbocker Press), 12:197.

2   *a lethal electrical charge and a turkey*: The turkey, alas, did not survive the encounter.

2   *"A short, fat, trunched"*: The visitor was Manasseh Cutler, cited in Harold Bloom, ed., *Benjamin Franklin* (New York: Infobase Publishing, 2008), 17.

3   *"A calm lethargic state succeeded"*: Kevin Hayes and Isabelle Bour, eds. *Franklin in His Own Time* (Iowa City: University of Iowa Press, 2011), 122.

3   *"he quietly expired"*: Ibid., 122.

3   *the greatest happiness of the greatest number*: The formulation is the brainchild of the philosopher (and Franklin contemporary) Jeremy Bentham.

4   *David Eagleman calls a "possibilian"*: Eagleman first used the term in an NPR interview. *Talk of the Nation*, February 17, 2009.

TWO: BABY BEN

7   *born on January 17, 1706*: At the time, Franklin's birthday was recorded on January 6, but in 1752 England and its colonies switched from the Julian to the Gregorian calendar, causing Franklin's birthday to shift to January 17.

8   *a neighbor had sketched the house*: William Thackara, on a visit to Boston, converted the pencil sketch into a drawing.

8   *a sturdy green-steepled*: This rendition of the Old South Meeting Hall was built in 1729. The original, where Franklin was baptized, was made of cedar wood.

8   *"the blame and shame of it"*: The judge was Samuel Sewall. Quoted in Arthur Bernon Tourtellot, *Benjamin Franklin: The Shaping of Genius: The Boston Years* (Garden City, NY: Doubleday, 1977), 6.

9   *"to the service of the church"*: Ibid., 145.

9   *"Private virtue assured a public role"*: Ormond Seavey, *Becoming Benjamin Franklin: The Autobiography and the Life* (University Park: Penn State University Press, 1990), 105.

11 *"Seest thou a man diligent"*: Joyce Chaplin, ed., *Benjamin Franklin's Autobiography* (New York: Norton, 2012), 76.

11 *stand before four kings*: Franklin stood before Kings George II and George III of England, and Louis XV and Louis XVI of France. He dined with Denmark's King Christian VII.

12 *Eli Whitney's cotton gin*: Whitney was born in colonial America. By the time he invented the cotton gin, in 1794, the colonies (now states) had gained their independence.

13 *"The morals of our people"*: John Adams, *The Diary and Autobiography of John Adams* (Cambridge, MA: Belknap, 1961), 2:150, 27.

13 *And a surprising number chose to join*: Seavey, *Becoming Benjamin Franklin*, 115.

14   *"[Bostonians] dressed as elegantly"*: Claude-Anne Lopez and Eugenia Herbert, *The Private Franklin: The Man and His Family* (New York: Norton, 1975), 7.

14   *Near the Franklin house*: When Benjamin was six years old, the Franklins moved to a much larger house, about five blocks north.

16   *"I think father if you said grace"*: Paul M. Zall, ed., *Ben Franklin Laughing* (Berkeley: University of California Press, 1980), 98.

16   *"the quackery of literature"*: As recalled by Benjamin Rush in Harold Bloom, ed., *Benjamin Franklin* (New York: Infobase Publishing, 2008), 17.

THREE: BOOKISH BEN

17   *"Be not fools"*: Cotton Mather, *Essays to Do Good* (New York: Kindle, 2012), 462.

18   *"What description of men"*: Paul M. Zall, ed., *Ben Franklin Laughing* (Berkeley: University of California Press, 1980), 131.

19   *"Books are useful"*: Daniel Defoe, *An Essay upon Projects* (New York: AMS Press, 1999), 12.

19   *"slough of despond"*: John Bunyan, *The Pilgrim's Progress* (London: Penguin Classics, 2008), 17.

20   *"the virtues of these great men"*: *Plutarch's Lives,* translated by John Dryden (New York: Modern Library, 2001), 325.

20   *"change and shift"*: Ibid., 201.

21   *He once ran an ad*: "The Person that borrow'd B. Franklin's Law-Book of this Province, is hereby desired to return it, he having forgot to whom he lent it," *Pennsylvania Gazette,* July 24, 1735.

23   *not the town's medical establishment*: There was one exception among the doctors. Zabdiel Boylston enthusiastically embraced the new inoculation. See Eric Weiner, "How 18th Century Boston Countered Vaccine Hesitancy," *Medium,* September 20, 2021.

23   *"No religion has ever been"*: Arthur Bernon Tourtellot, *Benjamin Franklin: The Shaping of Genius: The Boston Years* (Garden City, NY: Doubleday, 1977), 188.

23   *"He is unworthy"*: Mather, *Essays to Do Good,* 64.

23   *"It is an invaluable honor"*: Ibid., 96.

24   *"a workless faith"*: Ibid., 282.

24   *"Perhaps thou art one"*: Ibid., 208.

24   *"Let this be a caution to you"*: Benjamin Franklin, *The Papers of Benjamin Franklin* (New Haven: Yale University Press, 1959), 20:286.

FOUR: EMPIRICAL BEN

26   *"The past is a foreign"*: Leslie Hartley, *The Go-Between* (New York: New York Review Books, 1953), 17.

27   *The Romans had an expression*: Stanley Finger, *Doctor Franklin's Medicine* (Philadelphia: University of Pennsylvania Press, 2006), 44.

29   *"But what, sir"*: The anecdote, relayed by Franklin's friend André Morellet, is cited

in Paul M. Zall, ed., *Ben Franklin Laughing* (Berkeley: University of California Press, 1980), 101.

31   *"I pushed the edges of these forward"*: In a letter to Jacques Barbeu-Dubourg, cited in Sarah Pomeroy, *Benjamin Franklin, Swimmer: An Illustrated History* (Philadelphia: American Philosophical Society Press, 2021), 6.

32   *"I was drawn along the surface"*: Ibid., 8.

FIVE: MASKED BEN

34   *"There is much difference"*: Benjamin Franklin, *Poor Richard's Almanack* (New York: Barnes & Noble, 2004), 62.

36   *"expose the vices and follies"*: *New England Courant*, August 7, 1721.

36   *"a notorious, scandalous paper"*: J. A. Leo Lemay, *The Life of Benjamin Franklin* (Philadelphia: University of Pennsylvania Press, 2006), 1:111.

38   *"a play upon possibility"*: Ralph Ellison, *Shadow and Act* (New York: Vintage International), 54.

39   *"look where they pleased"*: Quoted in Jennifer Van Horn, *The Power of Objects in Eighteenth-Century British America* (Chapel Hill: University of North Carolina Press, 2017), 251.

39   *"androgynous imagination"*: John Updike, "Many Bens," *New Yorker*, February 22, 1988.

41   *"Here's the king of Prussia"*: James Sappenfield, *A Sweet Instruction: Franklin's Journalism as a Literary Apprenticeship* (Carbondale: Southern Illinois University Press, 1973), 20:436.

41   *"it relieved readers"*: Ibid., 16–17.

41   *"never at a loss for something to say"*: Cited in ibid., 15.

42   *"Who can do more than guess"*: Edmund Morgan, *Benjamin Franklin* (New Haven: Yale University Press, 2012), 146.

42   *"cult of authenticity"*: Theodor Adorno, *The Jargon of Authenticity* (London: Routledge Classics, 2003), 3.

43   *"genuine fake"*: Alan Watts, *The Book: On the Taboo against Knowing Who You Are* (New York: Vintage, 1989), 53.

SIX: GROUNDED BEN

46   *"the wisest man among us"*: Pauline Maier, "Boston and New York in the 18th Century," *American Antiquarian Society*, October 21, 1981, https://www.americanantiquarian .org/proceedings/44517672.pdf.

49   *"They became homesick"*: David Anderson, "The Soldiers Who Died of Homesickness," *Conversation*, September 30, 2016, https://theconversation.com/the-soldiers -who-died-of-homesickness-65910.

49   *"The idea that you might"*: Salman Rushdie, *Joseph Anton: A Memoir* (New York: Random House, 2012), 430.

50   *"the pineal gland"*: In a letter to Thomas Jefferson, February 3, 1814, https://founders .archives.gov/documents/Jefferson/03-07-02-0140.

50 *"The air proveth sweet"*: Cited in Andrew Murphy, *William Penn: A Life* (New York: Oxford University Press, 2018), 159.

51 *150 enslaved Africans*: The first White protests against slavery occurred four years later, in 1688, led by four German immigrants.

51 *By 1700, one Philadelphian in ten*: The rate of enslavement remained more or less constant for much of the eighteenth century. Historian Gary Nash estimates that on the eve of the American Revolution, one in twelve Philadelphians was enslaved and about one out of five households enslaved someone. See Gary Nash, "Franklin and Slavery," *Proceedings of the American Philosophical Society* 150, no. 4 (2006), 618–635.

51 *"would be astonished"*: Russell Weigley, ed., *Philadelphia: A 300-Year History* (New York: Norton, 1982), 14.

52 *"I was shaved by"*: Alexander Hamilton, *Gentleman's Progress: The Itinerarium of Dr. Alexander Hamilton* (New York: Alejandro's Libros, 2012), 623.

52 *"We are a people, thrown together"*: William Smith, cited in Carl Bridenbaugh and Jessica Bridenbaugh, *Rebels and Gentlemen: Philadelphia in the Age of Franklin* (New York: Oxford University Press, 1962), 16.

52 *One visitor said an hour*: The visitor was William Black, cited in Alan Houston, *Benjamin Franklin and the Politics of Improvement* (New Haven: Yale University Press, 2008), 75.

52 *"Filthy-dirty"*: Billy Smith, "Benjamin Franklin, Civic Improver," in Page Talbott, ed., *Benjamin Franklin: In Search of a Better World* (New Haven: Yale University Press, 2005), 98.

55 *There, Mungo led a happy life*: Writing to Georgiana, Franklin lamented the passing of Mungo, exceptional for his species. "Few squirrels were better accomplish'd; for he had had a good education, had travell'd far, and seen much of the world."

SEVEN: WANDERING BEN

58 *logging 42,000 miles*: Percy Adams, "Benjamin Franklin and the Travel Writing Tradition" in J. A. Leo Lemay, ed., *The Oldest Revolutionary: Essays on Benjamin Franklin* (Philadelphia: University of Pennsylvania Press, 1976), 34.

59 *"Old Conjurer"*: Adams, *The Diary and Autobiography of John Adams* (Cambridge: Belknap Press, 1961), 369.

60 *Ben wondered why*: Karma soon caught up with Governor Keith. Hounded by his creditors, he sailed from America to England. He spent time in a debtors' prison and died in the Old Bailey jail in 1749.

60 *"a great and monstrous thing"*: Daniel Defoe, *A Tour through the Whole Island of Great Britain* (New Haven: Yale University Press, 1991), 135.

EIGHT: RESILIENT BEN

62 *"gnats' blood, Inuit sun visors"*: Kathryn Hughes, "Hans Sloane's 'Nicknackatory' and the Founding of the British Museum," *Guardian*, June 16, 2017.

63 *the moxie to meet bigwigs*: Franklin almost met his hero, Isaac Newton, but it was not to be.

64 *"like skeletons of buildings"*: William Stow, cited in White, *A Great and Monstrous Thing: London in the Eighteenth Century* (Cambridge, MA: Harvard University Press, 2013), 7.

64 *"a very proper name for it"*: White, *A Great and Monstrous Thing*, 6.

64 *"the bitter black drink called coffee"*: Samuel Pepys, quoted in Anthony Clayton, *The Coffee Houses of London: A Stimulating Story* (London: Historical Publications, 2003), 7.

66 *"[Americans] are a race of convicts"*: James Boswell, *The Life of Samuel Johnson* (London: Penguin Classics, 2008), 430.

67 *"Where Benjamin Franklin Learned His Trade"*: That is not quite accurate. He learned the printing trade in Boston and Philadelphia. He refined it in London.

68 *with brown eyes*: While the historic consensus, based mostly on reports from portrait painters, is that Franklin's eyes were brown, a few contemporaries described them as hazel or even gray. Nothing is straightforward when it comes to Benjamin Franklin.

69 *A wealthy nobleman*: Sir William Wyndham, a former chancellor of the exchequer.

NINE: HOMEWARD BEN

70 *"the beauty of sudden seeing"*: Robert Grudin, *The Grace of Great Things: Creativity and Innovation* (New York: Ticknor & Fields, 1990), 65.

71 *Who can resist*: Franklin was seduced by speed. As a teenager fleeing Puritan Boston, the ship couldn't sail fast enough. Later, he dreamed up ways to expedite ocean crossings, and, as deputy postmaster, accelerated colonial mail service.

71 *"Thus being esteem'd"*: Franklin also advised a young tradesman, "The sound of your hammer at five in the morning or nine at night, heard by a creditor, makes him easy six months longer." Franklin, *Papers*, 37:304.

73 *"Old buildings are like"*: Cited in Thompson Mayes, *Why Old Places Matter* (London: Rowman & Littlefield, 2013), 7.

73 *"he found it more pleasant"*: Carl Van Doren, *Benjamin Franklin* (New York: Viking, 1938), 292.

74 *"Perhaps if we could examine"*: A French friend, Pierre Cabanis, said Franklin possessed "a politeness of the heart." Kevin Hayes and Isabelle Bour, eds., *Franklin in His Own Time* (Iowa City: University of Iowa Press, 2011), 166.

76 *"There is no real advance in human reason"*: Jean-Jacques Rousseau, *Emile, or On Education* (Mineola, NY: Dover, 2013), 369.

79 *"Truth is what works"*: William James, "Pragmatism: A New Name for Some Old Ways of Thinking, Lecture II" (Project Gutenberg, 2004), https://www.gutenberg.org/files/5116/5116-h/5116-h.htm.

TEN: FLUID BEN

83 *"I have seen your epitaph"*: Franklin, *The Papers of Benjamin Franklin* (New Haven: Yale University Press, 1959), 5:475.

ELEVEN: SOCIAL BEN

86   *"was always a feast to me"*: Kevin Hayes and Isabelle Bour, eds., *Franklin in His Own Time* (Iowa City: University of Iowa Press, 2011), 24.

86   *"Whenever one found him"*: Ibid., 165.

88   *every Friday evening*: Perhaps out of a need for more privacy (or less ale), the Junto later moved to the house of one of its members, Robert Grace.

90   *"Hath anybody"*: Benjamin Franklin, *The Papers of Benjamin Franklin* (New Haven: Yale University Press, 1959), 1:255.

91   *He was planting*: Those seeds continue to flower to this day. Several dozen "Ben Franklin Circles" are active throughout the United States. See Andrew Marantz, "Benjamin Franklin Invented the Chat Room," *New Yorker*, April 2, 2018.

TWELVE: HABITUAL BEN

95   *"perseverance, kindness, gratitude, courage and honesty"*: Pelin Kesebir and Selin Kesebir, "The Cultural Salience of Moral Character and Virtue Declined in Twentieth Century America," *Journal of Positive Psychology* 7 (2012), 471–480.

96   *his own list of Thirteen Virtues*: Joyce Chaplin, ed., *Benjamin Franklin's Autobiography* (New York: Norton, 2012), 79–80.

97   *"overbearing and rather insolent"*: Ibid., 87.

THIRTEEN: TEXTUAL BEN

101   *He invented words, too*: For a comprehensive list of words invented by Franklin, see David Yerkes, "Franklin's Vocabulary," in J. A. Leo Lemay, ed., *Reappraising Benjamin Franklin* (Newark: University of Delaware Press, 1993), 396–411.

102   *Franklin has just opened*: Franklin partnered with his friend Hugh Meredith, whose family helped bankroll the two.

103   *It was, like Franklin himself*: Said his French friend André Morellet: "While founding an empire, he can be seen drinking and laughing; serious and playful, such is our Benjamin." Kevin Hayes and Isabelle Bour, eds., *Franklin in His Own Time* (Iowa City: University of Iowa Press, 2011), 151.

103   *"the highest happiness"*: Cited in Lemay, *The Life of Benjamin Franklin*, 65.

105   *the Bible and Poor Richard's Almanack*: Franklin regularly sold 10,000 copies of *Poor Richard's Almanack*. At the time, the population of Pennsylvania was only 15,000.

106   *most borrowed and revised*: Franklin biographer Leo Lemay estimates only 10 percent of the proverbs that appear in *Poor Richard* are original.

FOURTEEN: CURIOUS BEN

109   *"Evil stalks the land"*: Voltaire, "Poem on the Lisbon Disaster," in *Toleration and Other Essays by Voltaire*, translated by Joseph McCabe (New York: Knickerbocker Press, 1912), 86.

109   *collide with Isabel Miller*: That is not her real name. In a Franklinian gesture, she asked that I use a pseudonym.

110   *There is no evidence Franklin was ever unfaithful*: Historian Edmund Morgan sums up
      the state of knowledge on this aspect of Franklin's life. "We will never know whether
      he remained sexually faithful during his long absences." Edmund Morgan, *Benjamin
      Franklin* (New Haven: Yale University Press, 2012), 45.

113   *Many of the era's greatest*: Notes historian Ritchie Robertson: "Anyone who chose
      to exercise his brain and powers of observation could learn something new about
      almost any subject, and countless important contributions to science were made by
      amateurs without special training." Robertson, *The Enlightenment*, 5.

113   *"a strikingly useless commodity"*: James Delbourgo, *A Most Amazing Scene of Wonders:
      Electricity and Enlightenment in Early America* (Cambridge, MA: Harvard University
      Press, 2006), 148.

115   *"Genius, in truth"*: William James, *Principles of Psychology* (New York: Dover, 1950),
      2:110.

115   *"I've found out so much"*: Cited in J. A. Leo Lemay, *The Life of Benjamin Franklin* (Phil-
      adelphia: University of Pennsylvania Press, 2009), 3:65.

116   *"To know was to feel"*: Delbourgo, *A Most Amazing Scene of Wonders*, 9.

119   *"that great artillery of God Almighty"*: William Temple, cited in Ritchie Robertson,
      The Enlightenment: The Pursuit of Happiness (New York: HarperCollins, 2021), 14–15.

120   *"William raised the kite"*: Lemay, *The Life of Benjamin Franklin*, 3:105.

120   *Franklin's kite experiment*: Franklin thought he was the first to prove that lightning
      was electricity, but unbeknownst to him a French scientist had done so several
      months earlier, conducting an experiment designed by Franklin.

121   *"What good is a newborn baby?"*: Franklin's comment, spoken in French, was recorded
      by Baron Frédéric-Melchior von Grimm. See Benjamin Franklin, *The Papers of Ben-
      jamin Franklin* (New Haven: Yale University Press, 1959), 40:544–547.

121   *"If it hadn't been for that Franklin the whole house would have gone"*: As recalled by
      Isaac Jefferson, an enslaved person at Monticello. Kevin Hayes and Isabelle Bour,
      eds., *Franklin in His Own Time* (Iowa City: University of Iowa Press, 2011), 151.

121   *"snatched the lightning from"*: Cited in Carla Mulford, *Benjamin Franklin and the Ends
      of Empire* (Oxford: Oxford University Press), 289.

121   *"is universally believed"*: John Adams, diary entry June 3, 1779, Massachusetts Histori-
      cal Society, http://www.masshist.org/digitaladams/.

123   *"'til at length they entirely left me"*: Cited in Stanley Finger, *Dr. Franklin's Medicine*
      (Philadelphia: University of Pennsylvania Press, 2006), 106.

FIFTEEN: FUNNY BEN

125   *"Dialogue between the Gout and Mr. Franklin"*: Benjamin Franklin, *Autobiography,
      Poor Richard, and Later Writings* (New York: Library of America, 1987), 203–210.

126   *"He that is conscious of a stink"*: Cited in Jill Lepore, "What Poor Richard Cost Benja-
      min Franklin," *New Yorker*, January 20, 2008.

126   *"fetid smell"*: Cited in Carl Japikse, *Fart Proudly: Writings of Benjamin Franklin You
      Never Read in School* (Berkeley, CA: Frog Books, 1990), 15.

126 *"shall render the natural discharges"*: Ibid.

127 *"left to slaves and hired aliens"*: Cited in John Morreall, "Philosophy of Humor," *The Stanford Encyclopedia of Philosophy* (2023), https://plato.stanford.edu/archives/sum2023/entries/humor/.

127 *"Most people enjoy"*: Ibid.

128 *"a great share of inoffensive"*: Stephen Sayre, cited in Kevin Hayes and Isabelle Bour, eds., *Franklin in His Own Time* (Iowa City: University of Iowa Press, 2011), xiii.

129 *"had wit at will"*: John Adams, "From John Adams to Boston Patriot, November 8, 1810," Founders Online, National Archives, https://founders.archives.gov/documents/Adams/99-02-02-5574.

SIXTEEN: BUDDHA BEN

133 *"May I be the doctor"*: Shantideva, *A Guide to the Bodhisattva's Way of Life* (Dharamsala: Library of Tibetan Works and Archives, 1979), 20.

135 *an obscure academic paper*: Ryan Aponte, "Dharma of the Founders: Buddhism within the Philosophies of Benjamin Franklin, Thomas Jefferson, and Elihu Palmer," master's thesis (Georgetown University, 2012).

136 *"a beneficial intention"*: Shantideva, *A Guide to the Bodhisattva's Way of Life*, 4.

138 *One day, a Quaker man*: The anecdote is relayed by Franklin's friend Abbé Lefebvre de la Roche and cited in Paul M. Zall, ed., *Ben Franklin Laughing: Anecdotes from Original Sources by and about Benjamin Franklin* (Berkeley: University of California Press, 1980), 111.

140 *"Frequently there is more danger"*: Quoted in Stanley Finger, *Doctor Franklin's Medicine* (Philadelphia: University of Pennsylvania Press, 2006), 4.

141 *"the religion of the heart"*: Polly Stevenson, under her married name, Mary Hewson, quoted in Jared Sparks, *The Life of Benjamin Franklin* (Boston: Tappan, Whittemore, and Mason, 1850), 532.

142 *admitted its first patient*: The hospital opened at the home of Philadelphia resident John Kinsey. Several years later, the dedicated building was completed.

142 *Consider a classic Buddhist parable*: *The Lotus Sutras*, translated by Burton Watson (New York: Columbia University Press, 1994), 61.

143 *"flexibility, compromise, negotiation"*: Alan Houston, *Benjamin Franklin and the Politics of Improvement* (New Haven: Yale University Press, 2008), 69.

SEVENTEEN: NAKED BEN

148 *"injurious to the interests of the Crown"*: Benjamin Franklin, *The Papers of Benjamin Franklin* (New Haven: Yale University Press, 1959), 7:106.

149 *"the most cautious man"*: The visitor was Thomas Coombe. Quoted in Julie Flavell, *When London Was Capital of America* (New Haven: Yale University Press, 2010), 223.

149 *"cold and reserved"*: Kevin Hayes and Isabelle Bour, eds., *Franklin in His Own Time* (Iowa City: University of Iowa Press, 2011), 53.

150   *"putrid atmospheres"*: Stanley Finger, *Doctor Franklin's Medicine* (Philadelphia: University of Pennsylvania Press, 2006), 172.

150   *In one of the more amusing episodes*: Adams recalls the episode in a diary entry on September 9, 1776. *John Adams Autobiography, Vol. 1*, Massachusetts Historical Society. http://www.masshist.org/digitaladams/.

153   *When workers were excavating*: Colin Schultz, "Why Was Benjamin Franklin's Basement Filled with Skeletons?" *Smithsonian*, October 3, 2013.

EIGHTEEN: ANGRY BEN

160   *more than 15,000 letters*: Claire Rydell Arcenas and Caroline Winterer, "The Correspondence Network of Benjamin Franklin: the London Decades," Stanford University Online Project, http://republicofletters.stanford.edu/publications/franklin/.

161   *"I trust too sir"*: Franklin, *Papers*, 26:220.

162   *"The best revenge"*: Marcus Aurelius, *Meditations*, translated by Diskin Clay (London: Penguin Classics, 2006), 66.

166   *"music of angels"*: Cited in Stanley Finger and William Zeitler, "Benjamin Franklin and his glass armonica: from music as therapeutic to pathological," *Progress in Brain Research* 216 (2015), 93–125.

169   *"perpetual anarchy and disobedience"*: Franklin, *Papers*, 20:570.

169   *"an abridgement of what are called English liberties"*: In a letter from Thomas Hutchinson dated January 20, 1769. Founders Online, National Archives, https://founders.archives.gov/documents/Franklin/01-20-02-0282-0007.

169   *"invited as to a bull-baiting"*: Franklin, *Papers*, 21:112.

169   *"has forfeited all the respect of societies and of men"*: Franklin, *Papers*, 21:37.

169   *"conspicuously erect"*: Edward Bancroft, cited in Michael Warner, "Franklin and the Letters of the Republic," *Representations* 16 (1986), 110–130.

170   *"I will make your master"*: Franklin's supposed threat was reported nearly a decade after the Cockpit hearing in a London magazine. Most historians do not give it much credibility. Cited in Paul M. Zall, *Ben Franklin Laughing: Anecdotes from Original Sources by and About Benjamin Franklin* (Berkeley: University of California Press, 1980), 77.

NINETEEN: REFLECTIVE BEN

172   *"His temper is grown so very reserved"*: Benjamin Franklin, *The Papers of Benjamin Franklin* (New Haven: Yale University Press, 1959), 18:65.

173   *"Hearing him preach"*: Quoted in Peter Hoffer, *When Benjamin Franklin Met the Reverend Whitefield: Enlightenment, Revival and the Power of the Printed Word* (Baltimore: John Hopkins University Press, 2011), 16.

178   *"He speaks of himself"*: Cited in Ormond Seavey, *Becoming Benjamin Franklin: The Autobiography and the Life* (University Park: Penn State University Press, 1990), 39.

178   *"A mighty maze"*: Alexander Pope, "An Essay on Man Epistle 1," The Poetry Foundation, https://www.poetryfoundation.org/poems/44899/an-essay-on-man-epistle-i.

178   *He never smoked*: Franklin shared his views on tobacco with Benjamin Rush. See Har-
      old Bloom, *Benjamin Franklin* (New York: Infobase Publishing, 2008), 14.

179   *"one might have suppos'd a transmigration"*: Joyce Chaplin, ed., *Benjamin Franklin's Au-
      tobiography* (New York: Norton, 2012), 11.

179   *"humans are history-bearing"*: Elisabeth Lasch-Quinn, "Pastlessness," *Hedgehog Re-
      view* (Summer 2022), https://hedgehogreview.com/issues/the-use-and-abuse-of
      -history/articles/pastlessness.

180   *"a cerebral disease"*: Constantine Sedikides et al., "Nostalgia: Conceptual Issues and
      Existential Functions," in Jeff Greenberg, ed. *Handbook of Experimental Existential
      Psychology* (New York: Guilford Press, 2004), 201.

180   *"What makes old age hard"*: Somerset Maugham, *Points of View* (New York: Double-
      day, 1959), 70.

180   *a groundbreaking 1963*: Robert Butler, "The Life Review: An Interpretation of Remi-
      niscence in the Aged," *Psychiatry* 26, no. 1 (1963), 65–76.

180   *"My life is in the background"*: Ibid.

181   *found the secret ingredient*: Bin Li, Qin Zhu, and Rubo Cui, "Can Good Memories of
      the Past Instill Happiness? Nostalgia Improves Subjective Well-Being by Increasing
      Gratitude," *Journal of Happiness Studies* 24 (2023), 699–715.

TWENTY: DECISIVE BEN

185   *Endings carry greater weight*: Donald Redelmeier, Joel Katz, and Daniel Kahne-
      man, "Memories of Colonoscopy: A Randomized Trial," *Pain* 104, no. 1 (2003),
      187–194.

185   *fifteen-year mission*: Ben actually spent seventeen years in London, from 1757 to 1774,
      but his stay was interrupted by an eighteen-month visit to Philadelphia in 1763 and
      1764.

185   *"go from one end of America"*: Franklin relayed the comments to his friend William
      Strahan in a letter dated August 19, 1785.

188   *Only one example of Ben's moral algebra*: Franklin, *Papers*, 20:336. Franklin also re-
      ferred to this practice as "prudential algebra."

189   *"These are bad symptoms in advanced life"*: Benjamin Franklin, *The Papers of Benjamin
      Franklin* (New Haven: Yale University Press, 1959), 16:152.

189   *"my poor old mother"*: Ibid., 21:42.

189   *"I heartily wish you had"*: Ibid.

190   *"the tears literally running"*: Hayes and Bour, *Franklin in His Own Time*, 43.

TWENTY-ONE: BUSY BEN

195   *busy people are happier*: Marissa A. Sharif, "How Having Too Little or Too Much
      Time Is Linked to Lower Subjective Well-Being," *Journal of Personality and Social Psy-
      chology* 121, no. 4 (2021), 933–947.

195   *a more modern example*: Richard Larson, "Perspectives on Queues: Social Justice and
      the Psychology of Queueing," *Operations Research* 35, no. 6 (1987), 895–905.

196   *"The great affair"*: Robert Louis Stevenson, *Travels with a Donkey in the Cevennes* (Boston: Roberts Brothers, 1879), 81.

196   *"a suspicious person"*: Thomas Hutchinson, *The Diary and Letters of Thomas Hutchinson* (New York: Burt Franklin, 1971), 237.

196   *"a disposition entirely American"*: Kevin Hayes and Isabelle Bour, eds., *Franklin in His Own Time* (Iowa City: University of Iowa Press, 2011), 53.

198   *"ended in shouting matches"*: Gordon Wood, *The Americanization of Benjamin Franklin* (New York: Penguin, 2004), 162.

200   *"in the evening of life"*: William Strahan in a 1775 letter to Franklin. See Benjamin Franklin, *The Papers of Benjamin Franklin* (New Haven: Yale University Press, 1959), 20:220.

203   *"the Golden Age of Gout"*: W. S. C. Copeman, *A Short History of the Gout* (Berkeley: University of California Press, 1964), 80.

203   *"When I was a young man"*: Cited in Stanley Finger, *Doctor Franklin's Medicine* (Philadelphia: University of Pennsylvania Press, 2006), 287.

204   *"I do not repine at my malady"*: Carl Van Doren, ed., *Letters of Benjamin Franklin and Jane Mecom* (Princeton: Princeton University Press, 2015), 340.

205   *Some people maintain*: Clay Routledge et al., "Nostalgia as a Resource for Psychological Health and Well-Being," *Social and Personality Psychology Compass* 7, no. 11 (2013), 808–818.

205   *even in the face of adversity*: Gerben J. Westerhof and Syl Slatman, "In Search of the Best Evidence for Life Review Therapy to Reduce Depressive Symptoms in Older Adults: A Meta-Analysis of Randomized Controlled Trials," *Clinical Psychology: Science and Practice* 26, no. 4 (2019), 26 e12301.

206   *"two or three unlucky expressions"*: J. Jefferson Looney, ed., *The Papers of Thomas Jefferson* (Princeton: Princeton University Press, 2016), 13:464.

207   *"John Thompson, Hatter"*: Hayes and Bour, *Franklin in His Own Time*, 136.

208   *"We hold these truths to be sacred"*: P. Boyd, ed., *The Papers of Thomas Jefferson* (Princeton: Princeton University Press, 1950), 1:243.

208   *An assertive pen stroke*: Van Doren, *Benjamin Franklin*, 552.

208   *"it is impossible for the same thing to be and not to be"*: John Locke, *An Essay Concerning Human Understanding* (Hertfordshire: Wordsworth Editions, 2014), 27.

209   *"discovered himself to be an enemy"*: Larry R. Gerlach, ed., "New Jersey in the American Revolution, 1763–1783: A Documentary History" (Trenton: New Jersey Historical Commission, 1975), 210.

209   *"I suffer so much"*: Cited in *Proceedings of the New Jersey Historical Society* (Trenton: New Jersey Historical Society, 1918), 3:47.

210   *"If I have said, or done anything"*: Benjamin Franklin, *The Papers of Benjamin Franklin* (New Haven: Yale University Press, 1959), 22:551.

211   *"each one of us took"*: Cited in Henri Doniol, *Histoire de la Participation de la France à l'Etablissement des États-Unis d'Amerique* (Paris: Imprimerie Nationale, 1886), 1:267.

212   *"Everyone here is a soldier"*: Ibid.

214 "keep totally secret where you are bound": David Schoenbrun, Triumph in Paris: The Exploits of Benjamin Franklin (New York: Harper, 1976), 50.

214 "Don't go, pray don't": Franklin, Papers, 22:104.

TWENTY-TWO: FULL BEN

216 a wretched place: William Bell Clark, Lambert Wickes, Sea Raider and Diplomat: The Story of a Naval Captain of the Revolution (New Haven: Yale University Press, 1932), 100.

216 "with that senile ambition": Harold Bloom, ed., Benjamin Franklin (New York: Infobase Publishing, 2008), 19.

218 "Some think we are of a French extract": Benjamin Franklin, The Papers of Benjamin Franklin (New Haven: Yale University Press, 1959), 2:229.

222 "a wicked old man": Cited in Thomas Fleming, "Franklin Charms Paris," American Heritage (Spring 2010).

222 "There is no shred of evidence": Claude-Anne Lopez and Eugenia Herbert, The Private Franklin: The Man and His Family (New York: Norton, 1975), 278.

222 "He had an instinctive knowledge": Lorraine Smith Pangle, The Political Philosophy of Benjamin Franklin (Baltimore: Johns Hopkins University Press, 2007), 69.

222 "projectors, speculators, and adventurers of all descriptions": William Temple Franklin, Memoirs of the Life and Writings of Benjamin Franklin (London: Henry Colburn, 1818), 1:329.

224 he negotiated two treaties: The Treaty of Amity and Commerce and the Treaty of Alliance, both signed in February 1778.

225 "without noticing that he understood little": Kevin Hayes and Isabelle Bour, eds., Franklin in His Own Time (Iowa City: University of Iowa Press, 2011), 127.

225 "Men at forty/Learn to close softly": Donald Justice, "Men at Forty," Poetry 108, no. 2 (May 1966).

226 He looks like a man: The painting is currently on display at the Philadelphia Museum of Art, where I sought it out. It is even more striking in person.

228 "come to have the honour to see the great Franklin": John Adams, John Adams Autobiography, 2:26. Massachusetts Historical Society, http://www.masshist.org/digitaladams/.

228 "once a handsome woman": Hayes and Bour, Franklin in His Own Time, 69.

228 "it may truly be said": Hayes and Bour, Franklin in His Own Time, 134.

229 "had the common sense not to annoy": Jonathan Dull, Franklin the Diplomat: The French Mission (Philadelphia: American Philosophical Society Press, 1982), 9.

231 recent studies confirm: Yu Niiya, "Does a Favor Request Increase Liking toward the Requester?," Journal of Social Psychology 156, no. 2 (2016), 211–221.

234 "was amazed to find so much genius": Hayes and Bour, Franklin in His Own Time, 130.

235 Most (not all) cells: The life span of individual cells varies widely. Those found in your colon, for instance, are replaced every few days, while muscle and fat cells may take seventy years to regenerate. Some cells, such as those found in the brain and eyes, remain unchanged throughout your life.

240 "My grandfather mounted his litter": Cited in Lopez and Herbert, The Private Franklin, 281.

240 "I picture you in the litter": Ibid., 282.

TWENTY-THREE: FLOATING BEN

243 "The Art of Procuring": The essay was contained in a letter Franklin sent to a friend, Catherine Shipley, who was suffering from insomnia. Benjamin Franklin, The Papers of Benjamin Franklin (New Haven: Yale University Press, 1959), May 2, 1786.

244 "Dear and Honoured Father": Letter from William Franklin to Benjamin Franklin, July 22, 1784.

TWENTY-FOUR: DOUBTING BEN

251 "The joy I received": Cited in Claude-Anne Lopez and Eugenia Herbert, The Private Franklin: The Man and His Family (New York: Norton, 1975), 287.

252 "It has always been my maxim": Franklin reportedly made the comment to Thomas Paine during a visit to Paris. Cited in John Epps, The Life of John Walker, MD (London: Whittaker, Treacher, 1832), 145.

253 "this Venerable Nestor": The phrase was scientist Andrew Ellicott's, cited in Kevin Hayes and Isabelle Bour, eds., Franklin in His Own Time (Iowa City: University of Iowa Press, 2011), 99.

253 "He was determined not to increase": Ibid., 100.

253 "the brightness of his memory": Harold Bloom, Benjamin Franklin (New York: Infobase Publishing, 2008), 19.

253 "an activity of mind equal to": Cited in Bernard Cohen, Science and the Founding Fathers (New York: Norton, 1995), 189.

254 "They listened to his suggestions": Hastings Lyon, The Constitution and the Men Who Made It (Boston: Houghton Mifflin, 1936), 73.

254 "They that govern most": John Selden, The Table Talk of John Selden (London: John Russell Smith, 1856), 120.

254 "looks out upon the noisy passersby": Franklin's observation is recalled by an acquaintance, the historian Constantine Volney. Cited in Zall, Ben Franklin Laughing, 142.

255 "with great pertinacity and effect": Cited in William Carr, The Oldest Delegate: Franklin in the Constitutional Convention (Newark: University of Delaware Press, 1990), 56.

257 "When a broad table": Franklin's comment was recalled by James Madison. See Max Farrand, ed., The Records of the Federal Convention of 1787, https://oll.libertyfund .org/title/farrand-the-records-of-the-federal-convention-of-1787-vol-1.

257 "manipulative, hands-on approach": Donald Meyer, in Melvin Buxbaum, ed., Critical Essays on Benjamin Franklin (Boston: G. K. Hall, 1987), 164.

260 *"necessary uneasiness"*: John William Ward, "Who Was Benjamin Franklin," *American Scholar* 32, no. 4 (Autumn 1963), 563.

261 *"Well, Doctor, what have we got"*: The alleged exchange was relayed by James McHenry, a delegate from Maryland. "Papers of Dr. James McHenry on the Federal Convention of 1787," *American Historical Review* 11, no. 3 (1906), 595–624.

TWENTY-FIVE: BELATED BEN

262 *Franklin enslaved at least seven*: Details about Franklin's enslavement are difficult to pin down. Explains historian Gary Nash: "Like most other northern slaveowners, [Franklin] did not keep a record of slave births, deaths, and marriages because slaveholding was not central to productive processes as it was in the plantation South." Nash, "Franklin and Slavery," *Proceedings of the American Philosophical Society*, 619.

262 *Jefferson enslaved more than*: Henry Wiencek, "The Dark Side of Thomas Jefferson," *Smithsonian Magazine*, October 2012.

263 *"The man who is so good at making an excuse"*: Cited in Anonymous, *Liber Facetiarum: Being a Collection of Curious and Interesting Anecdotes* (Newcastle upon Tyne: Dr. Akenhead and Sons, 1809), 182.

263 *"Two likely young Negroes"*: Franklin, *Papers*, 1:378.

263 *"There is to be sold"*: Ibid., 1:345.

263 *"being no more reluctant to advertise"*: Nash, "Franklin and Slavery," *Proceedings of the American Philosophical Society*, 621.

263 *"If these may be valued"*: Franklin, *Papers*, 1:217.

264 *"mother of all sins"*: Benjamin Lay, *All Slave Keepers That Keep the Innocent in Bondage, Apostates* (Philadelphia [Printed for the author], 1737), 106.

264 *"Thus shall God shed the blood"*: Cited in Marcus Redeker, "The 'Quacker Comet' was the Greatest Abolitionist You've Never Heard Of," *Smithsonian Magazine*, September 2017.

264 *Joseph, Jemima, Peter, Bob*: As early as 1735, while still in his twenties, Franklin enslaved a boy named Joseph. See Nash, "Franklin and Slavery," *Proceedings of the American Philosophical Society*, 619.

266 *"a very strong and disagreeable odour"*: Thomas Jefferson, *Notes on the State of Virginia* (Boston: Lilly and Wait, 1832), 145, https://tile.loc.gov/storage-services/service/gdc/lhbcb/04902/04902.pdf.

266 *"in reason much inferior"*: Ibid., 146.

266 *"are inferior to the whites"*: Ibid., 150.

266 *"empirical temper"*: I. Bernard Cohen, "The Empirical Temper," in Charles Sanford, ed., *Benjamin Franklin and the American Character* (Boston: D. C. Heath, 1955), 91.

267 *was an all-in abolitionist*: Not all historians are convinced Franklin had a genuine change of heart about slavery. For an opposing view, see David Waldstreicher, *Runaway America: Benjamin Franklin, Slavery, and the American Revolution* (New York: Hill and Wang, 2014).

267 *appointed president of the Pennsylvania*: The full name of the organization was the Pennsylvania Society for Promoting the Abolition of Slavery and the Relief of Free Negroes Unlawfully Held in Bondage.

267 *"of one flesh, all the children"*: Franklin, *Papers*, "From the Pennsylvania Abolition Society: Constitution," April 23, 1787.

TWENTY-SIX: ETERNAL BEN

270 *"kindly intended to wean him from"*: Cited in William Pepper, *The Medical Side of Benjamin Franklin* (Philadelphia: William J. Campbell, 1911), 114.

272 *"in great agony"*: Cited in Bigelow, *The Works of Benjamin Franklin*, vol. 12, 197.

273 *"it roused him to a display"*: Ibid.

273 *"die in a decent manner"*: Franklin's friend Benjamin Rush relayed the episode in a letter to Richard Price, April 24, 1790. Cited in Zall, *Ben Franklin Laughing*, 98.

Select Bibliography

Alsop, Susan Mary. *Yankees at the Court: The First Americans in Paris*. New York: Washington Square Press, 1982.

Anderson, Douglas. *The Radical Enlightenments of Benjamin Franklin*. Baltimore: Johns Hopkins University Press, 1997.

Barbour, Frances, ed. *A Concordance to the Sayings in Franklin's Poor Richard*. Detroit: Gale Research Company, 1974.

Battaly, Heather. *Virtue*. Cambridge, UK: Polity, 2015.

Becker, Carl L. *Benjamin Franklin*. Ithaca, NY: Cornell University Press, 1946.

Bloom, Harold, ed. *Benjamin Franklin*. New York: Infobase Publishing, 2008.

Bridenbaugh, Carl, and Jessica Bridenbaugh. *Rebels and Gentlemen: Philadelphia in the Age of Franklin*. New York: Oxford University Press, 1962.

Bunker, Nick. *Young Benjamin Franklin: The Birth of Ingenuity*. New York: Knopf, 2018.

Bunyan, John. *The Pilgrim's Progress*. London: Penguin Classics, 2008.

Buxbaum, Melvin, ed. *Critical Essays on Benjamin Franklin*. Boston: G. K. Hall, 1987.

Campbell, James. *Recovering Franklin: An Exploration of a Life of Science and Service*. Chicago: Open Court, 1999.

Carr, William. *The Oldest Delegate: Franklin in the Constitutional Convention*. Newark: University of Delaware Press, 1990.

Chaline, Eric. *Strokes of Genius: A History of Swimming*. London: Reaktion Books, 2017.

Chaplin, Joyce, ed. *Benjamin Franklin's Autobiography*. New York: Norton, 2012.

Clayton, Anthony. *The Coffee Houses of London: A Stimulating Story*. London: Historical Publications, 2003.

Cohen, I. Bernard. *Science and the Founding Fathers*. New York: Norton, 1995.

Conner, Paul W. *Poor Richard's Politicks: Benjamin Franklin and His New American Order*. New York: Oxford University Press, 1965.

Defoe, Daniel. *An Essay upon Projects*. New York: AMS Press, 1999.

Delbourgo, James. *A Most Amazing Scene of Wonders: Electricity and Enlightenment in Early America.* Cambridge, MA: Harvard University Press, 2006.

Dull, Jonathan R. *Franklin the Diplomat: The French Mission.* Philadelphia: American Philosophical Society Press, 1982.

———. *Benjamin Franklin and the American Revolution.* Lincoln: University of Nebraska Press, 2010.

Epstein, Daniel. *The Loyal Son: The War in the Franklin House.* New York: Ballantine Books, 2017.

Finger, Stanley. *Doctor Franklin's Medicine.* Philadelphia: University of Pennsylvania Press, 2006.

Flavell, Julie. *When London Was Capital of America.* New Haven: Yale University Press, 2010.

Franklin, Benjamin. *The Papers of Benjamin Franklin,* vols. 1–43. New Haven: Yale University Press, 1959.

———. *Autobiography, Poor Richard, and Later Writings.* New York: Library of America, 1987.

———. *Silence Dogood, the Busy-Body, and Early Writings.* New York: Library of America, 1987.

Gargaz, Pierre-André. *A Project of Universal and Perpetual Peace.* New York: Garland, 1973.

Goodwin, George. *Benjamin Franklin in London: The British Life of America's Founding Father.* New Haven: Yale University Press, 2016.

Hamilton, Alexander. *Gentleman's Progress: The Itinerarium of Dr. Alexander Hamilton.* New York: Alejandro's Libros, 2012.

Hayes, Kevin, and Isabelle Bour, eds. *Franklin in His Own Time: A Biographical Chronicle of His Life, Drawn from Recollections, Interviews, and Memories by Family, Friends, and Associates.* Iowa City: University of Iowa Press, 2011.

Hoffer, Peter. *When Benjamin Franklin Met the Reverend Whitefield: Enlightenment, Revival, and the Power of the Printed Word.* Baltimore: John Hopkins University Press, 2011.

Houston, Alan. *Benjamin Franklin and the Politics of Improvement.* New Haven: Yale University Press, 2008.

Huang, Nian-Sheng. *Benjamin Franklin in American Thought and Culture 1790–1990.* Philadelphia: American Philosophical Society, 1994.

Inglis, Lucy. *Georgian London: Into the Streets.* London: Penguin, 2013.

Isaacson, Walter. *Benjamin Franklin: An American Life.* New York: Simon & Schuster, 2003.

Japikse, Carl. *Fart Proudly: Writings of Benjamin Franklin You Never Read in School.* Berkeley, CA: Frog Books, 1990.

Kerry, Paul E., and Matthew S. Holland, eds. *Benjamin Franklin's Intellectual World.* Madison, NJ: Fairleigh Dickinson University Press, 2012.

Lemay, J. A. Leo, ed. *The Oldest Revolutionary: Essays on Benjamin Franklin.* Philadelphia: University of Pennsylvania Press, 1976.

———, ed. *Reappraising Benjamin Franklin.* Newark: University of Delaware Press, 1993.

———. *The Life of Benjamin Franklin,* vols. 1–3. Philadelphia: University of Pennsylvania Press, 2006.

Locke, John. *An Essay Concerning Human Understanding*. Hertfordshire: Wordsworth Editions, 2014.

Lopez, Claude-Anne. *Mon Cher Papa: Franklin and the Ladies of Paris*. New Haven: Yale University Press, 1990.

Lopez, Claude-Anne, and Eugenia Herbert. *The Private Franklin: The Man and His Family*. New York: Norton, 1975.

Mather, Cotton. *Essays to Do Good: Modern English Version*. New York: Kindle, 2012.

Mayes, Thompson. *Why Old Places Matter*. London: Rowman & Littlefield, 2013.

Menz, Steve. *Ocean*. New York: Bloomsbury Academic, 2020.

Morgan, David T. *The Devious Dr. Franklin, Colonial Agent: Benjamin Franklin's Years in London*. Macon, GA: Mercer University Press, 1999.

Morgan, Edmund. *Benjamin Franklin*. New Haven: Yale University Press, 2012.

Mulford, Carla, ed. *The Cambridge Companion to Benjamin Franklin*. Cambridge: Cambridge University Press, 2008.

Nunley, John, and Cara McCarty, eds. *Masks: Faces of Culture*. St. Louis: Harry Abrams, 1999.

Pangle, Lorraine Smith. *The Political Philosophy of Benjamin Franklin*. Baltimore: Johns Hopkins University Press, 2007.

Pomeroy, Susan. *Benjamin Franklin, Swimmer: An Illustrated History*. Philadelphia: American Philosophical Society Press, 2021.

Postman, Neil. *Building a Bridge to the 18th Century: How the Past Can Improve Our Future*. New York: Vintage, 1999.

Robertson, Ritchie. *The Enlightenment: The Pursuit of Happiness*. New York: HarperCollins, 2021.

Rossiter, Clinton. *Seedtime of the Republic: The Origin of the American Tradition of Political Liberty*. New York: Harcourt Brace, 1953.

Sanford, Charles, ed. *Benjamin Franklin and the American Character*. Boston: Heath, 1955.

Sappenfield, James. *A Sweet Instruction: Franklin's Journalism as a Literary Apprenticeship*. Carbondale: Southern Illinois University Press, 1973.

Schoenbrun, David. *Triumph in Paris: The Exploits of Benjamin Franklin*. New York: Harper, 1976.

Seavey, Ormond. *Becoming Benjamin Franklin: The Autobiography and the Life*. University Park: Penn State University Press, 1990.

Shantideva. *A Guide to the Bodhisattva's Way of Life*. Dharamsala: Library of Tibetan Works and Archives, 1979.

Slack, Kevin. *Benjamin Franklin, Natural Right, and the Art of Virtue*. Rochester, NY: University of Rochester Press, 2017.

Talbott, Page, ed. *Benjamin Franklin: In Search of a Better World*. New Haven: Yale University Press, 2005.

Tanford, Charles. *Ben Franklin Stilled the Waves*. Oxford: Oxford University Press, 2004.

Thane, Pat, ed. *A History of Old Age*. Los Angeles: J. Paul Getty Museum, 2005.

Tise, Larry, ed. *Benjamin Franklin and Women*. University Park: Penn State University Press, 2000.

Tourtellot, Arthur Bernon. *Benjamin Franklin: The Shaping of Genius: The Boston Years.* Garden City, NY: Doubleday, 1977.

Van Doren, Carl. *Benjamin Franklin.* New York: Book-of-the-Month Club, 1938.

Van Horn, Jennifer. *The Power of Objects in Eighteenth-Century British America.* Chapel Hill: University of North Carolina Press, 2017.

Walters, Kerry. *Benjamin Franklin and His Gods.* Chicago: University of Illinois Press, 1999.

Weigley, Russell, ed. *Philadelphia: A 300-Year History.* New York: Norton, 1982.

White, Jerry. *A Great and Monstrous Thing: London in the Eighteenth Century.* Cambridge, MA: Harvard University Press, 2013.

Winterer, Caroline: *American Enlightenments: Pursuing Happiness in the Age of Reason.* New Haven: Yale University Press, 2016.

Zall, Paul M., ed. *Ben Franklin Laughing: Anecdotes from Original Sources by and about Benjamin Franklin.* Berkeley: University of California Press, 1980.

———. *Benjamin Franklin's Humor.* Lexington: University Press of Kentucky, 2005.

Ziff, Larzer, ed. *The Portable Benjamin Franklin.* New York: Penguin Classics, 2005.

Index

ordinariness, 2

positivity, 3, 81–82, 168, 181, 184, 204, 205, 225, 270, 277–78

sense of humor, 125–30, 131, 207, 229, 259

sensitivity, 167, 190

serious and playful, 103, 160, 289n

sociability, 2, 44, 64–65, 83, 149, 154, 225

social caution, 85, 149, 291n

—CIVIC IMPROVEMENT AND:

BF's influence and, 49, 275

Junto Club, 87–91, 115, 289n

masking and, 41

Pennsylvania Hospital, 139–42, 143, 197–98, 275, 291n

public positions, 252

reading and, 18

usefulness and, xvi, 87–88, 107, 124, 197–98

—FRENCH MISSION, 212–24

abolitionism and, 267

aging and, 215–16, 217, 233, 235–36

Auray sojourn, 215, 216–18

Battle of Saratoga and, 223–24

charm and, 222–23

enemies and, 229–30

Louis XVI and, 234–35

Passy residence, 219–22

popularity and, 218–19, 222–23, 227–28, 232, 240

printing and, 101, 227

success of, 224, 226–33, 235

travel and, 213–14, 218, 238–40, 242–43, 245, 249–50, 251–52

womanizing reputation and, 222, 228

—IMAGES OF:

in Auray, 216

in Boston, 7, 14–15, 54

French popularity and, 227, 234, 236

French portraits, 226, 236, 295n

materialism and, 136–37, 138

ubiquity of, xiv

—INVENTIONS AND EXPERIMENTS:

bifocals, xvi, 82, 204, 283n

currency and, 61, 102, 195

distance from Europe and, 114–15

empiricism and, 29

experiential knowledge and, 116–17

experimentation and, 113

fame and, 121–22

final years and, 1, 2, 166

flexible catheter, 88, 166

generosity and, 137, 166

glass armonica, 164–68

kite experiment, 120, 189–90

life after death and, 272

lightning rod, xvi, 71, 119–20, 121, 122

magic squares, 253–54

matching grants, 141

medicine and, 88, 140, 166, 204

phonetic alphabet, 166

scientific writing and, 117–18

support for, 115

swimming and, 31–32

travel and, 192, 288n

unity and, 186

usefulness and, 87–88, 166

words, 101

See also electricity

—LONDON MISSION (1757–74), 157

British contempt and, 81–82, 169–70

colonial advocacy and, 187

Craven Street home, 145, 146–47, 151–54, 155, 190–91

elite rejection and, 185–86

end of, 190, 191, 192

homesickness and, 154–55

Hutchinson letters affair, 168–70, 292n

last-minute compromise proposals, 187

length of, 293n

moral algebra and, 187–88

pastoral fantasies and, 171

Pennsylvania taxes and, 147–48, 158, 159

Stamp Act and, 171–72

Twyford House visit, 173, 174, 177

—AS PRINTER, 84, 93

apprenticeships, 34, 44, 53, 57, 163, 288n

as assistant to Keimer, 53, 84

empathy and, 229

freedom of the press and, 103

French mission and, 101, 227

identity of, 101–2

London sojourn (1723–26) and, 60, 67, 163

About the Author

ERIC WEINER is author of the *New York Times* bestsellers *The Geography of Bliss* (now a docuseries featuring Rainn Wilson) and *The Geography of Genius*, as well as the critically acclaimed *Man Seeks God* and *The Socrates Express*. A former foreign correspondent for NPR, his work has appeared in the *Atlantic*, *National Geographic*, the *Washington Post*, the *Wall Street Journal*, and the anthology *The Best American Travel Writing*. He lives with his family and a menagerie of animals in the Washington, DC, area. For more information, visit EricWeinerBooks.com.